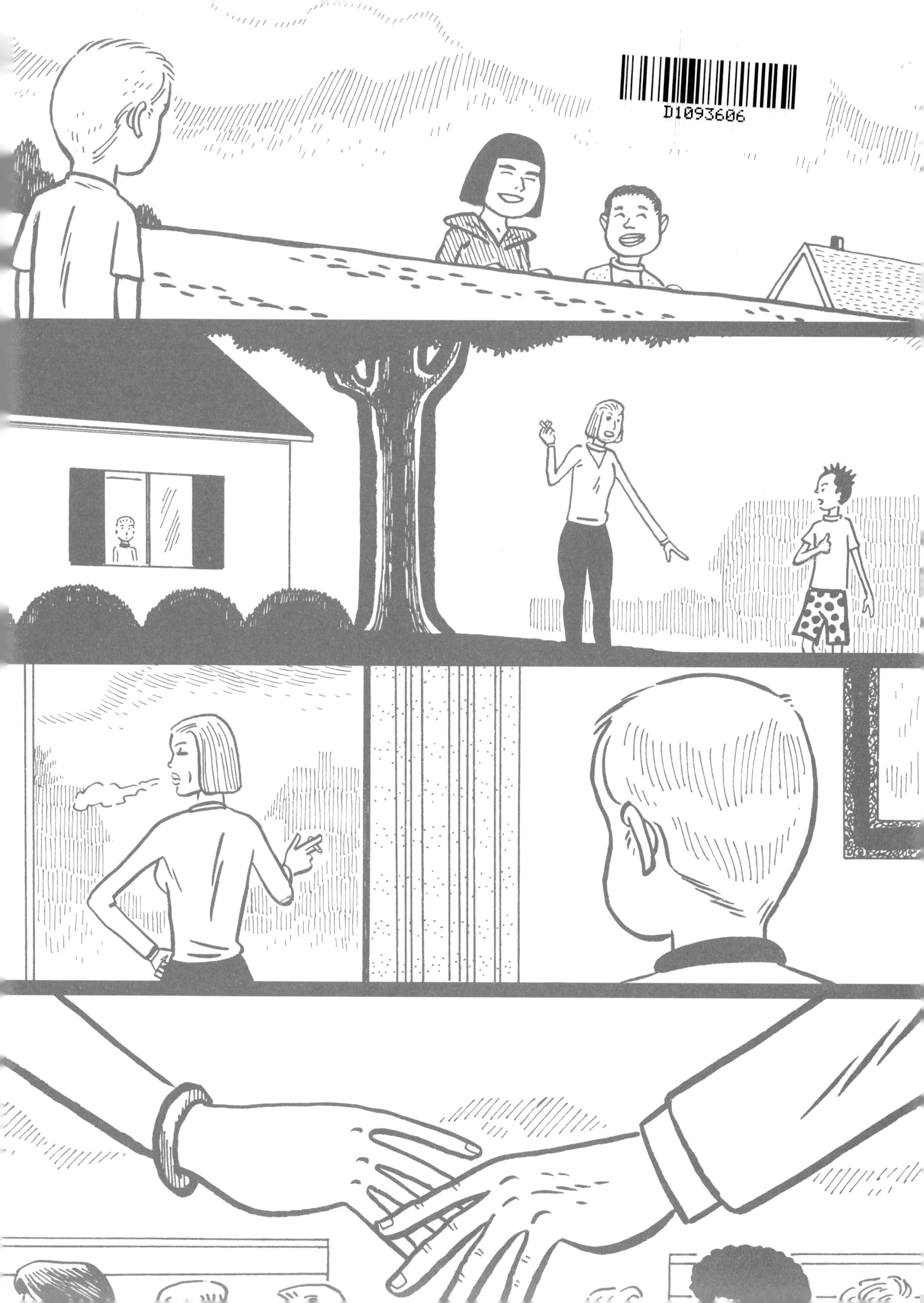

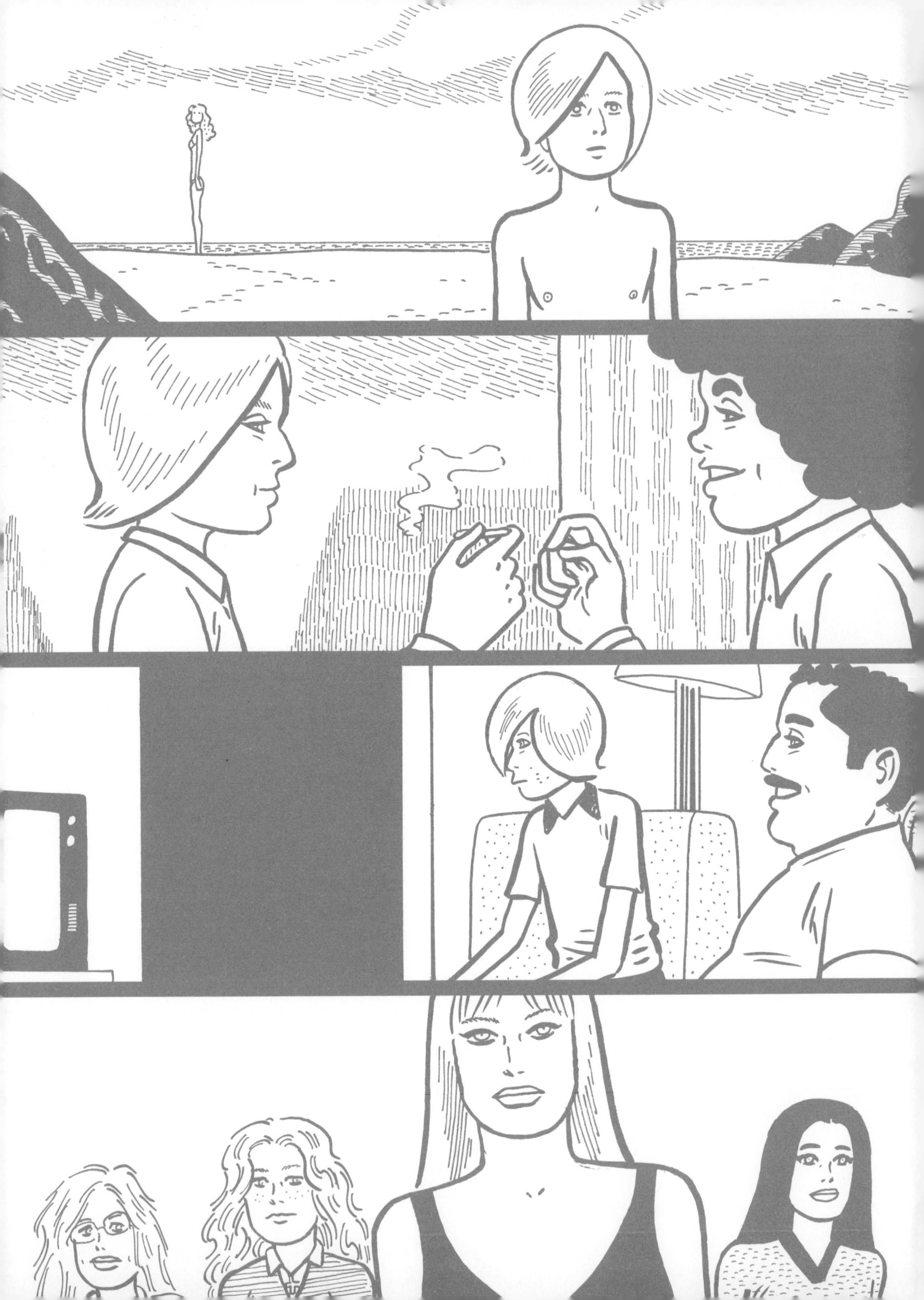

BUMPERHEAD

GILBERT HERNANDEZ

DRAWN & QUARTERLY

drawnandquarterly.com.

FIRST HARDCOVER EDITION: SEPTEMBER 2014. PRINTED IN CHINA.
10·9·8·7·6·5·4·3·2·1

LIBRARY AND ARCHIVES CANADA CATALOGUING IN PUBLICATION
Hernandez, Gilbert, author, illustrator
BUMPERHEAD/GILBERT HERNANDEZ. GILBERT HERNANDEZ.
ISBN 978-1-77046-165-9 (BOUND)
I. GRAPHIC NOVELS. I. TITLE
PN6727.H47B86 2014   741.5973   C2013-908472-X

PUBLISHED IN THE U.S. BY DRAWN & QUARTERLY, A CLIENT PUBLISHER OF FARRAR, STRAUS AND GIROUX. ORDERS: 888.330.8477
PUBLISHED IN CANADA BY DRAWN & QUARTERLY, A CLIENT PUBLISHER OF RAINCOAST BOOKS. ORDERS: 800.663.5714
PUBLISHED IN THE UK BY DRAWN & QUARTERLY, A CLIENT PUBLISHER OF PUBLISHERS GROUP UK. ORDERS: INFO@PGUK.CO.UK

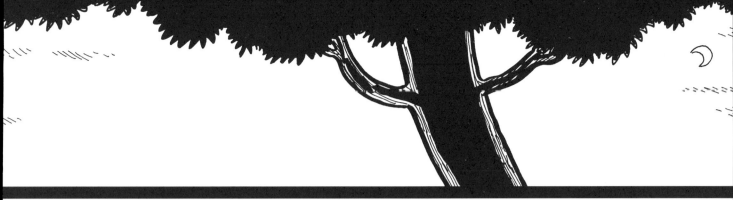

FOR CAROL AND NATALIA, MY DREAMS COME TRUE

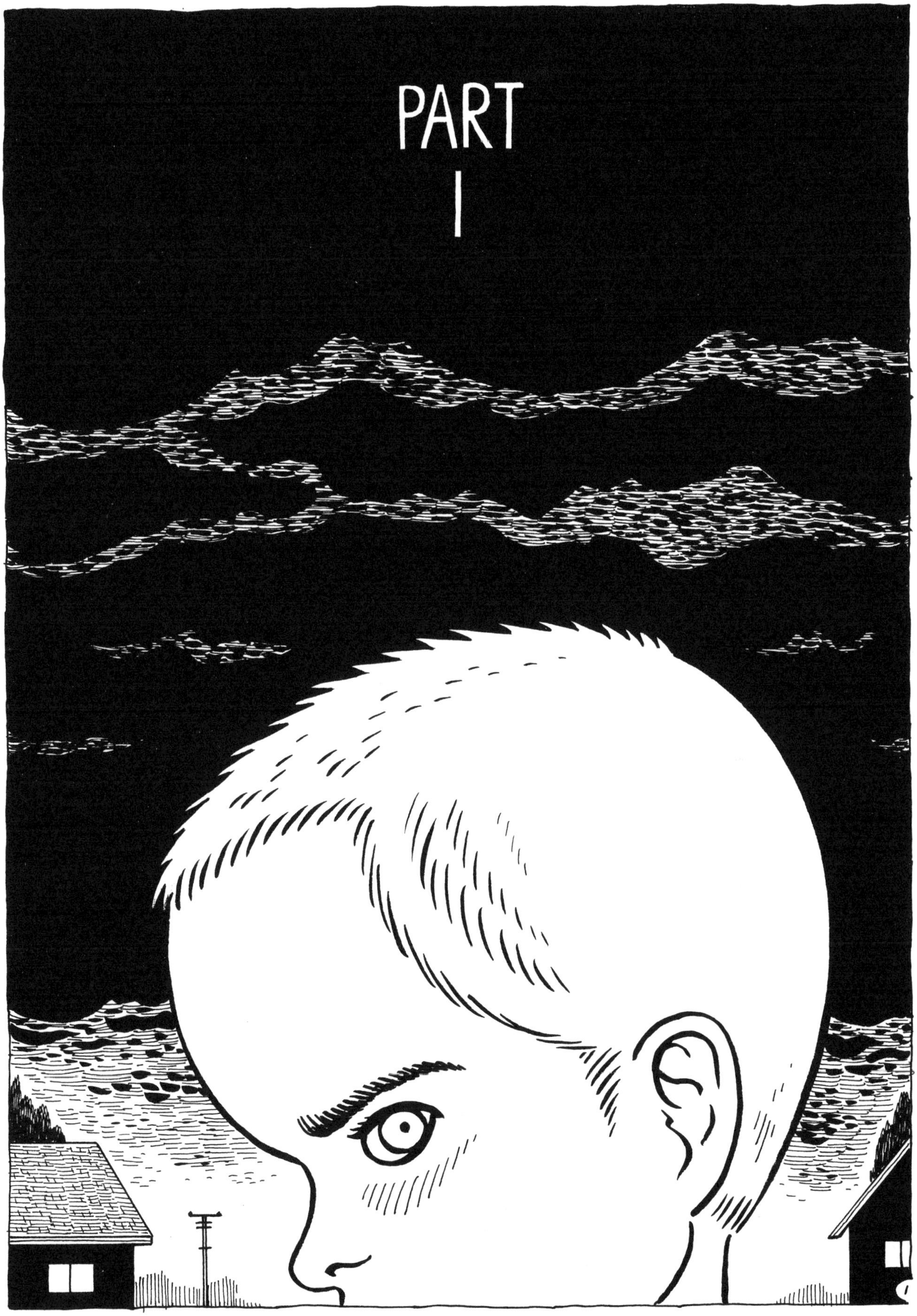
PART
I

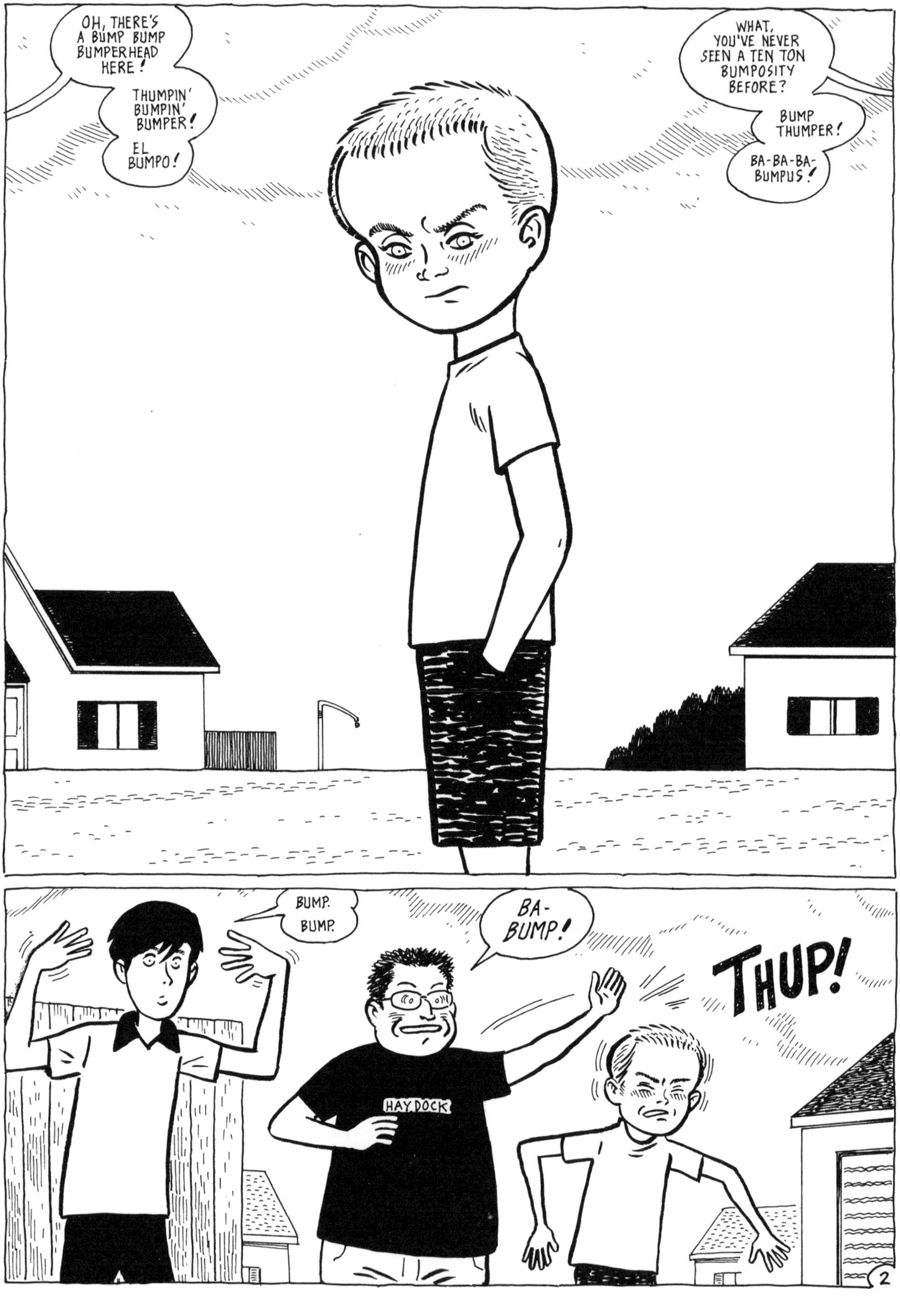
OH, THERE'S A BUMP BUMP BUMPERHEAD HERE!
THUMPIN' BUMPIN' BUMPER!
EL BUMPO!
WHAT, YOU'VE NEVER SEEN A TEN TON BUMPOSITY BEFORE?
BUMP THUMPER!
BA-BA-BA-BUMPUS!
BUMP. BUMP.
BA-BUMP!
HAYDOCK
THUP!

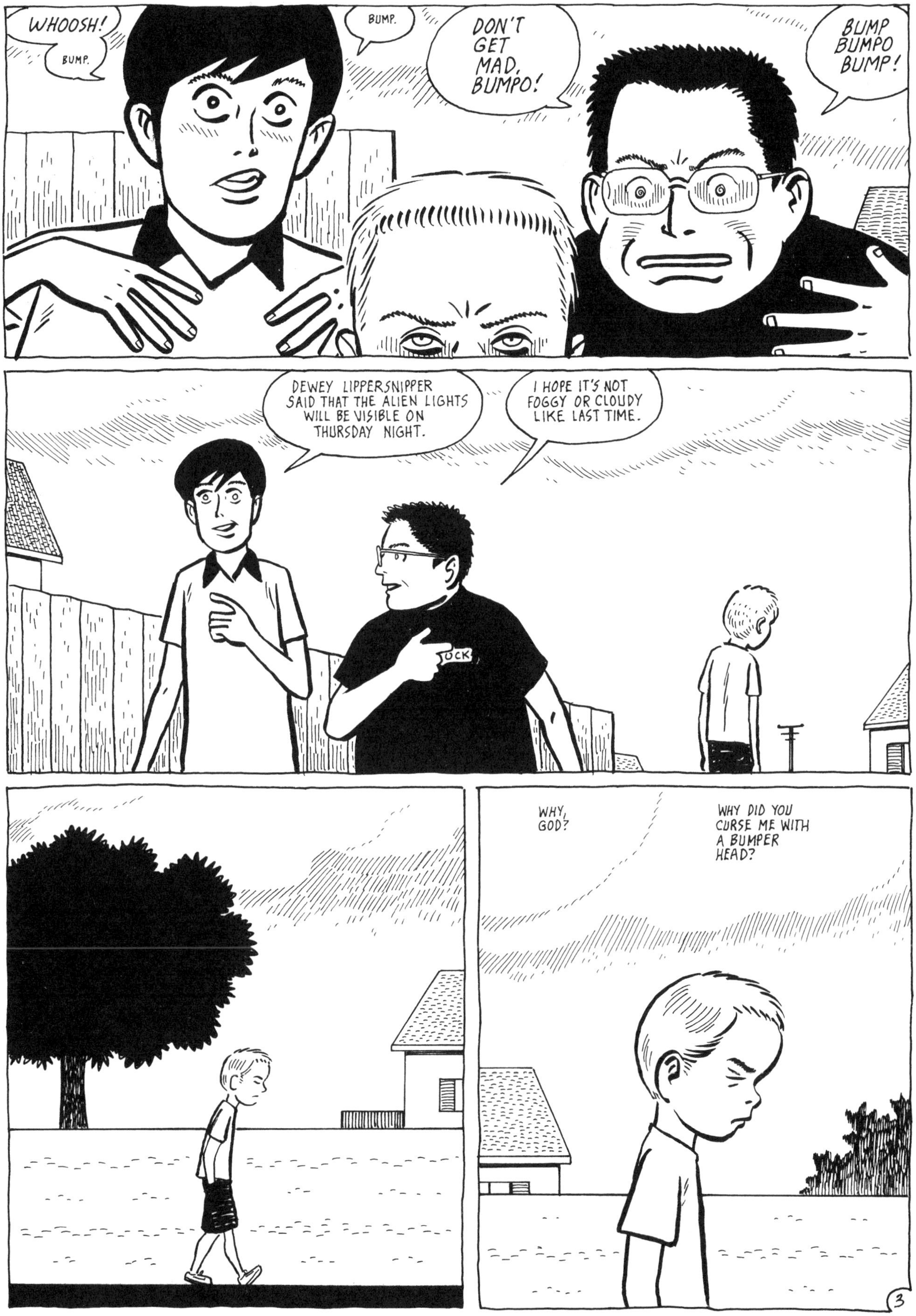
WHOOSH!
BUMP.
BUMP.
DON'T GET MAD, BUMPO!
BUMP BUMPO BUMP!
DEWEY LIPPERSNIPPER SAID THAT THE ALIEN LIGHTS WILL BE VISIBLE ON THURSDAY NIGHT.
I HOPE IT'S NOT FOGGY OR CLOUDY LIKE LAST TIME.
WHY, GOD?
WHY DID YOU CURSE ME WITH A BUMPER HEAD?

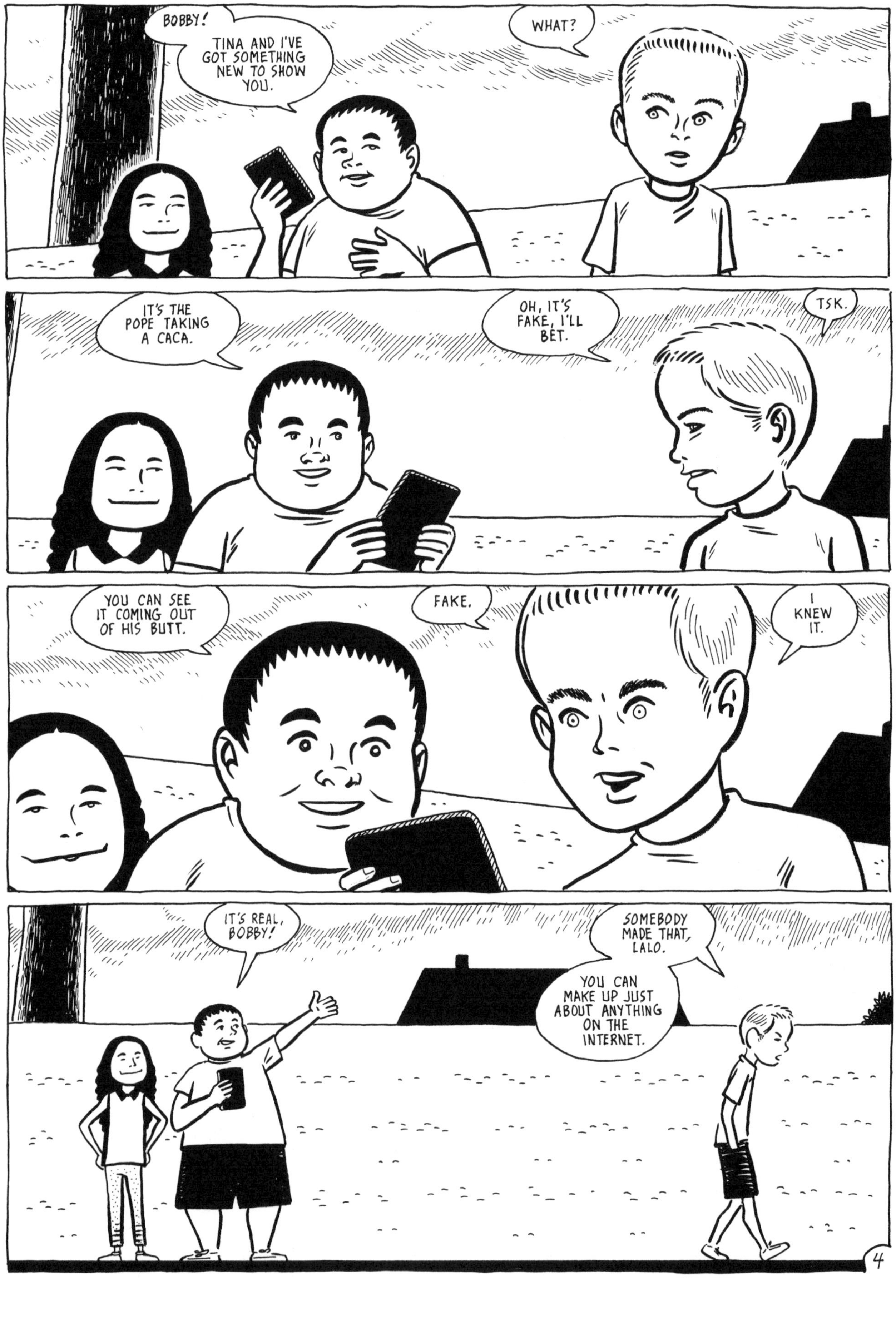

BOBBY!
TINA AND I'VE GOT SOMETHING NEW TO SHOW YOU.
WHAT?
IT'S THE POPE TAKING A CACA.
OH, IT'S FAKE, I'LL BET.
TSK.
YOU CAN SEE IT COMING OUT OF HIS BUTT.
FAKE.
I KNEW IT.
IT'S REAL, BOBBY!
SOMEBODY MADE THAT, LALO.
YOU CAN MAKE UP JUST ABOUT ANYTHING ON THE INTERNET.

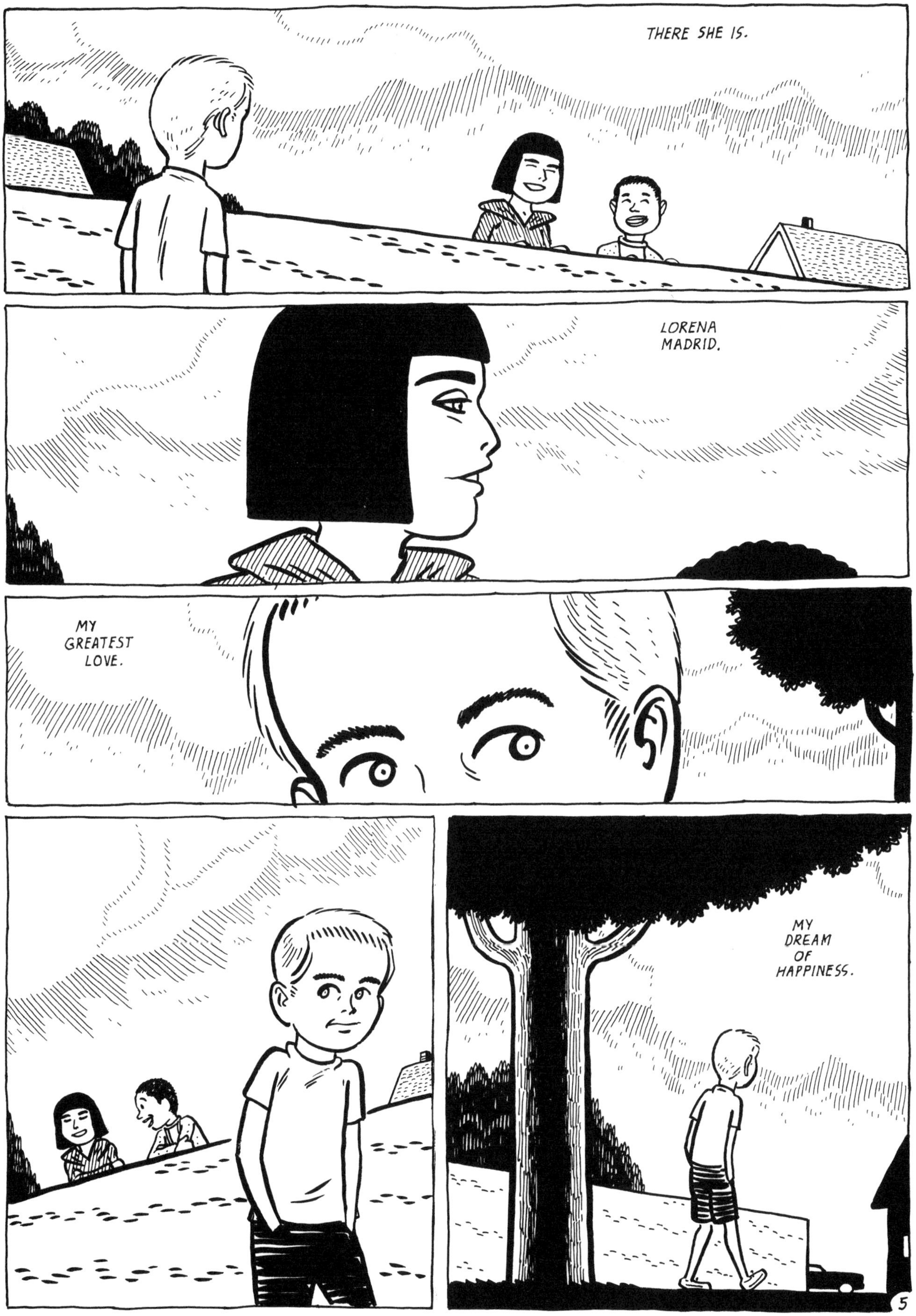
THERE SHE IS.
LORENA MADRID.
MY GREATEST LOVE.
MY DREAM OF HAPPINESS.

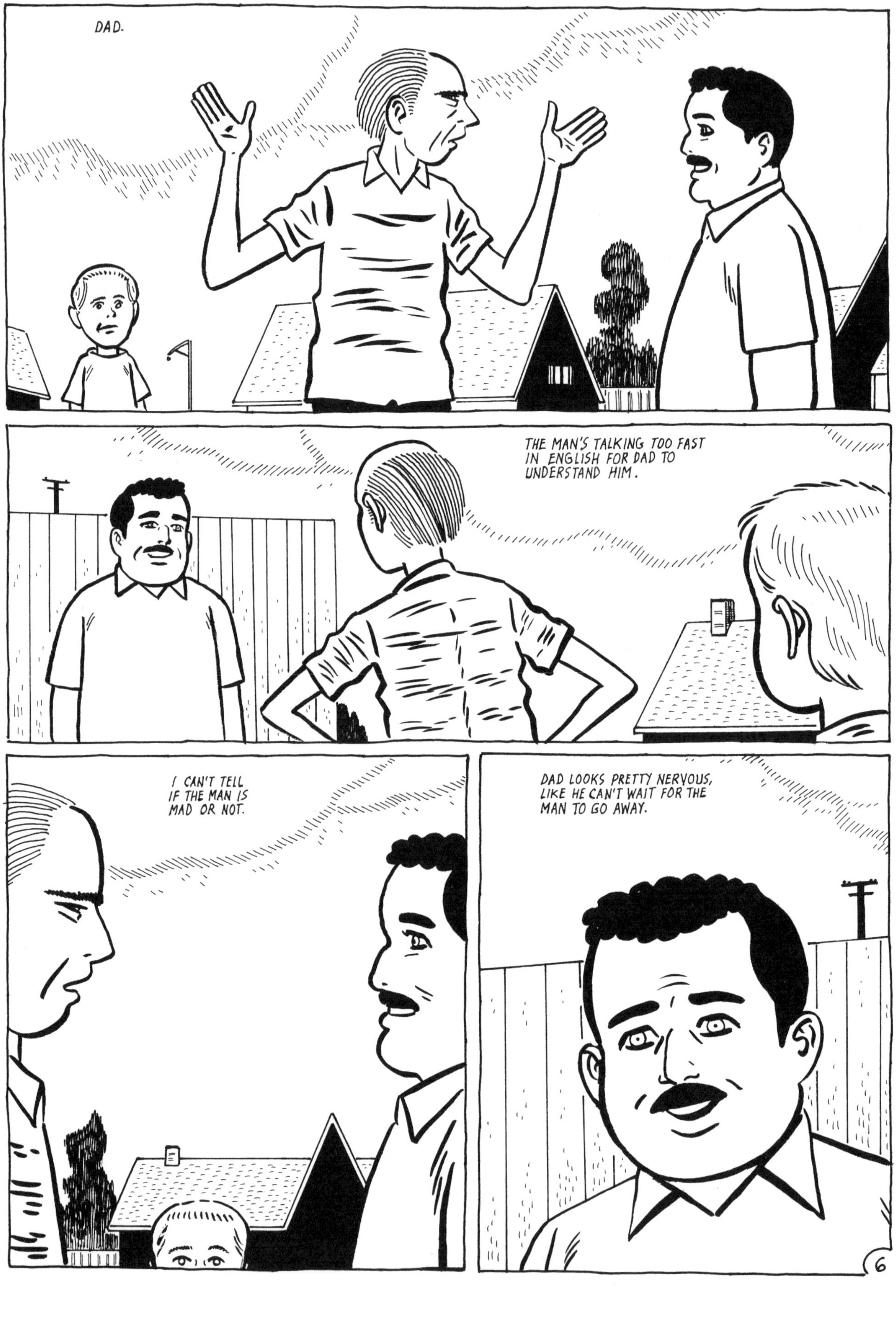
DAD.
THE MAN'S TALKING TOO FAST IN ENGLISH FOR DAD TO UNDERSTAND HIM.
I CAN'T TELL IF THE MAN IS MAD OR NOT.
DAD LOOKS PRETTY NERVOUS, LIKE HE CAN'T WAIT FOR THE MAN TO GO AWAY.

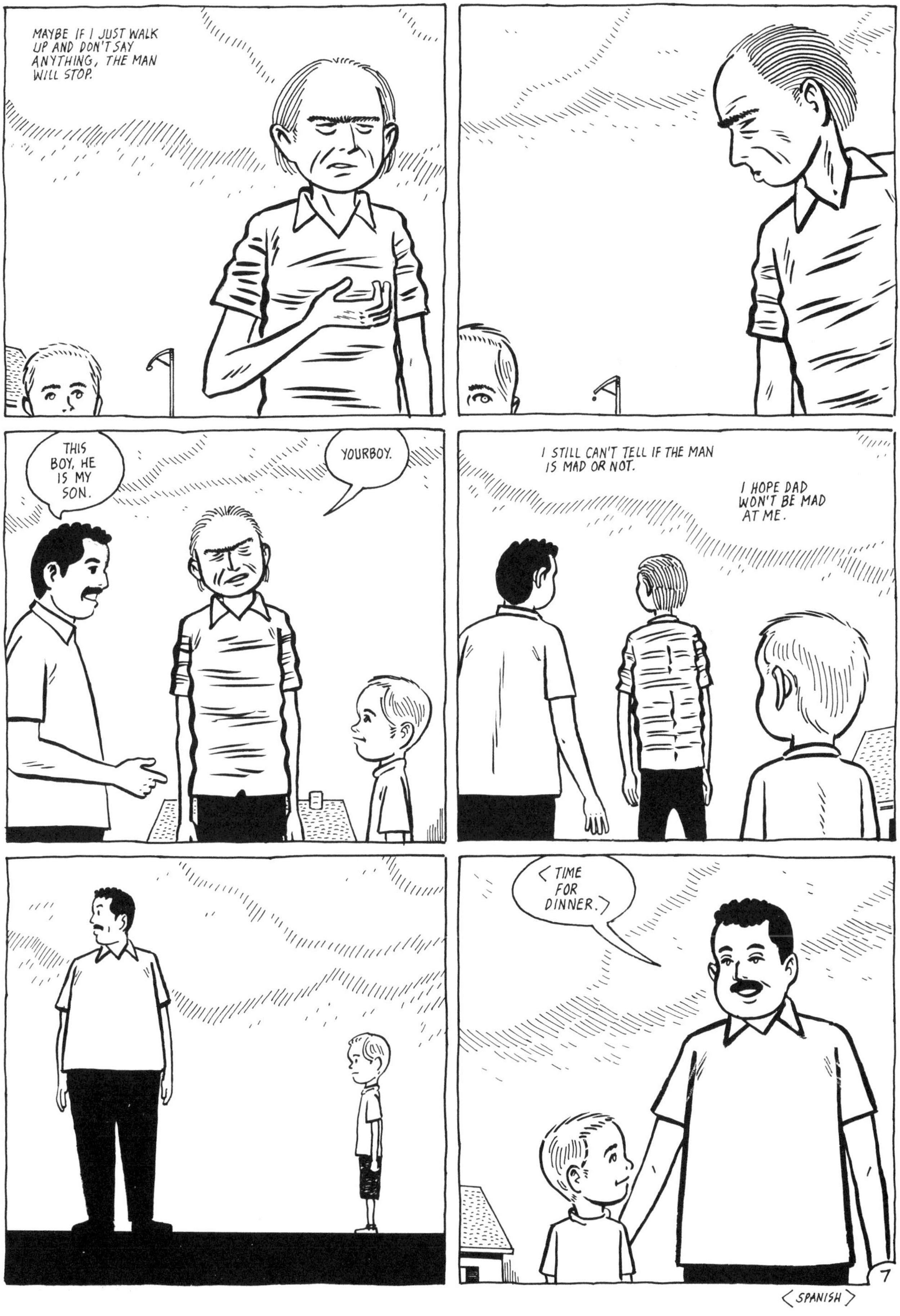
MAYBE IF I JUST WALK UP AND DON'T SAY ANYTHING, THE MAN WILL STOP.
THIS BOY, HE IS MY SON.
YOURBOY.
I STILL CAN'T TELL IF THE MAN IS MAD OR NOT.
I HOPE DAD WON'T BE MAD AT ME.
< TIME FOR DINNER. >

< SPANISH >

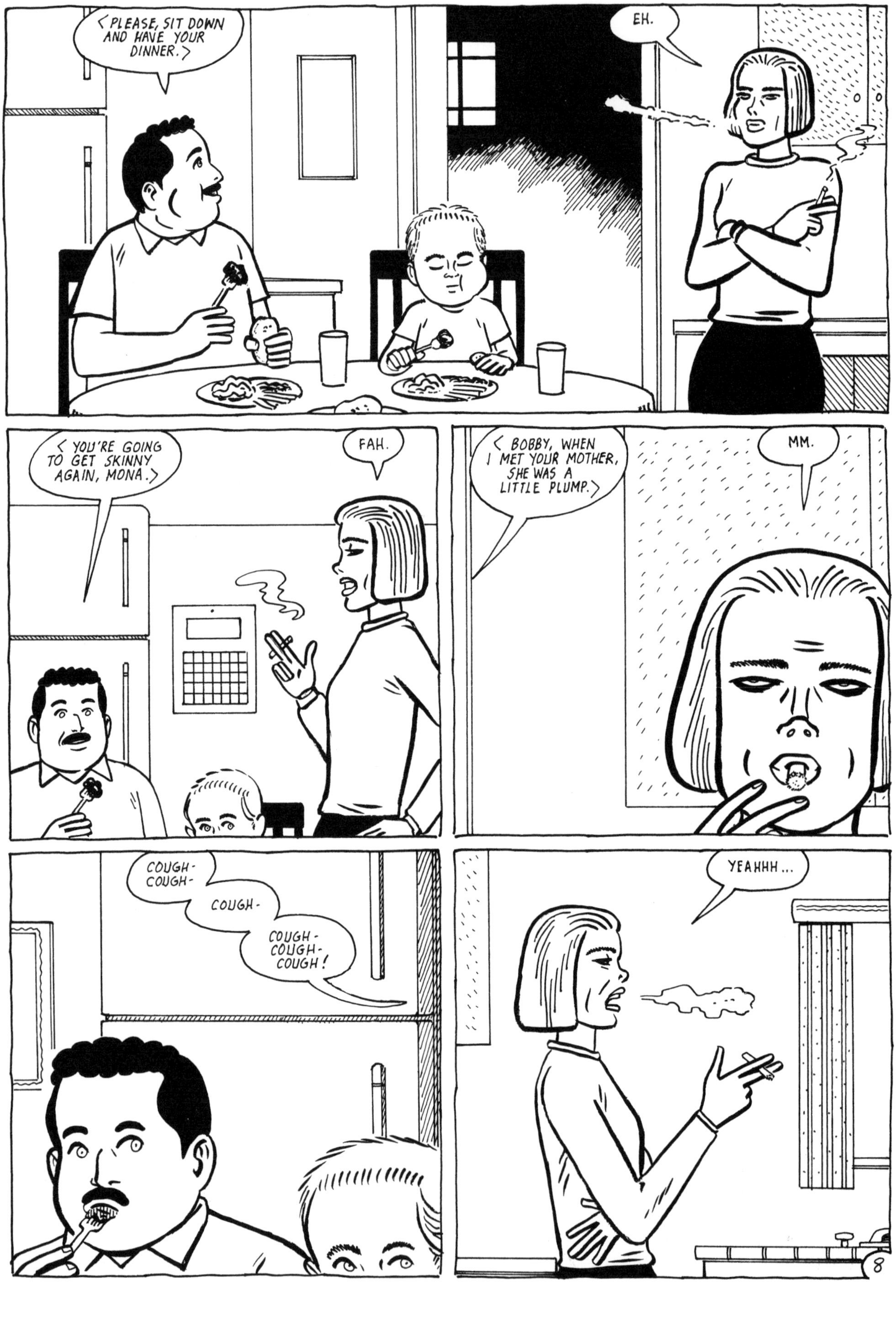
<PLEASE, SIT DOWN AND HAVE YOUR DINNER.>
EH.
<YOU'RE GOING TO GET SKINNY AGAIN, MONA.>
FAH.
<BOBBY, WHEN I MET YOUR MOTHER, SHE WAS A LITTLE PLUMP.>
MM.
COUGH-COUGH-
COUGH-
COUGH-COUGH-COUGH!
YEAHHH...

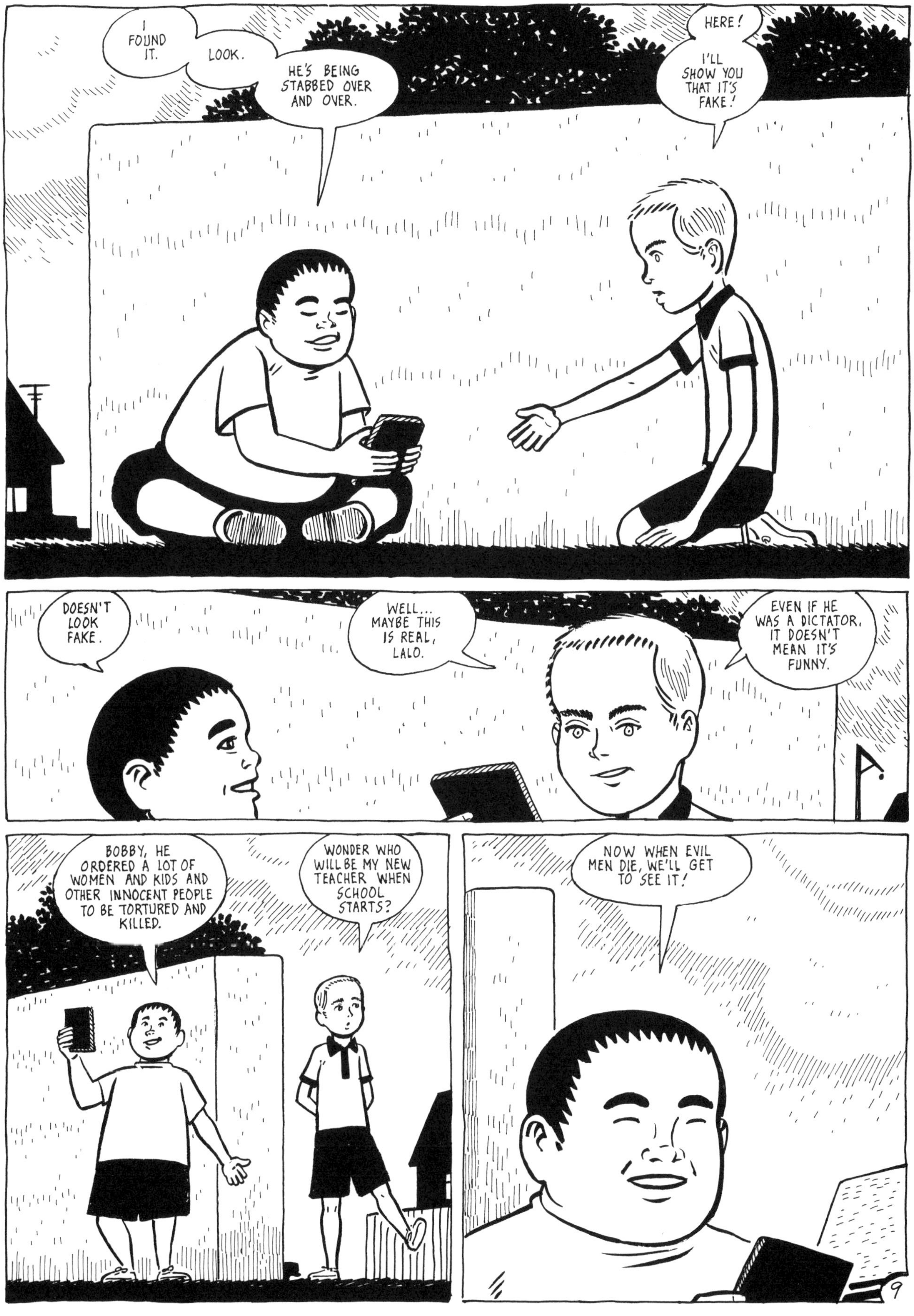
I FOUND IT.
LOOK.
HE'S BEING STABBED OVER AND OVER.
HERE!
I'LL SHOW YOU THAT IT'S FAKE!
DOESN'T LOOK FAKE.
WELL... MAYBE THIS IS REAL, LALO.
EVEN IF HE WAS A DICTATOR, IT DOESN'T MEAN IT'S FUNNY.
BOBBY, HE ORDERED A LOT OF WOMEN AND KIDS AND OTHER INNOCENT PEOPLE TO BE TORTURED AND KILLED.
WONDER WHO WILL BE MY NEW TEACHER WHEN SCHOOL STARTS?
NOW WHEN EVIL MEN DIE, WE'LL GET TO SEE IT!

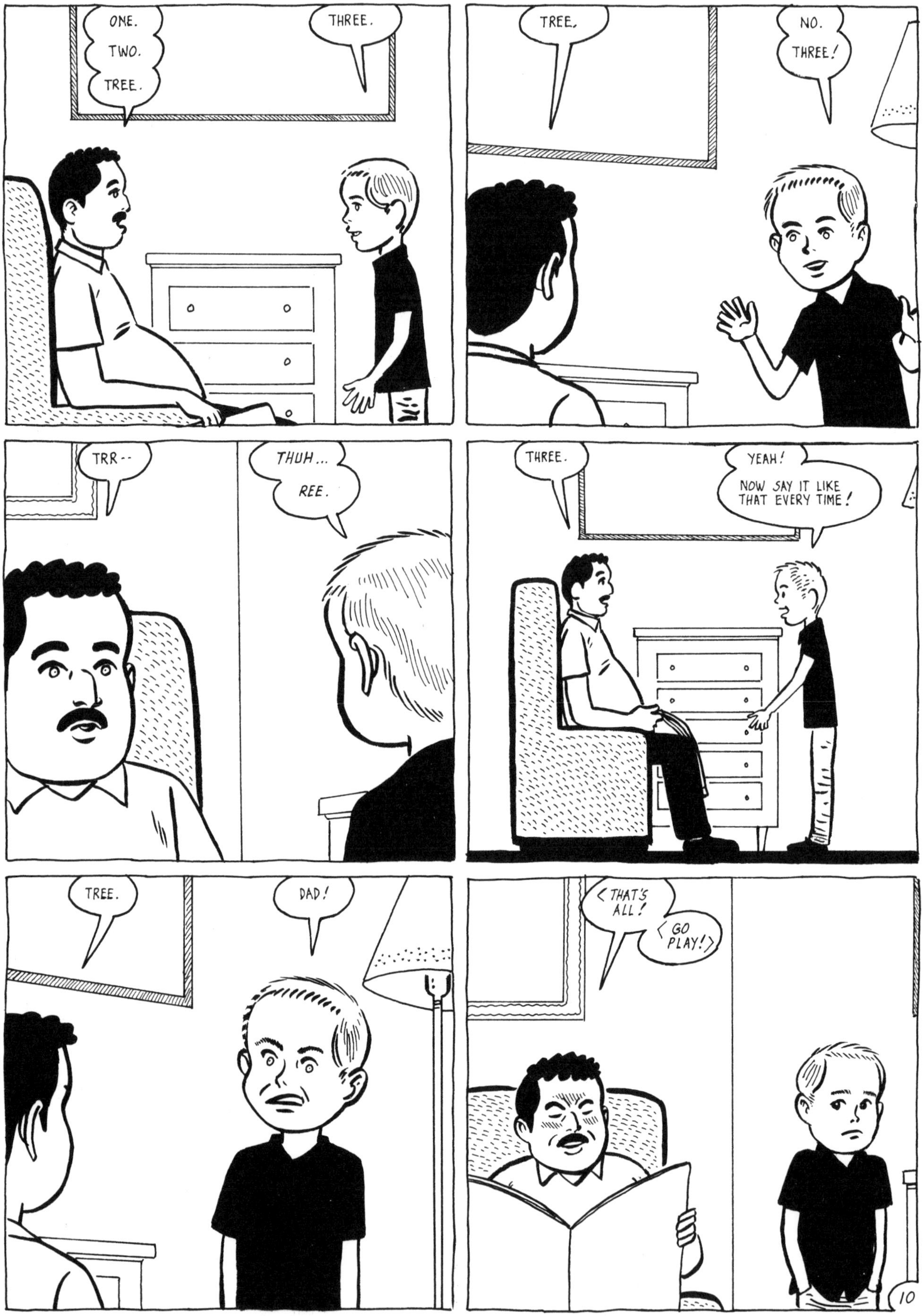
ONE.
TWO.
TREE.
THREE.
TREE.
NO.
THREE!
TRR--
THUH...
REE.
THREE.
YEAH!
NOW SAY IT LIKE THAT EVERY TIME!
TREE.
DAD!
<THAT'S ALL!
<GO PLAY!>

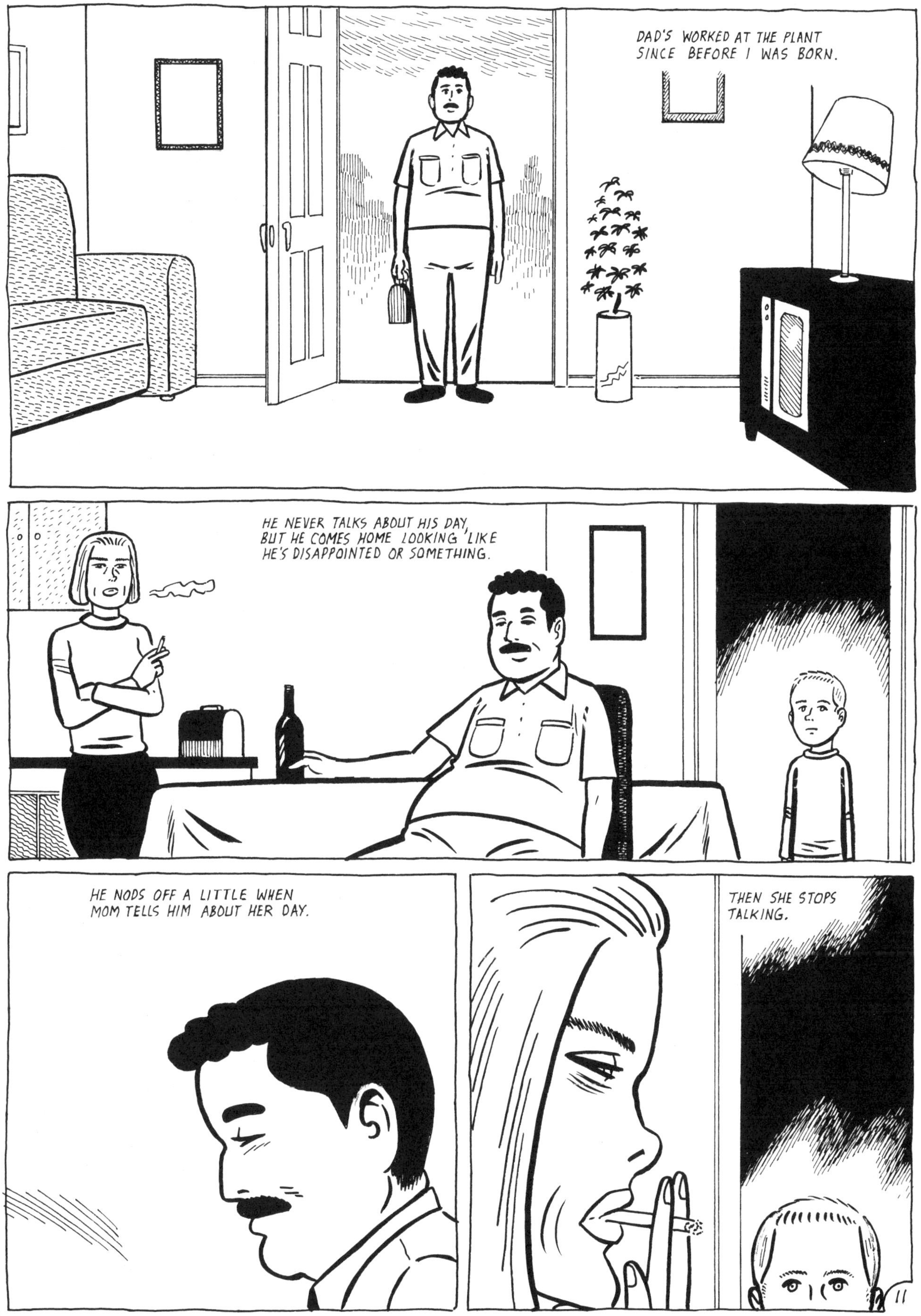
DAD'S WORKED AT THE PLANT SINCE BEFORE I WAS BORN.
HE NEVER TALKS ABOUT HIS DAY, BUT HE COMES HOME LOOKING LIKE HE'S DISAPPOINTED OR SOMETHING.
HE NODS OFF A LITTLE WHEN MOM TELLS HIM ABOUT HER DAY.
THEN SHE STOPS TALKING.

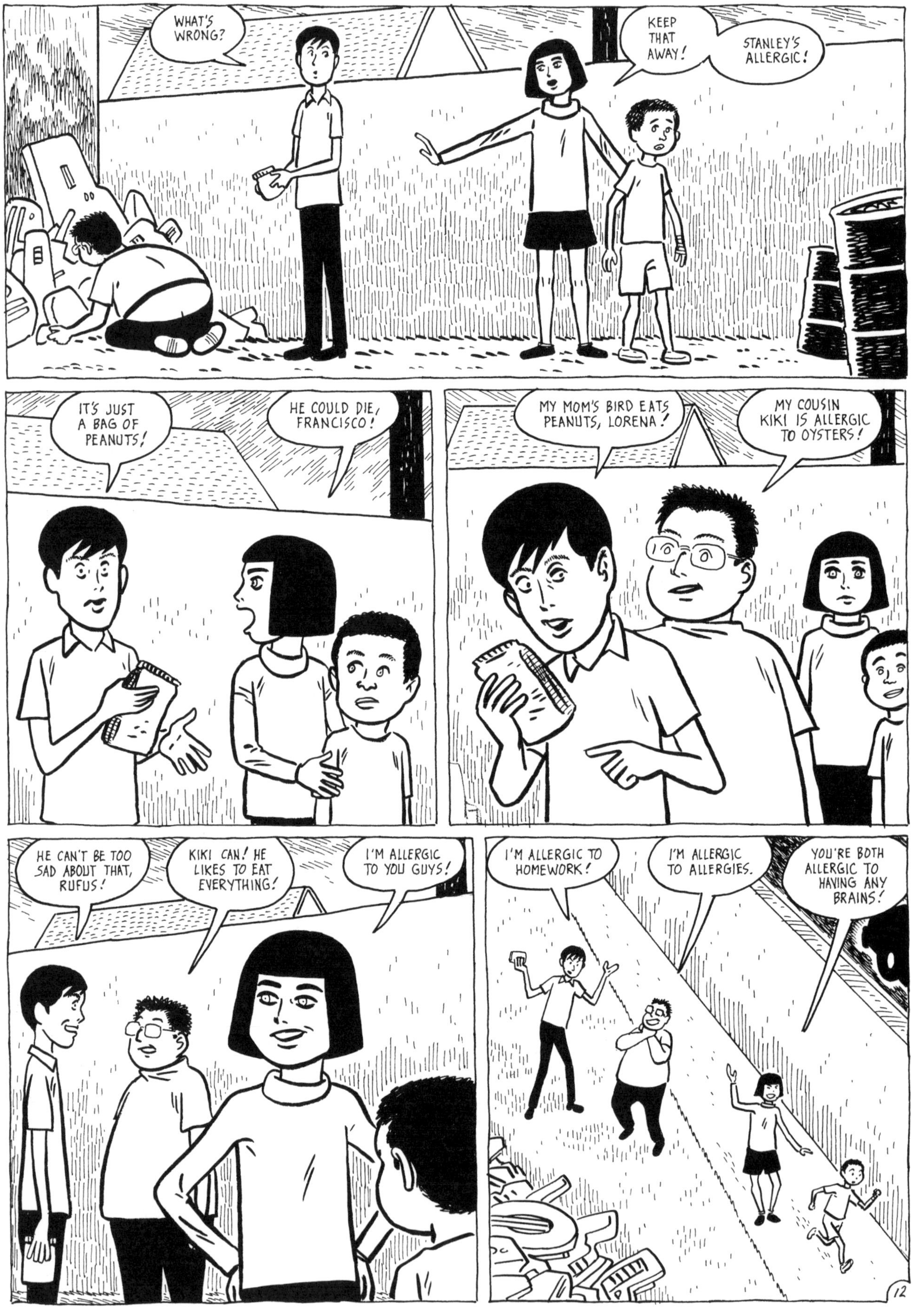
WHAT'S WRONG?
KEEP THAT AWAY!
STANLEY'S ALLERGIC!
IT'S JUST A BAG OF PEANUTS!
HE COULD DIE, FRANCISCO!
MY MOM'S BIRD EATS PEANUTS, LORENA!
MY COUSIN KIKI IS ALLERGIC TO OYSTERS!
HE CAN'T BE TOO SAD ABOUT THAT, RUFUS!
KIKI CAN! HE LIKES TO EAT EVERYTHING!
I'M ALLERGIC TO YOU GUYS!
I'M ALLERGIC TO HOMEWORK!
I'M ALLERGIC TO ALLERGIES.
YOU'RE BOTH ALLERGIC TO HAVING ANY BRAINS!

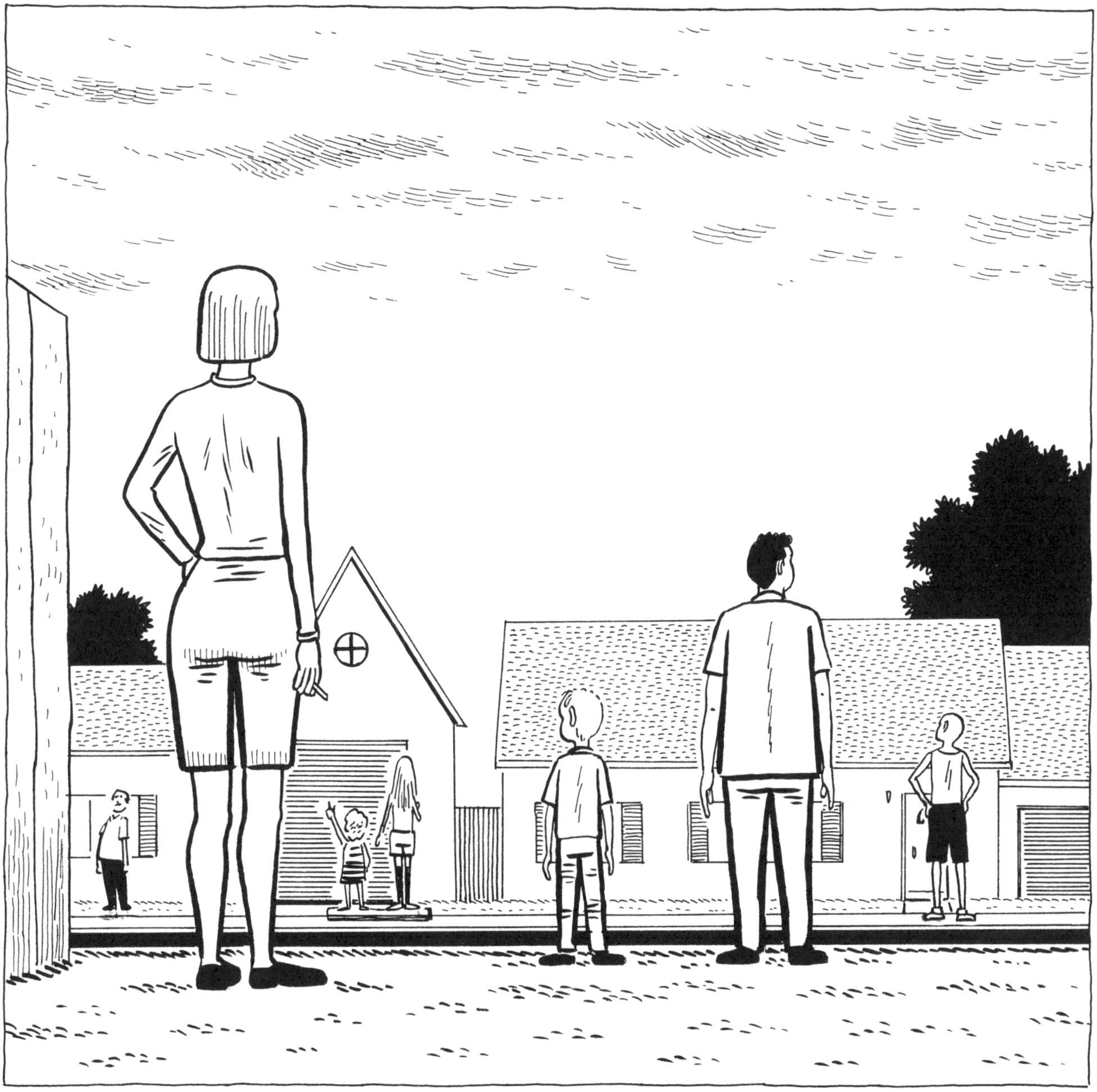

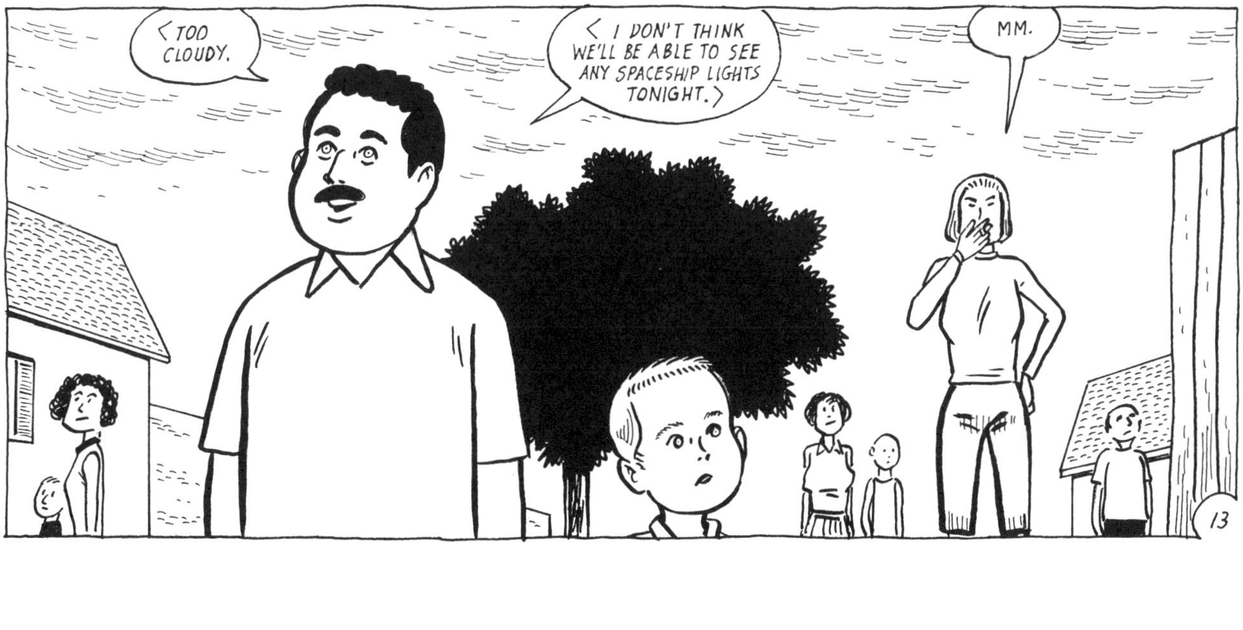

<TOO CLOUDY.
< I DON'T THINK WE'LL BE ABLE TO SEE ANY SPACESHIP LIGHTS TONIGHT.>
MM.

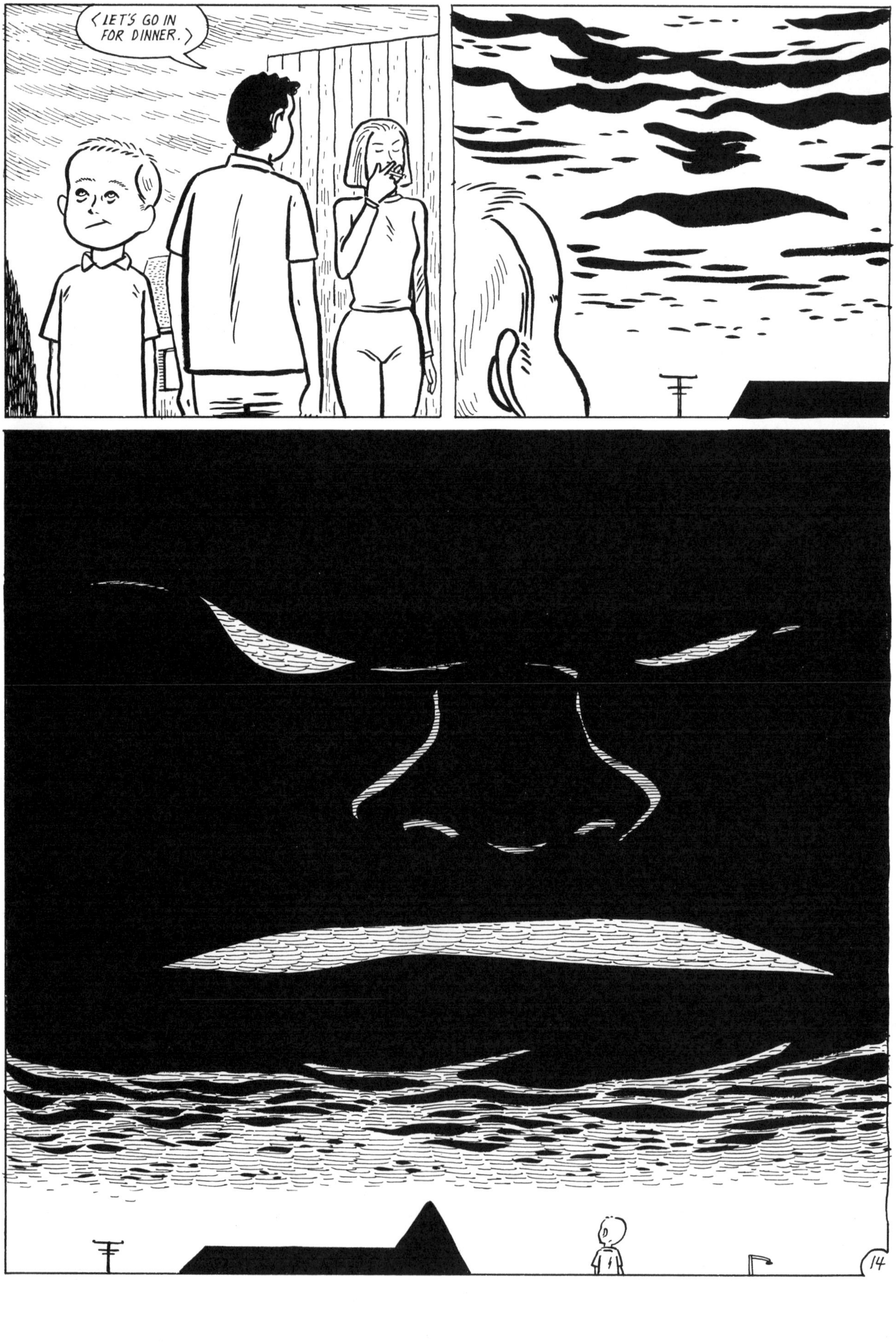
< LET'S GO IN FOR DINNER. >

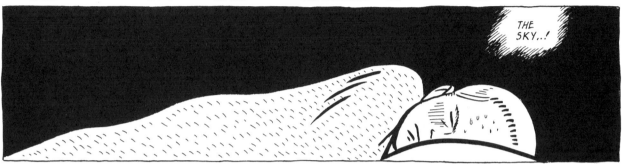

THE SKY..!

JUST A NIGHTMARE.

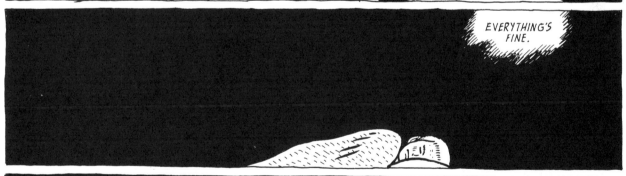

EVERYTHING'S FINE.

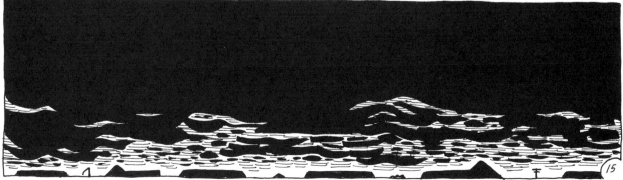

15

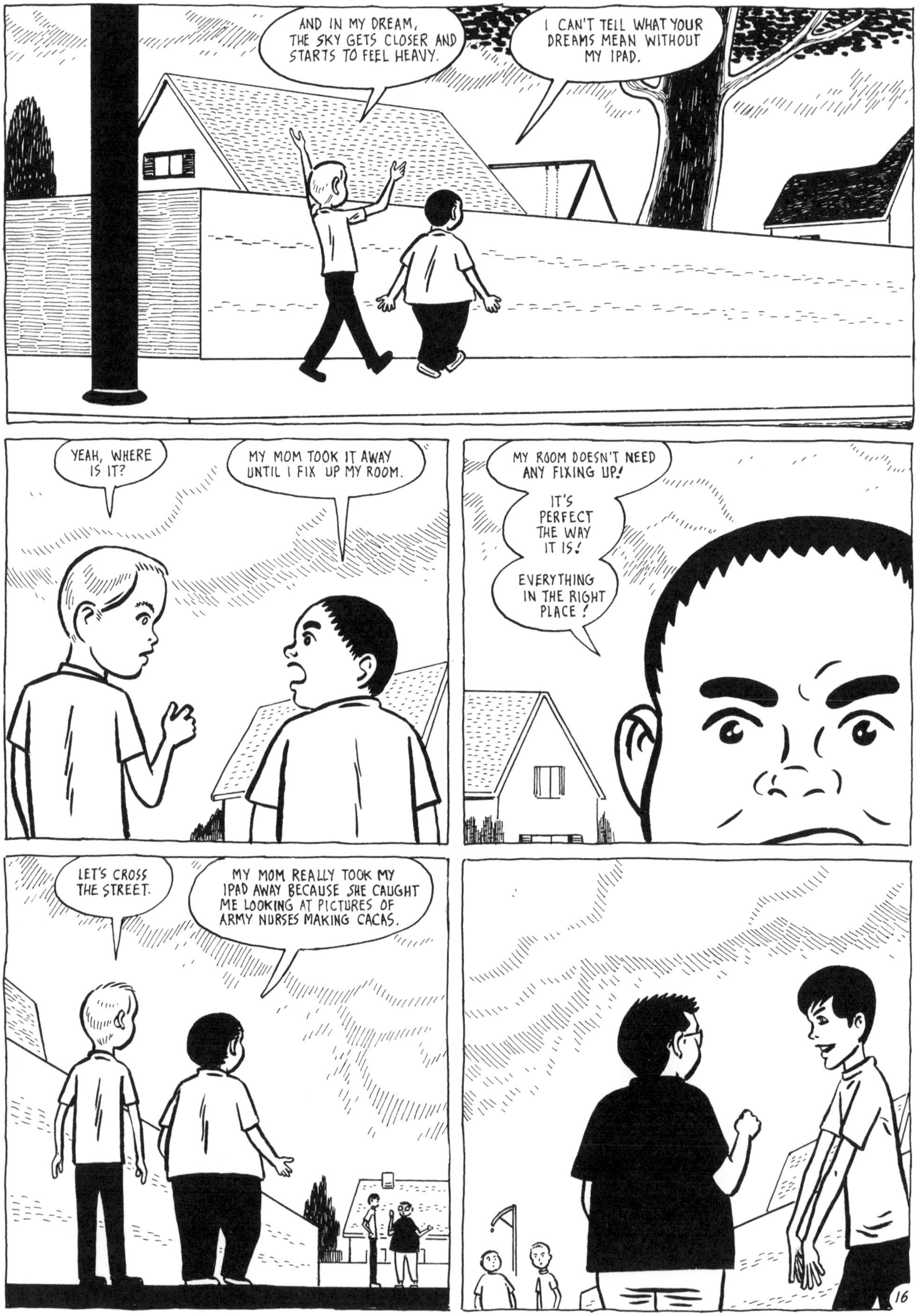
AND IN MY DREAM, THE SKY GETS CLOSER AND STARTS TO FEEL HEAVY.
I CAN'T TELL WHAT YOUR DREAMS MEAN WITHOUT MY IPAD.
YEAH, WHERE IS IT?
MY MOM TOOK IT AWAY UNTIL I FIX UP MY ROOM.
MY ROOM DOESN'T NEED ANY FIXING UP!
IT'S PERFECT THE WAY IT IS!
EVERYTHING IN THE RIGHT PLACE!
LET'S CROSS THE STREET.
MY MOM REALLY TOOK MY IPAD AWAY BECAUSE SHE CAUGHT ME LOOKING AT PICTURES OF ARMY NURSES MAKING CACAS.

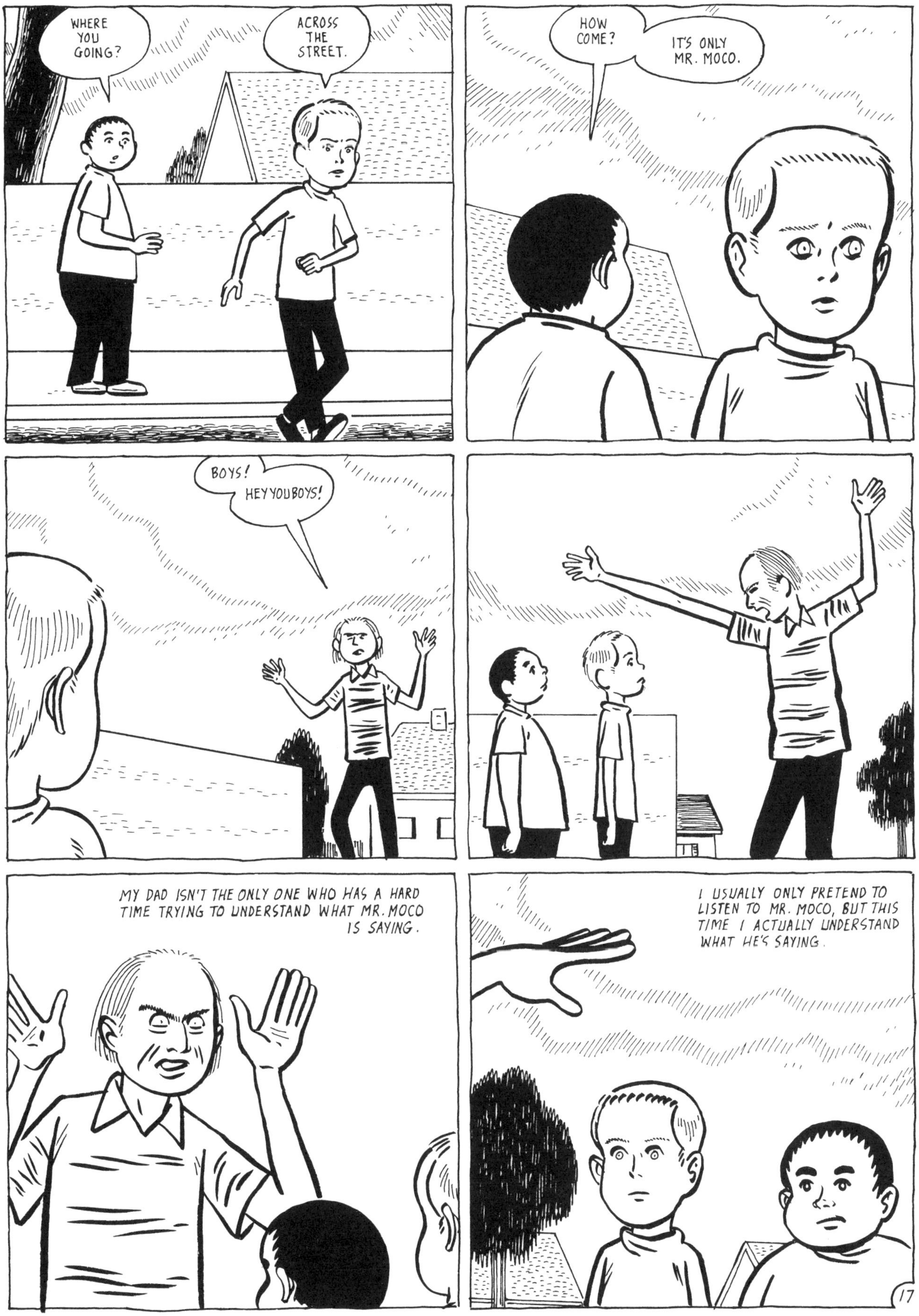

WHERE YOU GOING?
ACROSS THE STREET.
HOW COME?
IT'S ONLY MR. MOCO.
BOYS!
HEYYOUBOYS!
MY DAD ISN'T THE ONLY ONE WHO HAS A HARD TIME TRYING TO UNDERSTAND WHAT MR. MOCO IS SAYING.
I USUALLY ONLY PRETEND TO LISTEN TO MR. MOCO, BUT THIS TIME I ACTUALLY UNDERSTAND WHAT HE'S SAYING.

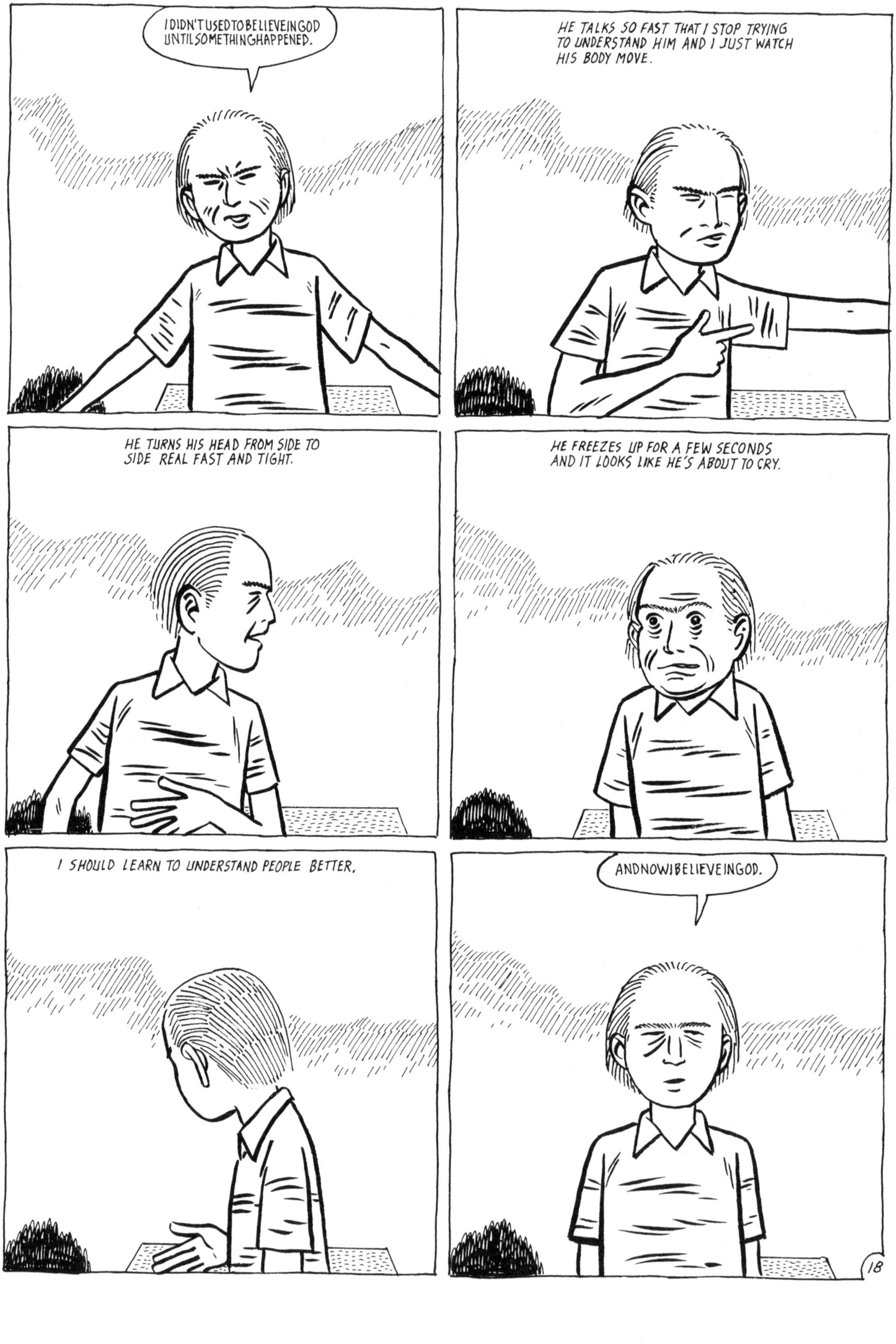
IDIDN'TUSEDTOBELIEVEINGOD UNTILSOMETHINGHAPPENED.
HE TALKS SO FAST THAT I STOP TRYING TO UNDERSTAND HIM AND I JUST WATCH HIS BODY MOVE.
HE TURNS HIS HEAD FROM SIDE TO SIDE REAL FAST AND TIGHT.
HE FREEZES UP FOR A FEW SECONDS AND IT LOOKS LIKE HE'S ABOUT TO CRY.
I SHOULD LEARN TO UNDERSTAND PEOPLE BETTER.
ANDNOWIBELIEVEINGOD.

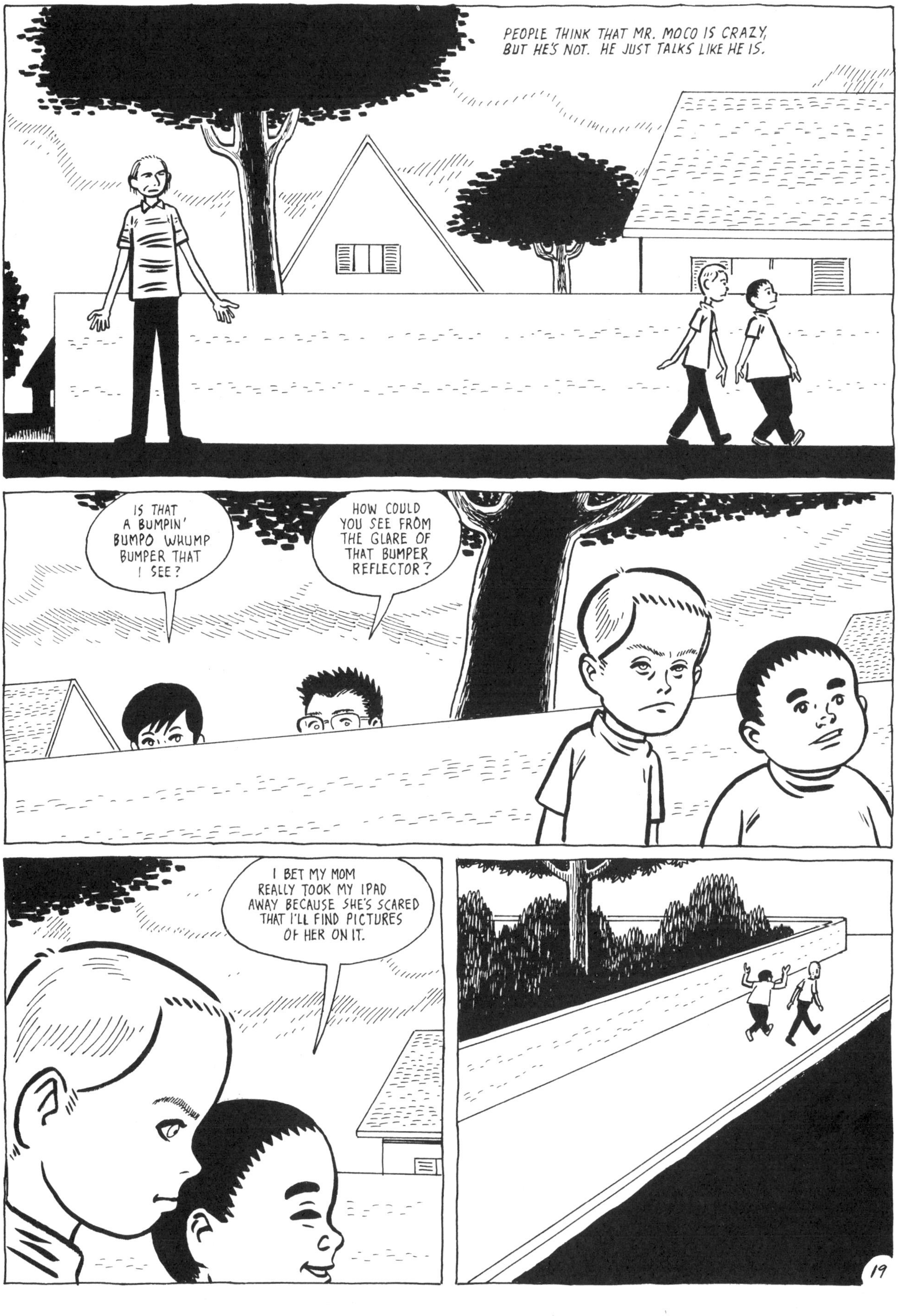
PEOPLE THINK THAT MR. MOCO IS CRAZY, BUT HE'S NOT. HE JUST TALKS LIKE HE IS.
IS THAT A BUMPIN' BUMPO WHUMP BUMPER THAT I SEE?
HOW COULD YOU SEE FROM THE GLARE OF THAT BUMPER REFLECTOR?
I BET MY MOM REALLY TOOK MY IPAD AWAY BECAUSE SHE'S SCARED THAT I'LL FIND PICTURES OF HER ON IT.

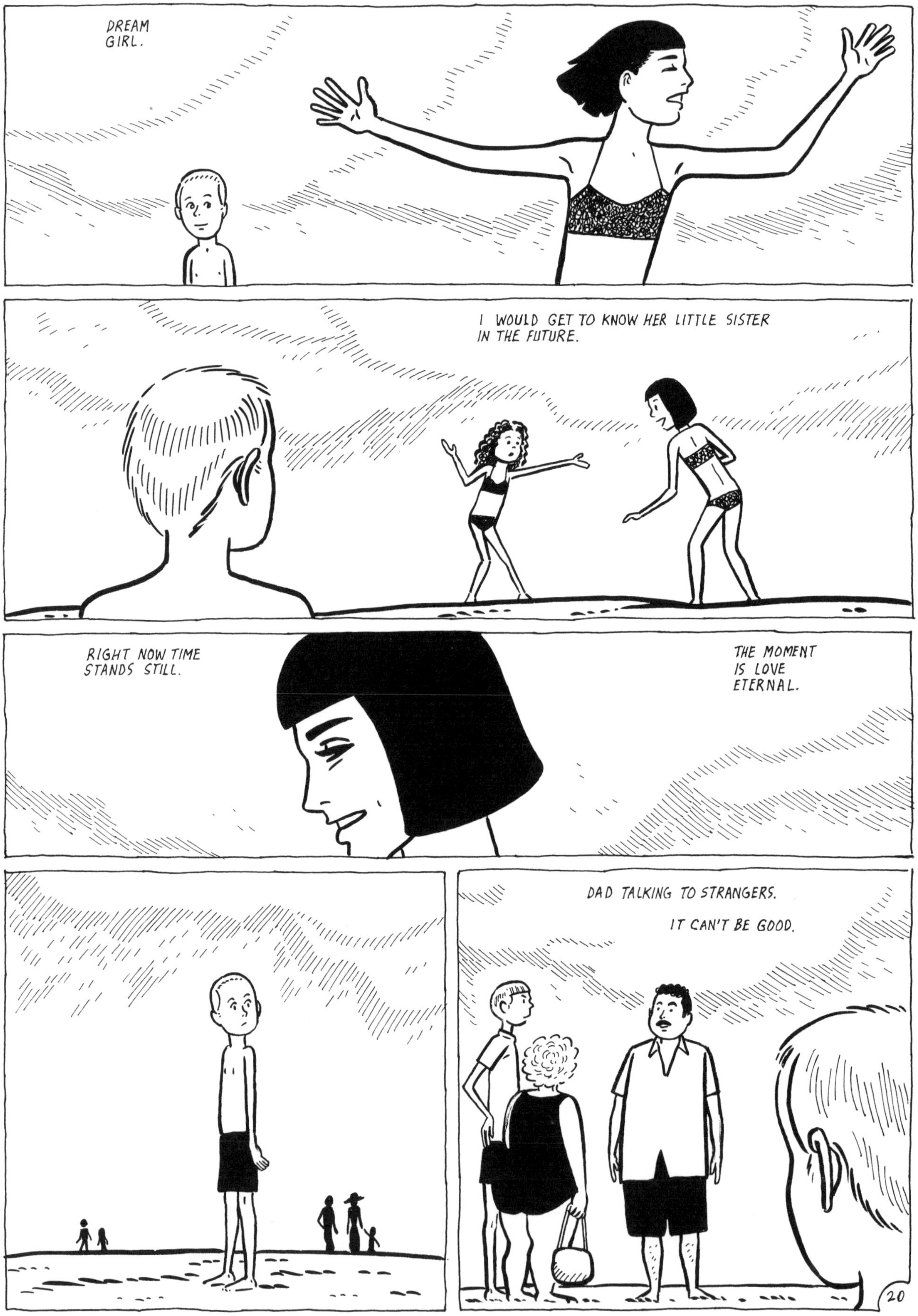
DREAM GIRL.
I WOULD GET TO KNOW HER LITTLE SISTER IN THE FUTURE.
RIGHT NOW TIME STANDS STILL.
THE MOMENT IS LOVE ETERNAL.
DAD TALKING TO STRANGERS.
IT CAN'T BE GOOD.

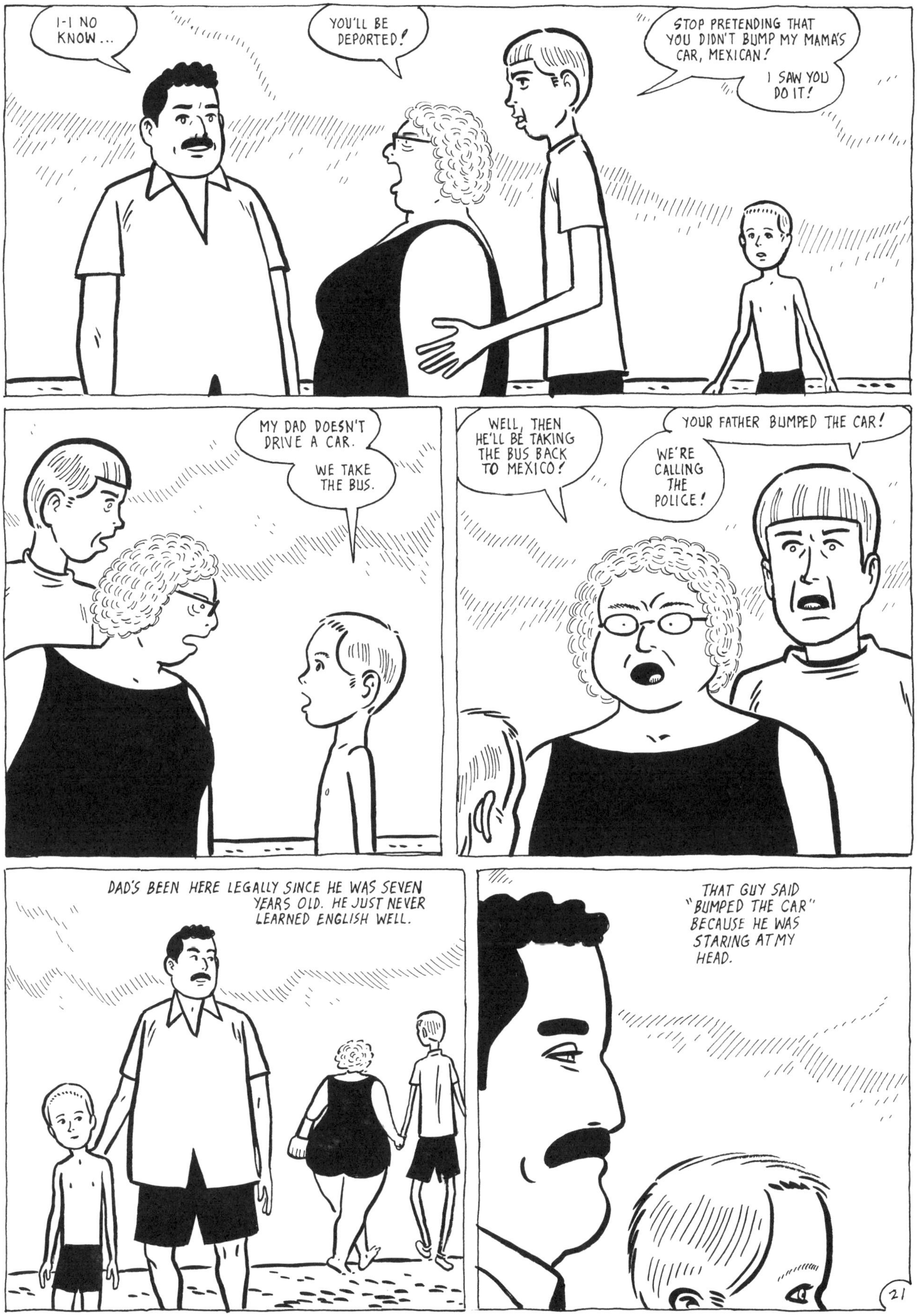
I-I NO KNOW...
YOU'LL BE DEPORTED!
STOP PRETENDING THAT YOU DIDN'T BUMP MY MAMA'S CAR, MEXICAN!
I SAW YOU DO IT!
MY DAD DOESN'T DRIVE A CAR.
WE TAKE THE BUS.
WELL, THEN HE'LL BE TAKING THE BUS BACK TO MEXICO!
YOUR FATHER BUMPED THE CAR!
WE'RE CALLING THE POLICE!
DAD'S BEEN HERE LEGALLY SINCE HE WAS SEVEN YEARS OLD. HE JUST NEVER LEARNED ENGLISH WELL.
THAT GUY SAID "BUMPED THE CAR" BECAUSE HE WAS STARING AT MY HEAD.

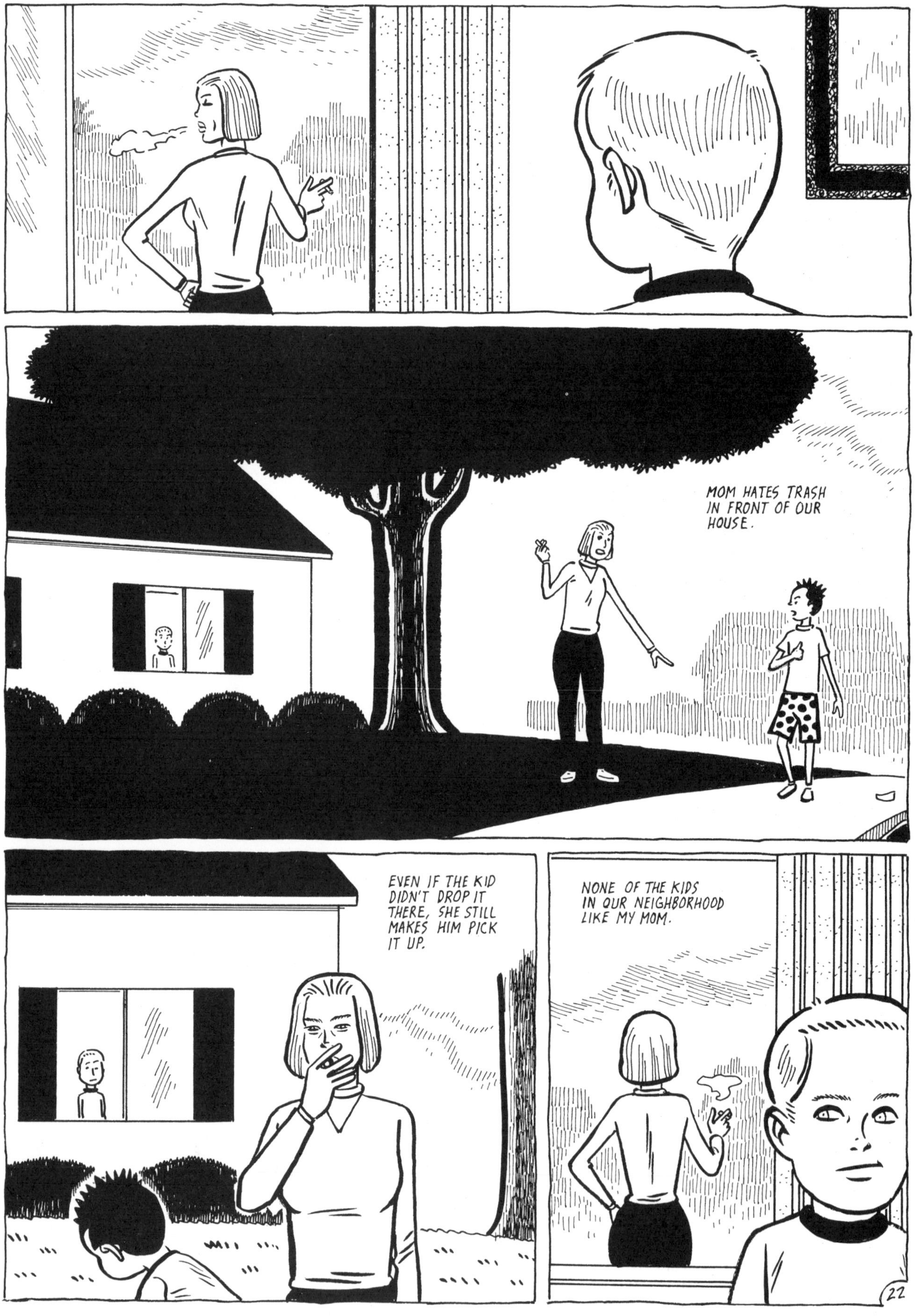
MOM HATES TRASH IN FRONT OF OUR HOUSE.
EVEN IF THE KID DIDN'T DROP IT THERE, SHE STILL MAKES HIM PICK IT UP.
NONE OF THE KIDS IN OUR NEIGHBORHOOD LIKE MY MOM.

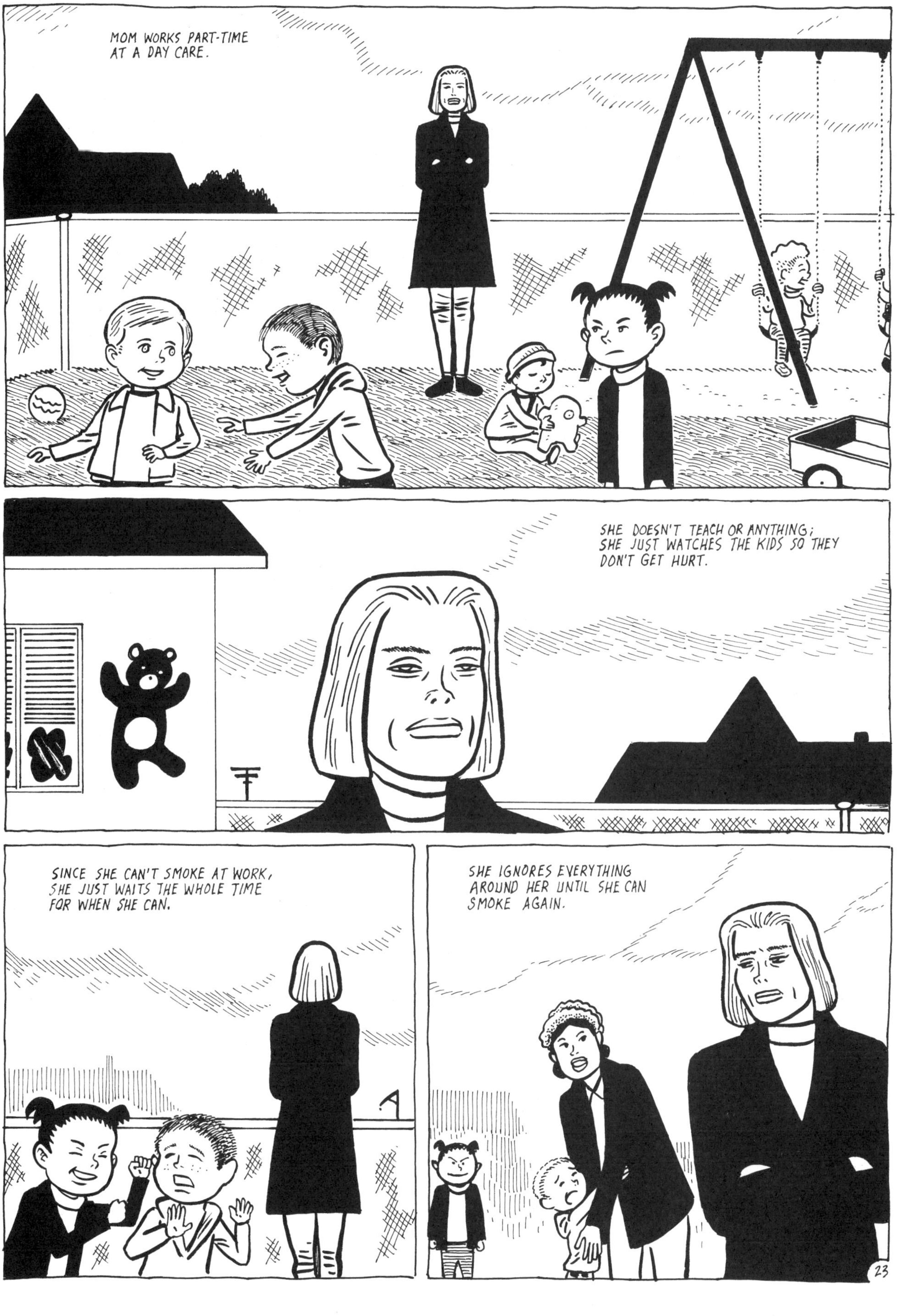
MOM WORKS PART-TIME AT A DAY CARE.
SHE DOESN'T TEACH OR ANYTHING; SHE JUST WATCHES THE KIDS SO THEY DON'T GET HURT.
SINCE SHE CAN'T SMOKE AT WORK, SHE JUST WAITS THE WHOLE TIME FOR WHEN SHE CAN.
SHE IGNORES EVERYTHING AROUND HER UNTIL SHE CAN SMOKE AGAIN.
23

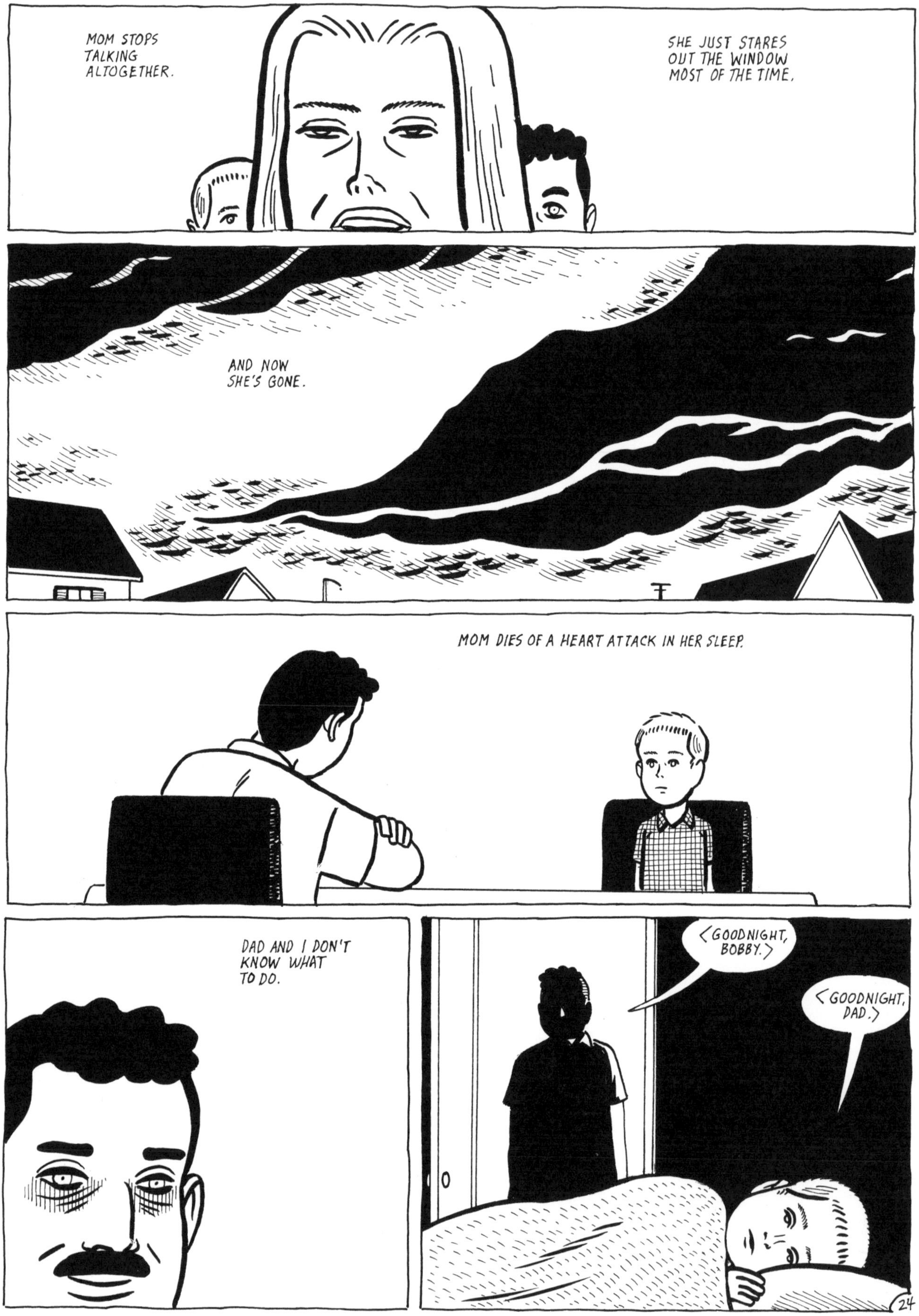
MOM STOPS TALKING ALTOGETHER.
SHE JUST STARES OUT THE WINDOW MOST OF THE TIME.
AND NOW SHE'S GONE.
MOM DIES OF A HEART ATTACK IN HER SLEEP.
DAD AND I DON'T KNOW WHAT TO DO.
<GOODNIGHT, BOBBY.>
<GOODNIGHT, DAD.>

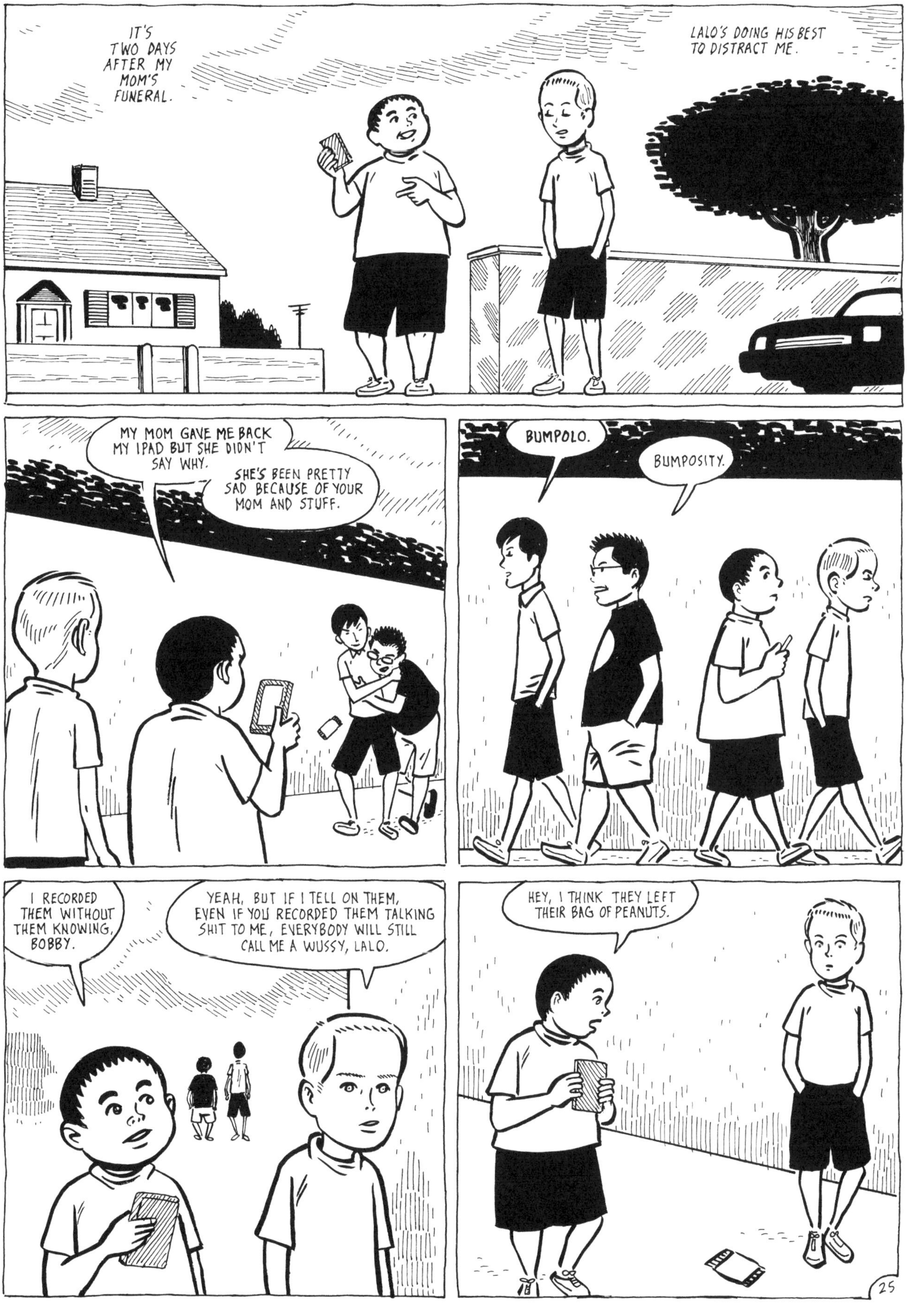

IT'S TWO DAYS AFTER MY MOM'S FUNERAL.
LALO'S DOING HIS BEST TO DISTRACT ME.
MY MOM GAVE ME BACK MY IPAD BUT SHE DIDN'T SAY WHY.
SHE'S BEEN PRETTY SAD BECAUSE OF YOUR MOM AND STUFF.
BUMPOLO.
BUMPOSITY.
I RECORDED THEM WITHOUT THEM KNOWING, BOBBY.
YEAH, BUT IF I TELL ON THEM, EVEN IF YOU RECORDED THEM TALKING SHIT TO ME, EVERYBODY WILL STILL CALL ME A WUSSY, LALO.
HEY, I THINK THEY LEFT THEIR BAG OF PEANUTS.

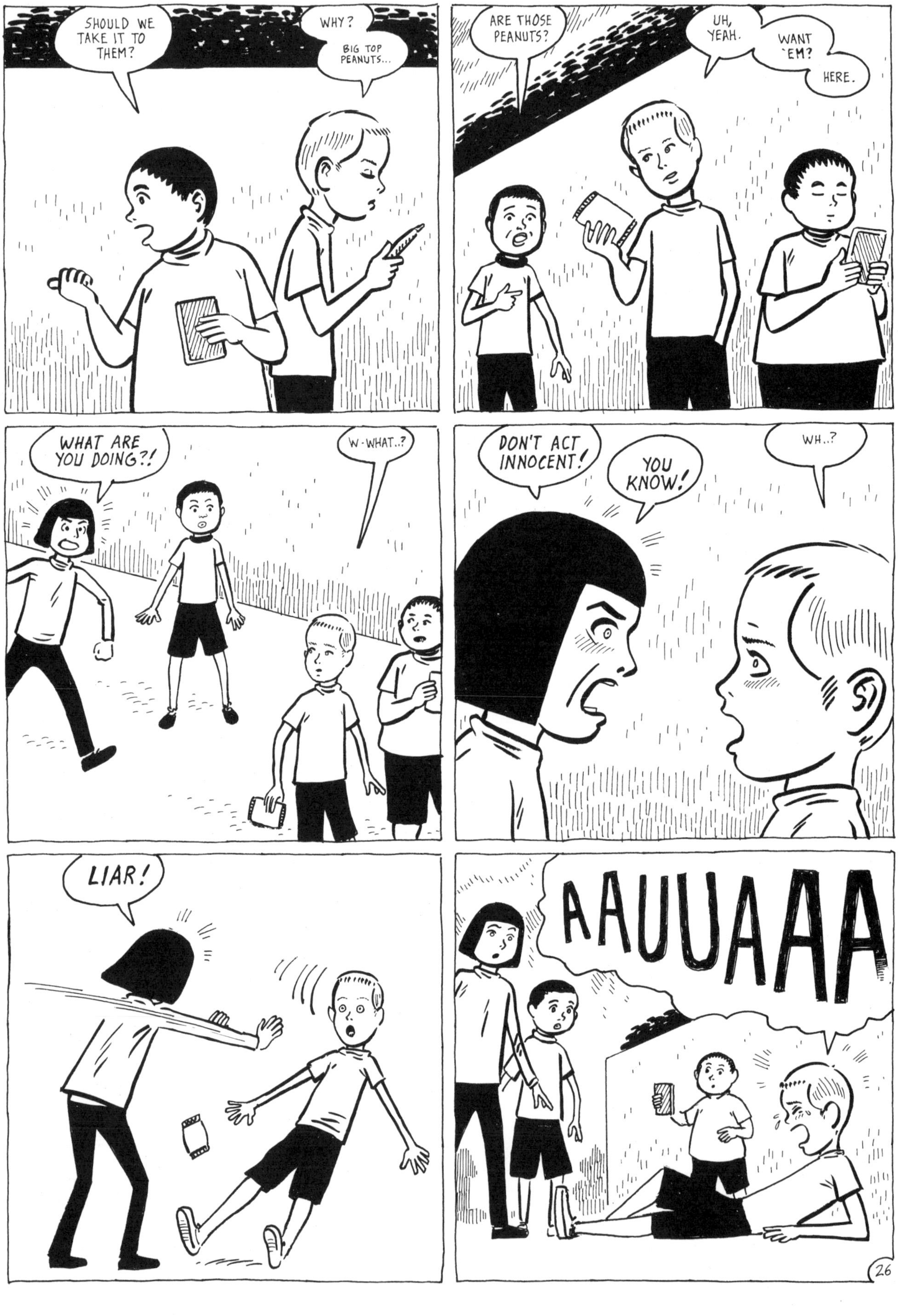
SHOULD WE TAKE IT TO THEM?
WHY?
BIG TOP PEANUTS...
ARE THOSE PEANUTS?
UH, YEAH.
WANT `EM?
HERE.
WHAT ARE YOU DOING?!
W-WHAT..?
DON'T ACT INNOCENT!
YOU KNOW!
WH..?
LIAR!
AAUUAAA

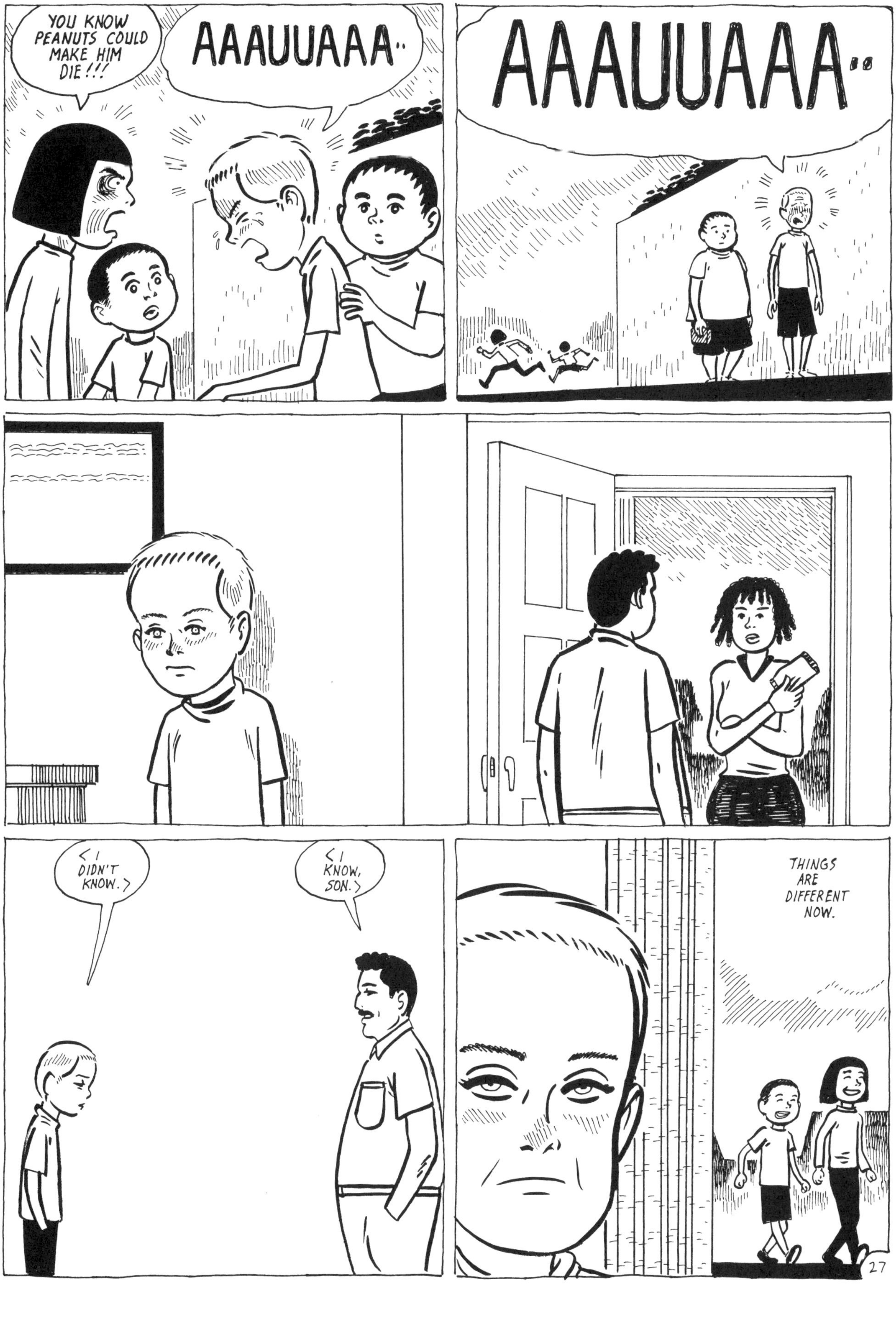
YOU KNOW PEANUTS COULD MAKE HIM DIE!!!
AAAUUAAA..
AAAUUAAA..
<I DIDN'T KNOW.>
<I KNOW, SON.>
THINGS ARE DIFFERENT NOW.

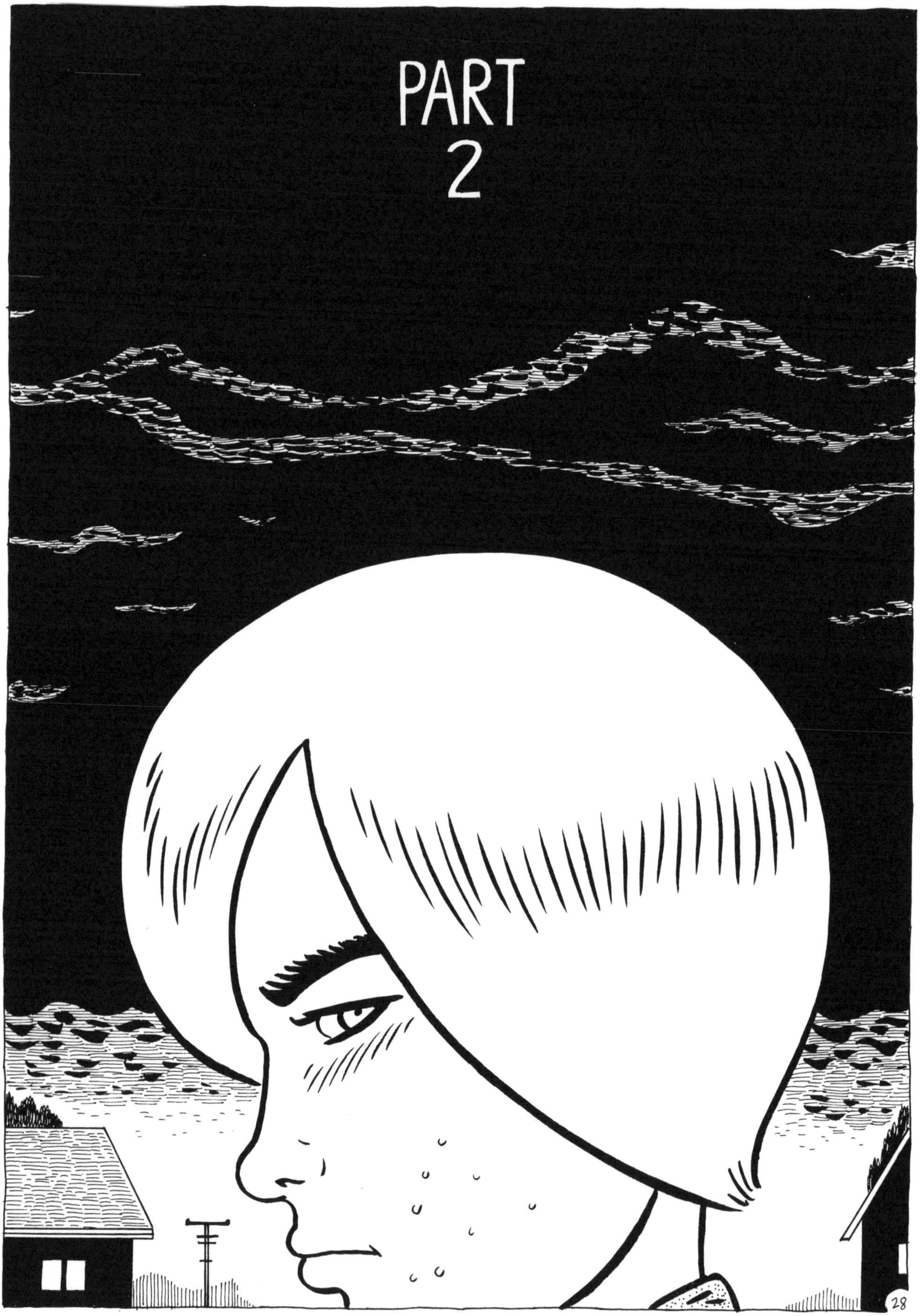
PART
2

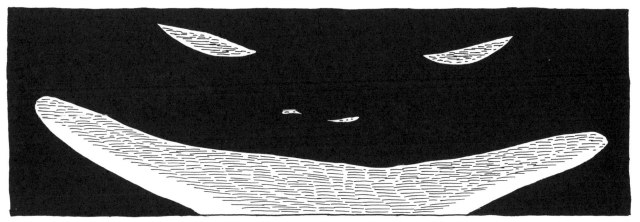

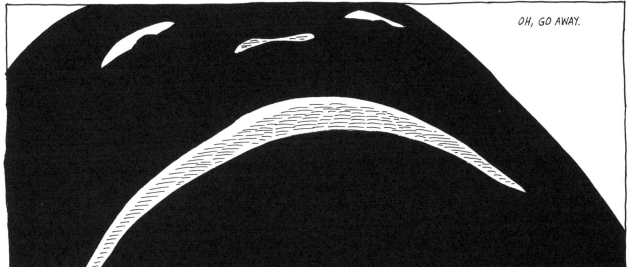

OH, GO AWAY.

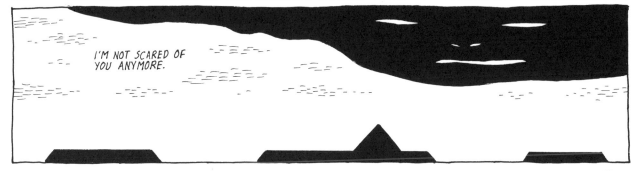

I'M NOT SCARED OF
YOU ANYMORE.

I'VE GOT A LIFE TO LIVE.

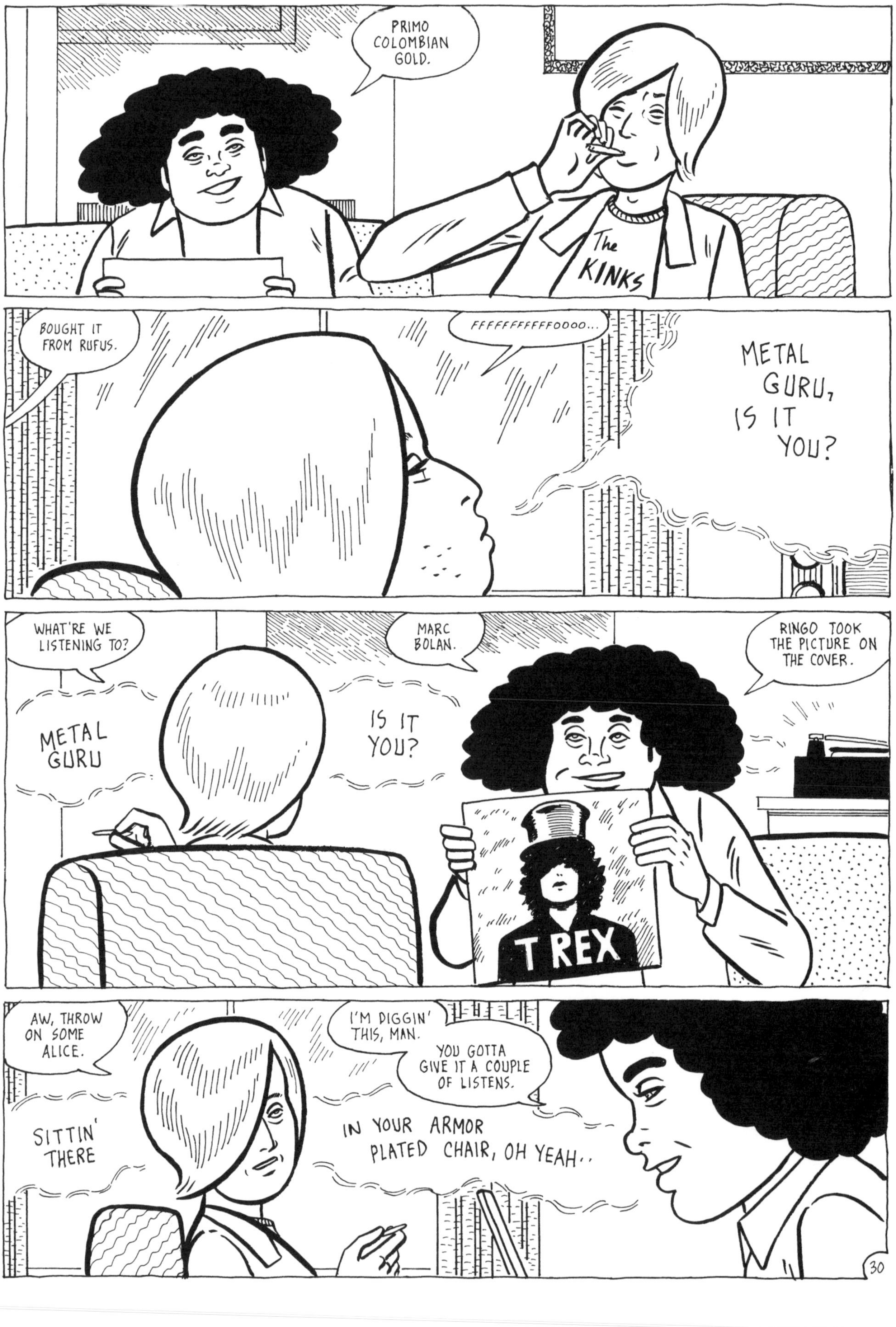
PRIMO COLOMBIAN GOLD.
The KINKS
BOUGHT IT FROM RUFUS.
FFFFFFFFFFFOOOO...
METAL GURU, IS IT YOU?
WHAT'RE WE LISTENING TO?
MARC BOLAN.
RINGO TOOK THE PICTURE ON THE COVER.
METAL GURU
IS IT YOU?
T REX
AW, THROW ON SOME ALICE.
I'M DIGGIN' THIS, MAN.
YOU GOTTA GIVE IT A COUPLE OF LISTENS.
SITTIN' THERE
IN YOUR ARMOR PLATED CHAIR, OH YEAH..

IN THE EARLY 1970S I'M REALLY INTO ALICE COOPER.

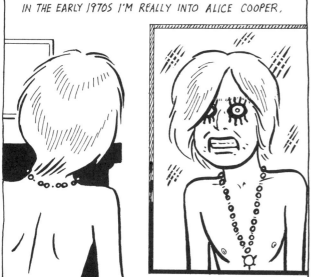

I CAN HARDLY CONTAIN MY ENTHUSIASM FOR JUST HOW INSPIRING HE IS TO ME.

< TURN DOWN THE MUSIC, BOBBY. >

< OK, DAD. >

DAD SEEMS TO BE PRETTY COOL WITH WHATEVER MUSIC I'M INTO.

I'M AN OUTSIDER AND I EXPRESS IT EVERY CHANCE I GET.

I SING... NO, SCREAM OUT ALICE COOPER'S 'UNDER MY WHEELS' FROM MY WINDOW AND THE NEIGHBORS CALL THE COPS.

31

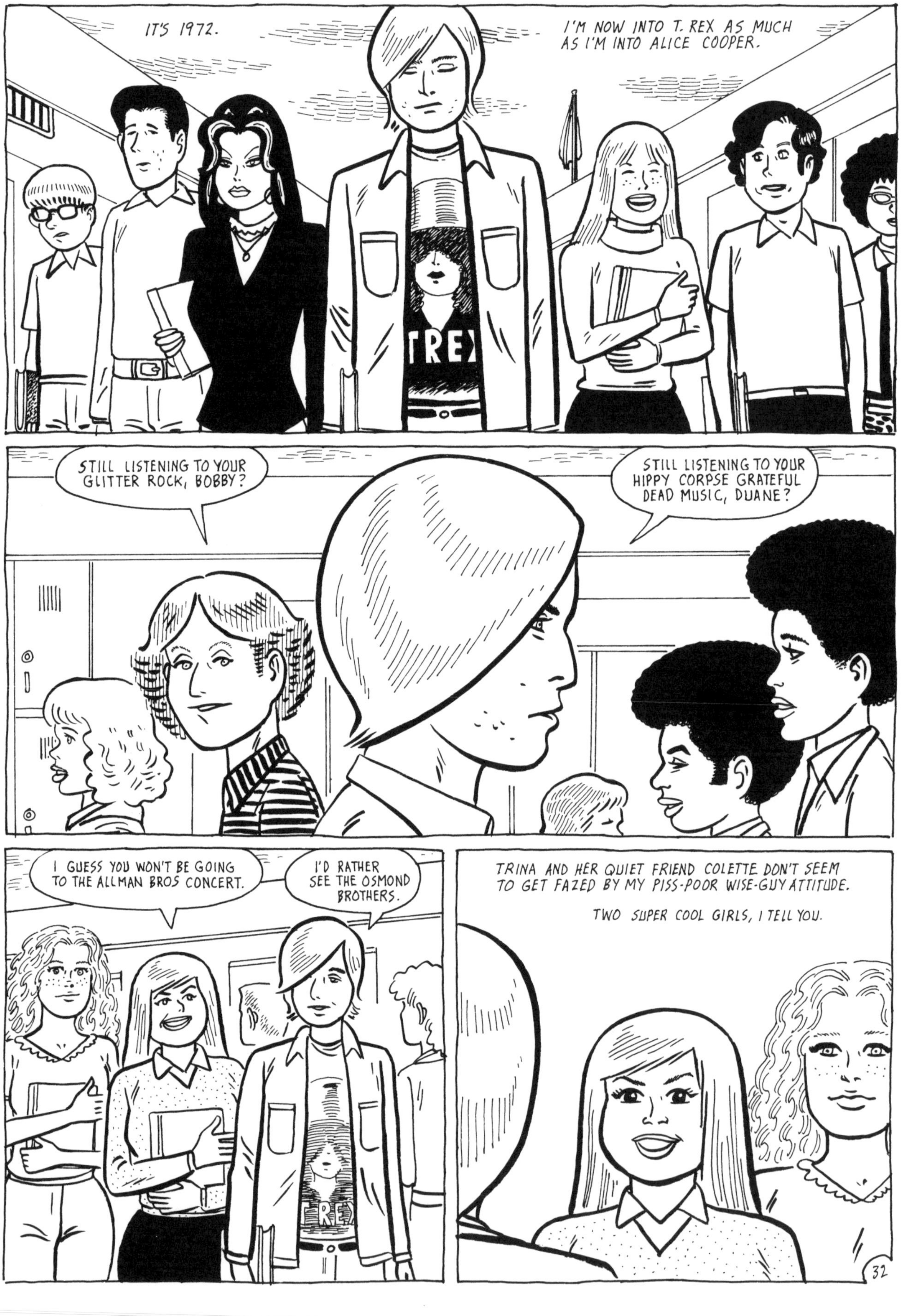
IT'S 1972.
I'M NOW INTO T. REX AS MUCH AS I'M INTO ALICE COOPER.
STILL LISTENING TO YOUR GLITTER ROCK, BOBBY?
STILL LISTENING TO YOUR HIPPY CORPSE GRATEFUL DEAD MUSIC, DUANE?
I GUESS YOU WON'T BE GOING TO THE ALLMAN BROS CONCERT.
I'D RATHER SEE THE OSMOND BROTHERS.
TRINA AND HER QUIET FRIEND COLETTE DON'T SEEM TO GET FAZED BY MY PISS-POOR WISE-GUY ATTITUDE.
TWO SUPER COOL GIRLS, I TELL YOU.

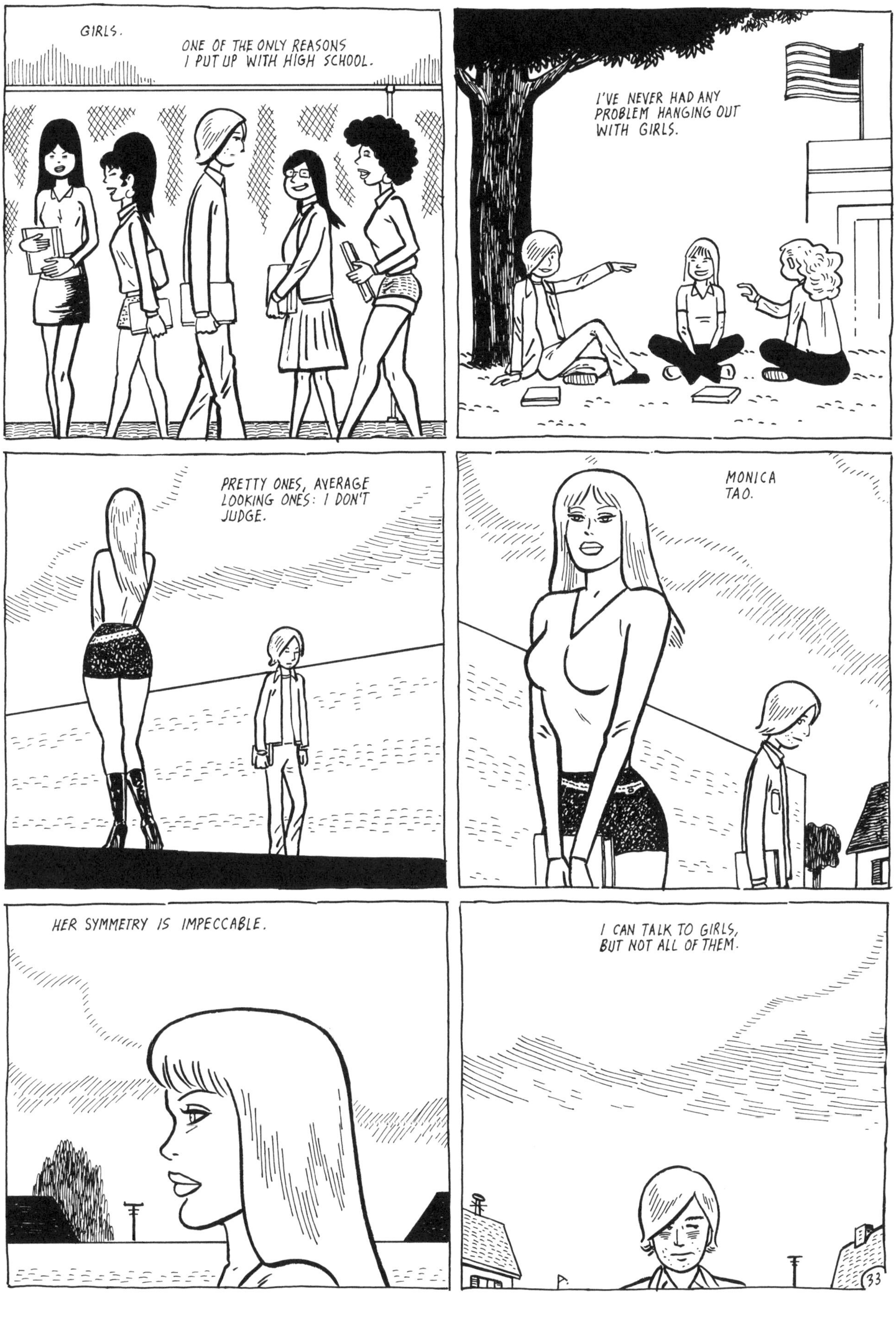
GIRLS.
ONE OF THE ONLY REASONS I PUT UP WITH HIGH SCHOOL.
I'VE NEVER HAD ANY PROBLEM HANGING OUT WITH GIRLS.
PRETTY ONES, AVERAGE LOOKING ONES: I DON'T JUDGE.
MONICA TAO.
HER SYMMETRY IS IMPECCABLE.
I CAN TALK TO GIRLS, BUT NOT ALL OF THEM.

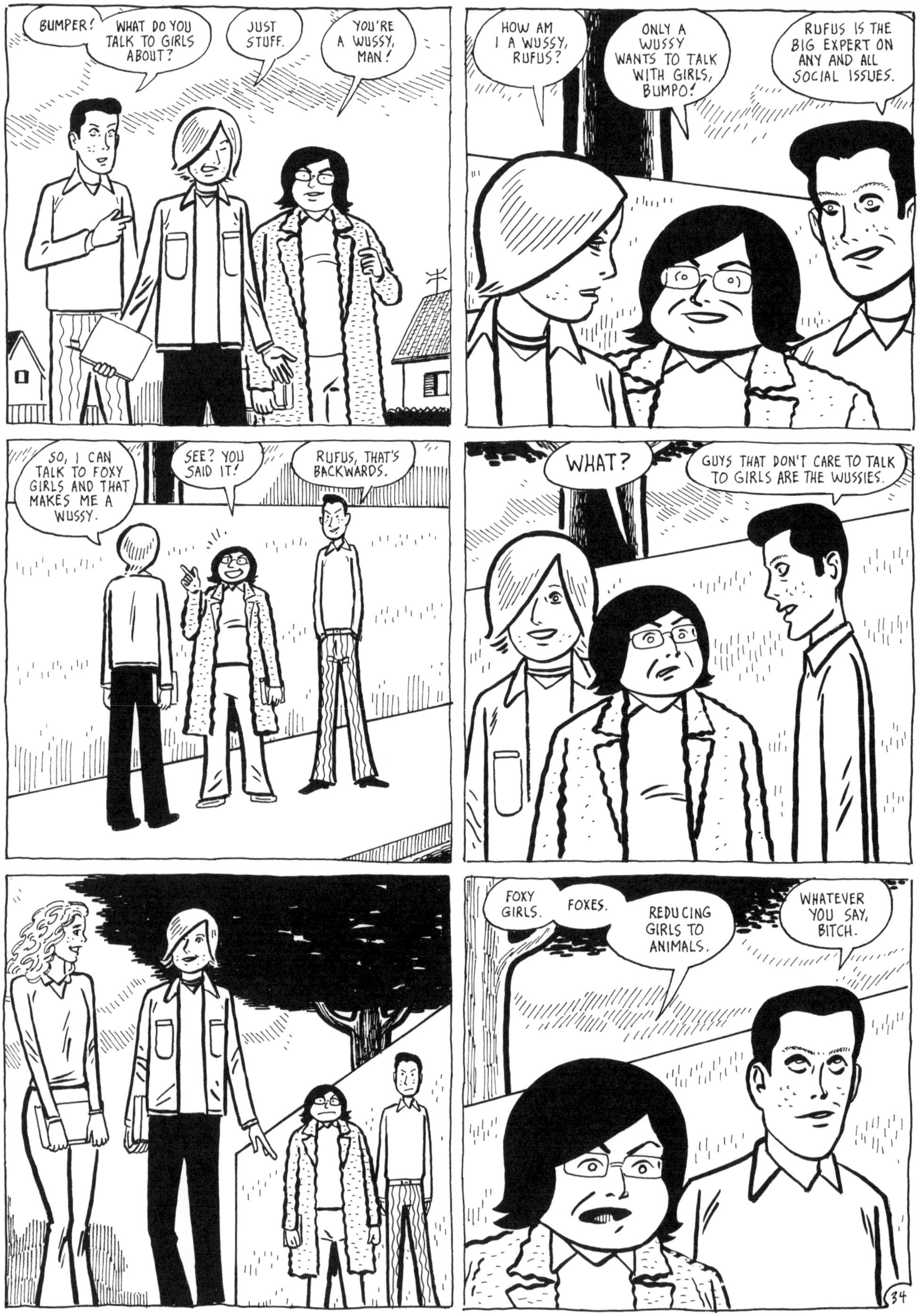
BUMPER!
WHAT DO YOU TALK TO GIRLS ABOUT?
JUST STUFF.
YOU'RE A WUSSY, MAN!
HOW AM I A WUSSY, RUFUS?
ONLY A WUSSY WANTS TO TALK WITH GIRLS, BUMPO!
RUFUS IS THE BIG EXPERT ON ANY AND ALL SOCIAL ISSUES.
SO, I CAN TALK TO FOXY GIRLS AND THAT MAKES ME A WUSSY.
SEE? YOU SAID IT!
RUFUS, THAT'S BACKWARDS.
WHAT?
GUYS THAT DON'T CARE TO TALK TO GIRLS ARE THE WUSSIES.
FOXY GIRLS.
FOXES.
REDUCING GIRLS TO ANIMALS.
WHATEVER YOU SAY, BITCH.
34

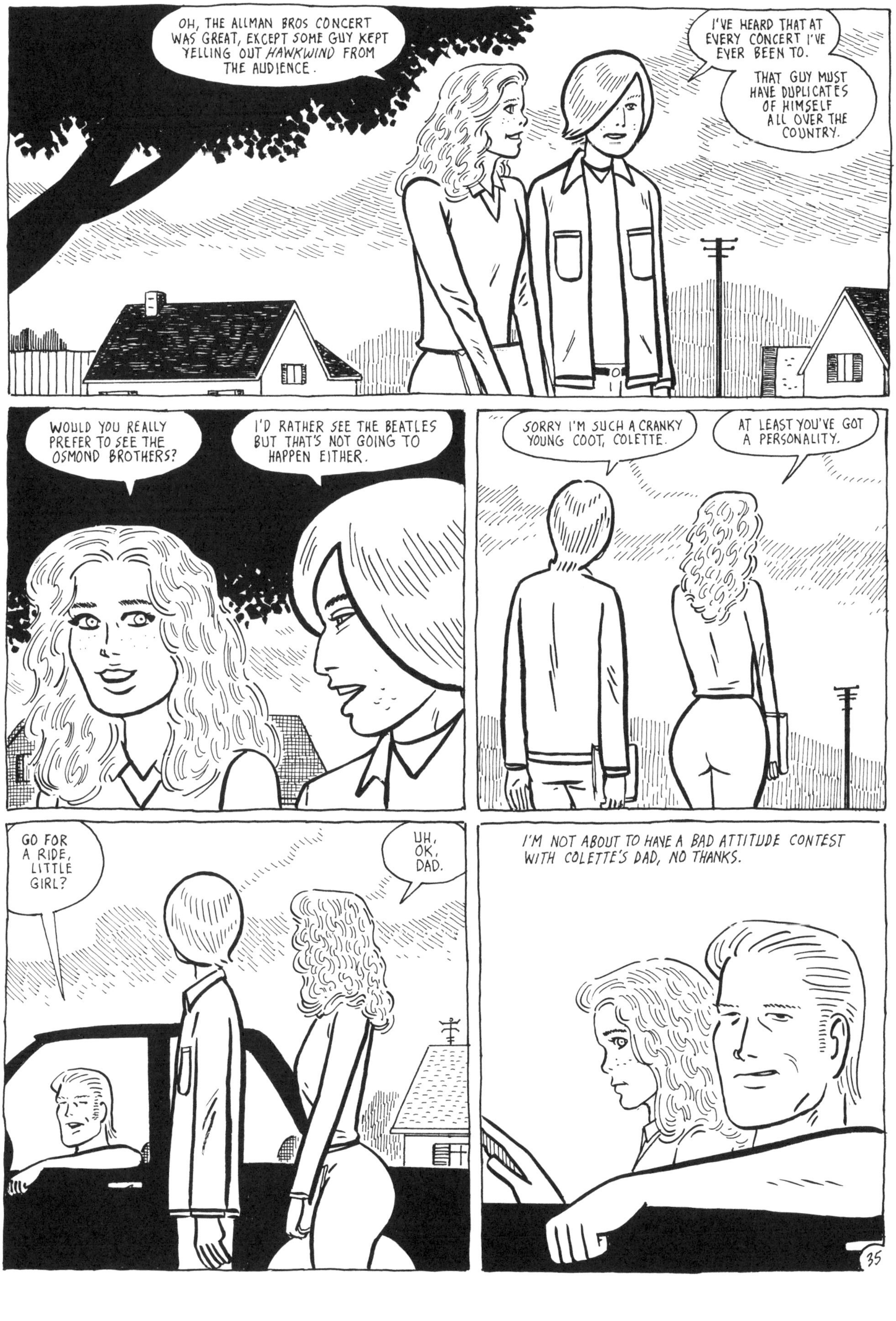
OH, THE ALLMAN BROS CONCERT WAS GREAT, EXCEPT SOME GUY KEPT YELLING OUT HAWKWIND FROM THE AUDIENCE.
I'VE HEARD THAT AT EVERY CONCERT I'VE EVER BEEN TO.
THAT GUY MUST HAVE DUPLICATES OF HIMSELF ALL OVER THE COUNTRY.
WOULD YOU REALLY PREFER TO SEE THE OSMOND BROTHERS?
I'D RATHER SEE THE BEATLES BUT THAT'S NOT GOING TO HAPPEN EITHER.
SORRY I'M SUCH A CRANKY YOUNG COOT, COLETTE.
AT LEAST YOU'VE GOT A PERSONALITY.
GO FOR A RIDE, LITTLE GIRL?
UH, OK, DAD.
I'M NOT ABOUT TO HAVE A BAD ATTITUDE CONTEST WITH COLETTE'S DAD, NO THANKS.

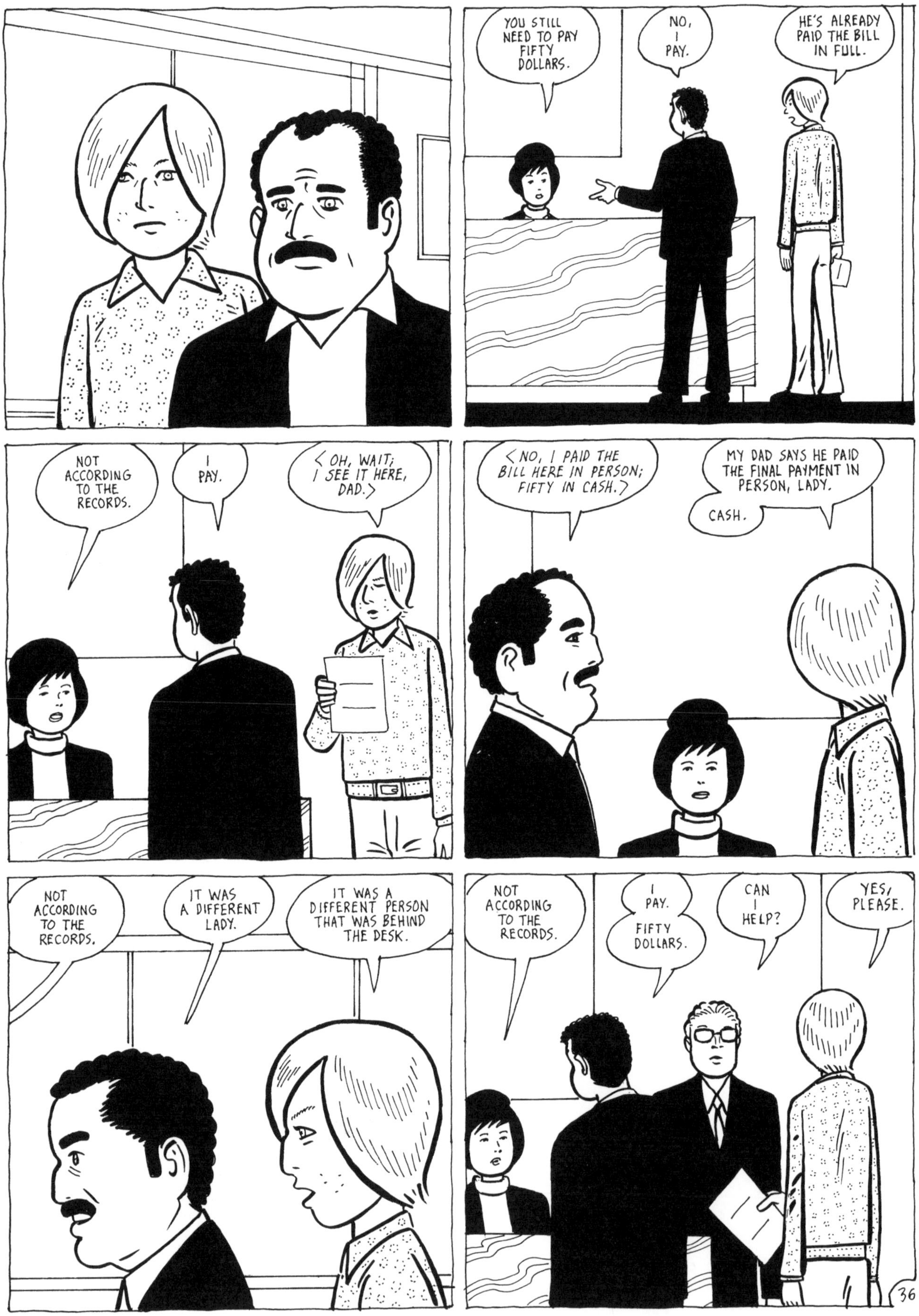
YOU STILL NEED TO PAY FIFTY DOLLARS.
NO, I PAY.
HE'S ALREADY PAID THE BILL IN FULL.
NOT ACCORDING TO THE RECORDS.
I PAY.
< OH, WAIT; I SEE IT HERE, DAD.>
< NO, I PAID THE BILL HERE IN PERSON; FIFTY IN CASH.>
MY DAD SAYS HE PAID THE FINAL PAYMENT IN PERSON, LADY.
CASH.
NOT ACCORDING TO THE RECORDS.
IT WAS A DIFFERENT LADY.
IT WAS A DIFFERENT PERSON THAT WAS BEHIND THE DESK.
NOT ACCORDING TO THE RECORDS.
I PAY.
FIFTY DOLLARS.
CAN I HELP?
YES, PLEASE.

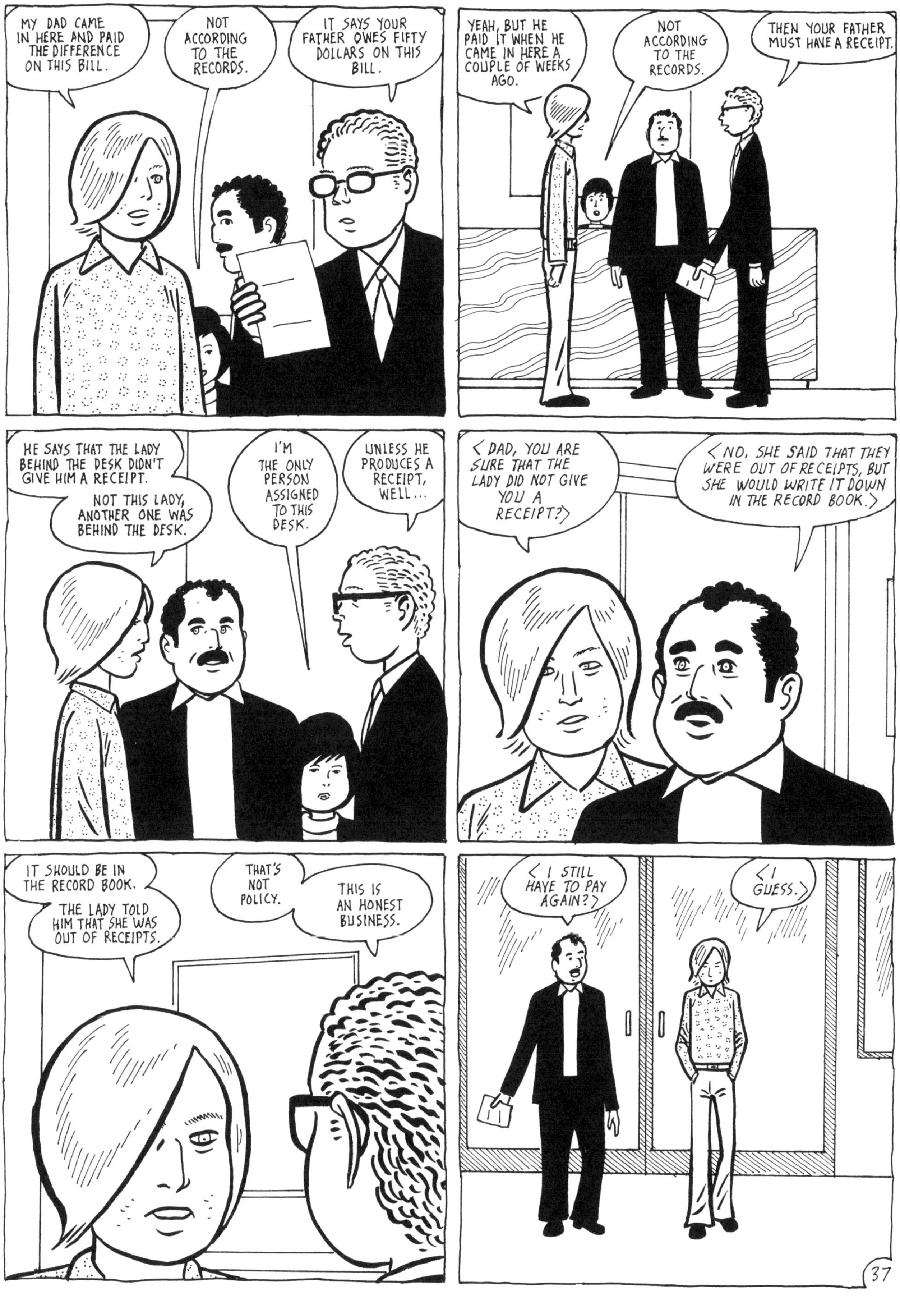
MY DAD CAME IN HERE AND PAID THE DIFFERENCE ON THIS BILL.
NOT ACCORDING TO THE RECORDS.
IT SAYS YOUR FATHER OWES FIFTY DOLLARS ON THIS BILL.
YEAH, BUT HE PAID IT WHEN HE CAME IN HERE A COUPLE OF WEEKS AGO.
NOT ACCORDING TO THE RECORDS.
THEN YOUR FATHER MUST HAVE A RECEIPT.
HE SAYS THAT THE LADY BEHIND THE DESK DIDN'T GIVE HIM A RECEIPT.
NOT THIS LADY, ANOTHER ONE WAS BEHIND THE DESK.
I'M THE ONLY PERSON ASSIGNED TO THIS DESK.
UNLESS HE PRODUCES A RECEIPT, WELL...
<DAD, YOU ARE SURE THAT THE LADY DID NOT GIVE YOU A RECEIPT?>
<NO, SHE SAID THAT THEY WERE OUT OF RECEIPTS, BUT SHE WOULD WRITE IT DOWN IN THE RECORD BOOK.>
IT SHOULD BE IN THE RECORD BOOK.
THE LADY TOLD HIM THAT SHE WAS OUT OF RECEIPTS.
THAT'S NOT POLICY.
THIS IS AN HONEST BUSINESS.
<I STILL HAVE TO PAY AGAIN?>
<I GUESS.>

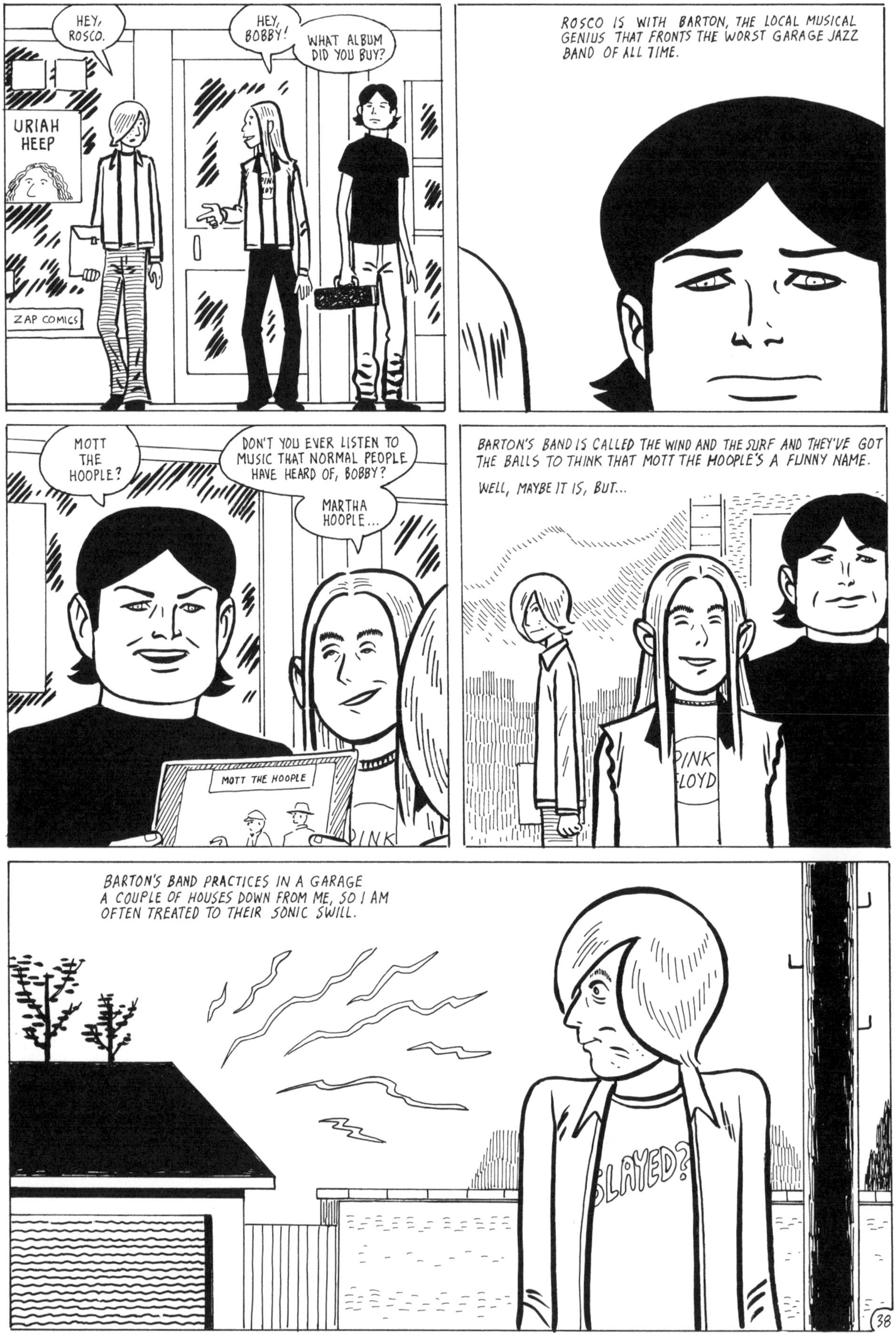
HEY, ROSCO.
HEY, BOBBY!
WHAT ALBUM DID YOU BUY?
URIAH HEEP
ZAP COMICS
ROSCO IS WITH BARTON, THE LOCAL MUSICAL GENIUS THAT FRONTS THE WORST GARAGE JAZZ BAND OF ALL TIME.
MOTT THE HOOPLE?
DON'T YOU EVER LISTEN TO MUSIC THAT NORMAL PEOPLE HAVE HEARD OF, BOBBY?
MARTHA HOOPLE...
MOTT THE HOOPLE
BARTON'S BAND IS CALLED THE WIND AND THE SURF AND THEY'VE GOT THE BALLS TO THINK THAT MOTT THE HOOPLE'S A FUNNY NAME.
WELL, MAYBE IT IS, BUT...
PINK FLOYD
BARTON'S BAND PRACTICES IN A GARAGE A COUPLE OF HOUSES DOWN FROM ME, SO I AM OFTEN TREATED TO THEIR SONIC SWILL.
SLAYED?

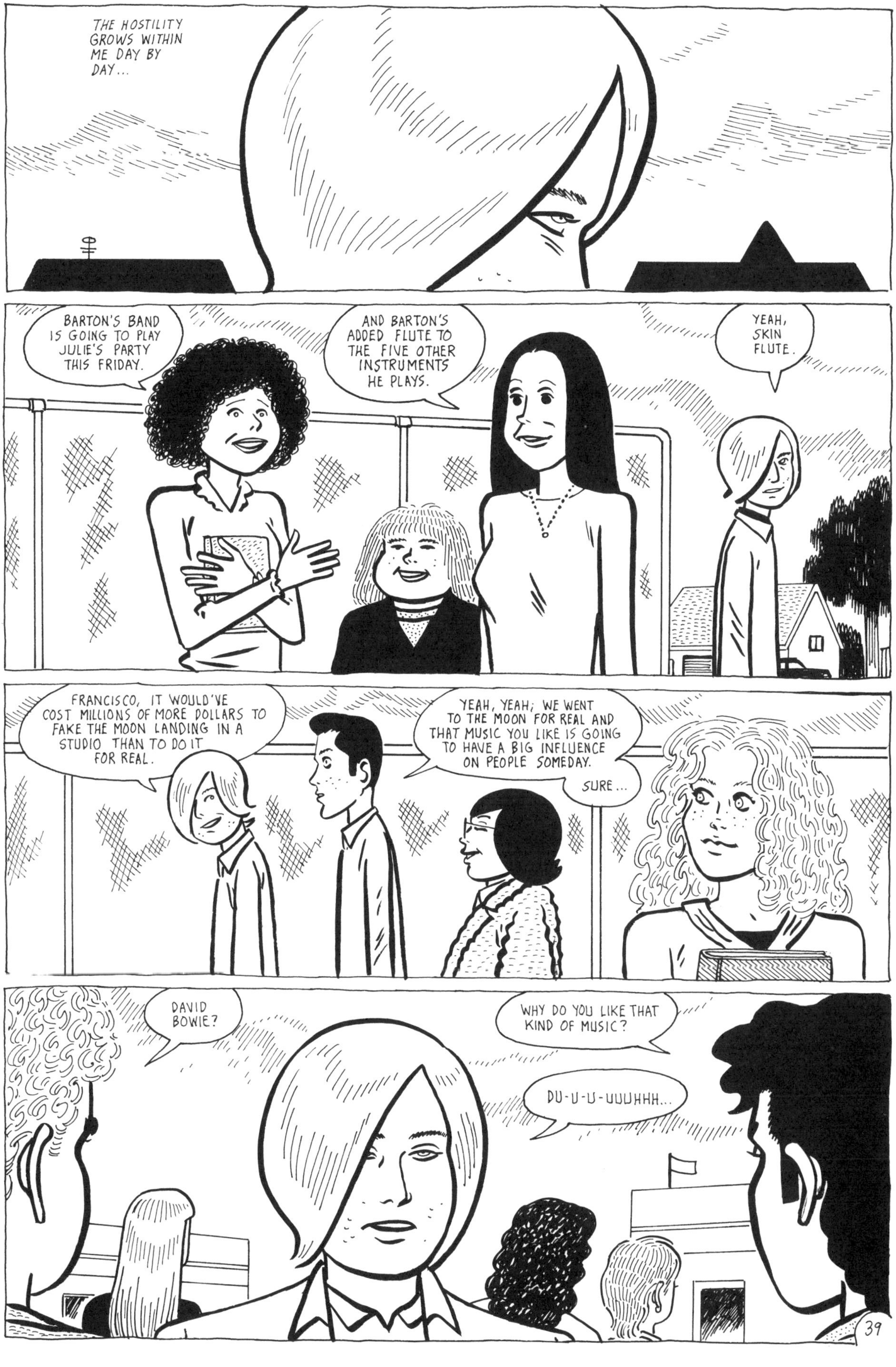
THE HOSTILITY GROWS WITHIN ME DAY BY DAY...
BARTON'S BAND IS GOING TO PLAY JULIE'S PARTY THIS FRIDAY.
AND BARTON'S ADDED FLUTE TO THE FIVE OTHER INSTRUMENTS HE PLAYS.
YEAH, SKIN FLUTE.
FRANCISCO, IT WOULD'VE COST MILLIONS OF MORE DOLLARS TO FAKE THE MOON LANDING IN A STUDIO THAN TO DO IT FOR REAL.
YEAH, YEAH; WE WENT TO THE MOON FOR REAL AND THAT MUSIC YOU LIKE IS GOING TO HAVE A BIG INFLUENCE ON PEOPLE SOMEDAY.
SURE...
DAVID BOWIE?
WHY DO YOU LIKE THAT KIND OF MUSIC?
DU-U-U-UUUHHH...

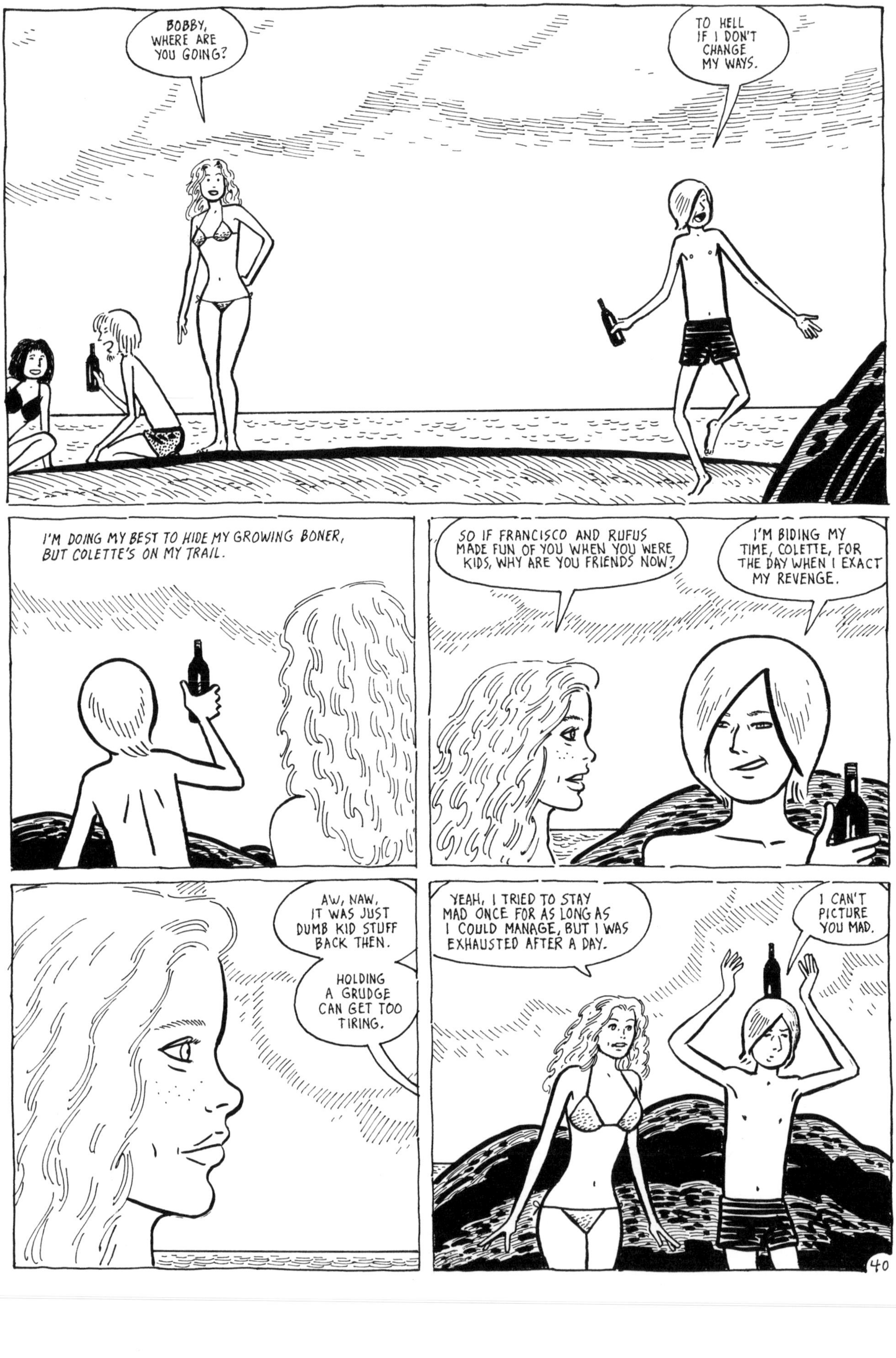
BOBBY, WHERE ARE YOU GOING?
TO HELL IF I DON'T CHANGE MY WAYS.
I'M DOING MY BEST TO HIDE MY GROWING BONER, BUT COLETTE'S ON MY TRAIL.
SO IF FRANCISCO AND RUFUS MADE FUN OF YOU WHEN YOU WERE KIDS, WHY ARE YOU FRIENDS NOW?
I'M BIDING MY TIME, COLETTE, FOR THE DAY WHEN I EXACT MY REVENGE.
AW, NAW, IT WAS JUST DUMB KID STUFF BACK THEN.
HOLDING A GRUDGE CAN GET TOO TIRING.
YEAH, I TRIED TO STAY MAD ONCE FOR AS LONG AS I COULD MANAGE, BUT I WAS EXHAUSTED AFTER A DAY.
I CAN'T PICTURE YOU MAD.

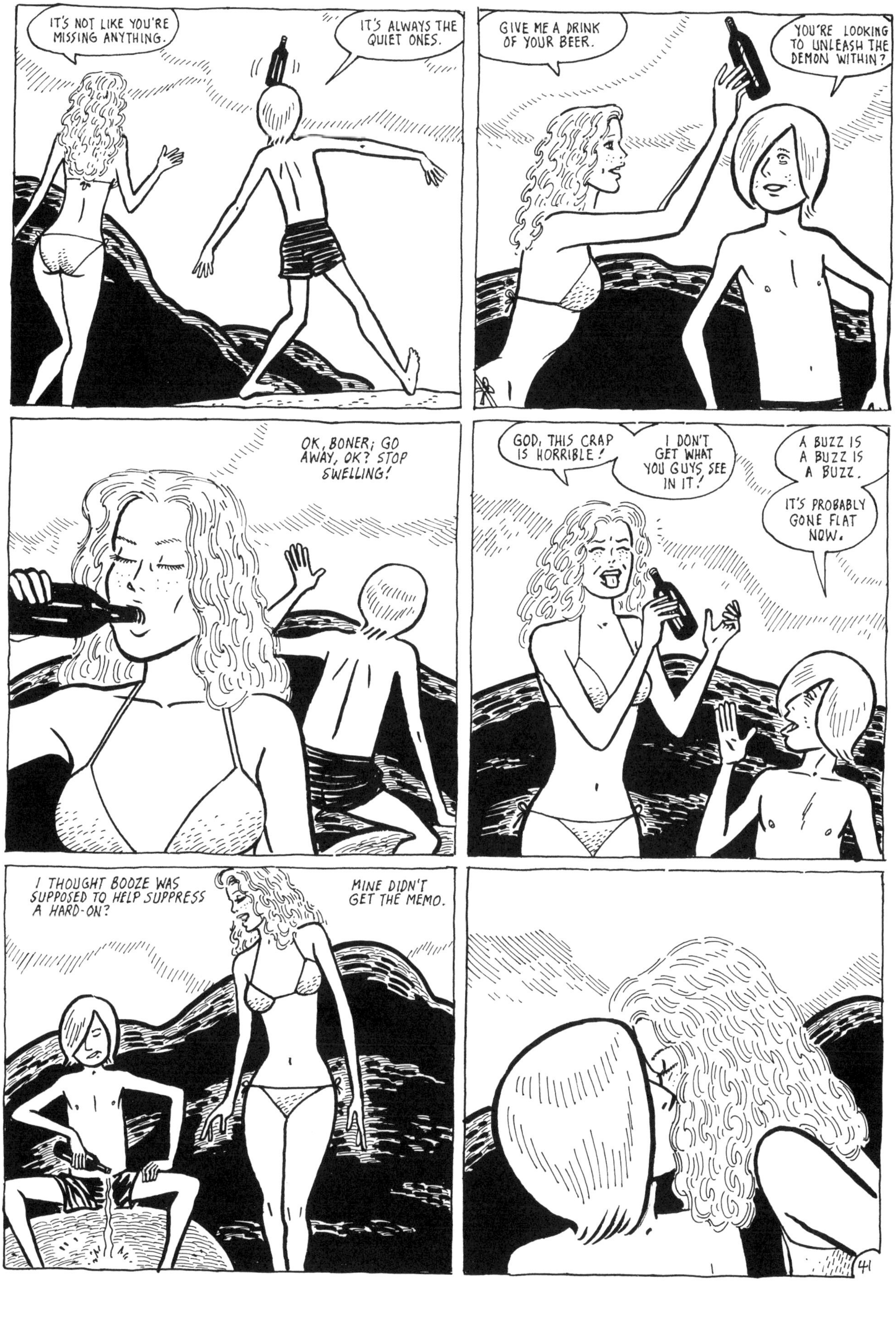
IT'S NOT LIKE YOU'RE MISSING ANYTHING.
IT'S ALWAYS THE QUIET ONES.
GIVE ME A DRINK OF YOUR BEER.
YOU'RE LOOKING TO UNLEASH THE DEMON WITHIN?
OK, BONER; GO AWAY, OK? STOP SWELLING!
GOD, THIS CRAP IS HORRIBLE!
I DON'T GET WHAT YOU GUYS SEE IN IT!
A BUZZ IS A BUZZ IS A BUZZ.
IT'S PROBABLY GONE FLAT NOW.
I THOUGHT BOOZE WAS SUPPOSED TO HELP SUPPRESS A HARD-ON?
MINE DIDN'T GET THE MEMO.
41

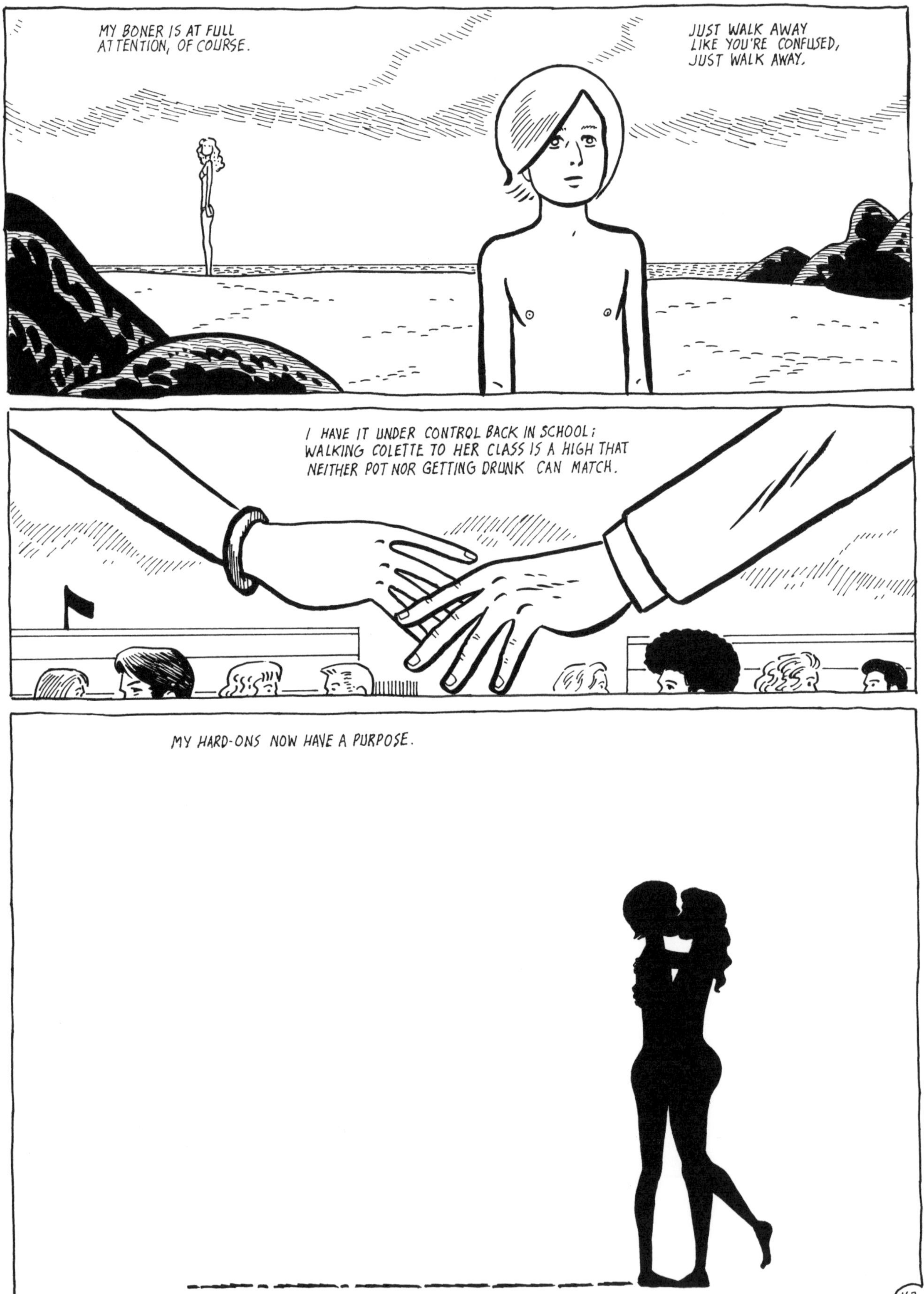
MY BONER IS AT FULL ATTENTION, OF COURSE.
JUST WALK AWAY LIKE YOU'RE CONFUSED, JUST WALK AWAY.
I HAVE IT UNDER CONTROL BACK IN SCHOOL; WALKING COLETTE TO HER CLASS IS A HIGH THAT NEITHER POT NOR GETTING DRUNK CAN MATCH.
MY HARD-ONS NOW HAVE A PURPOSE.

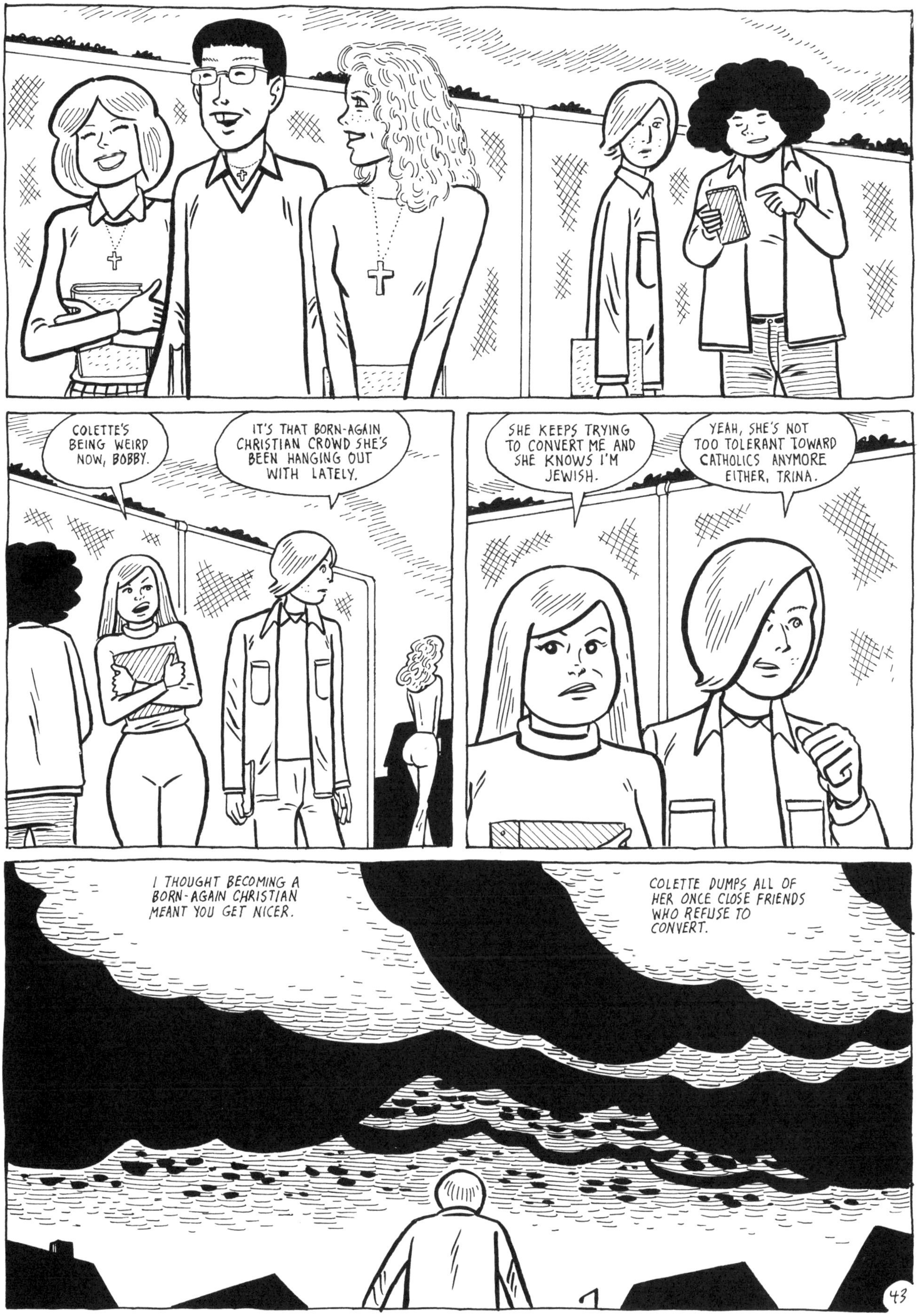

COLETTE'S BEING WEIRD NOW, BOBBY.
IT'S THAT BORN-AGAIN CHRISTIAN CROWD SHE'S BEEN HANGING OUT WITH LATELY.
SHE KEEPS TRYING TO CONVERT ME AND SHE KNOWS I'M JEWISH.
YEAH, SHE'S NOT TOO TOLERANT TOWARD CATHOLICS ANYMORE EITHER, TRINA.
I THOUGHT BECOMING A BORN-AGAIN CHRISTIAN MEANT YOU GET NICER.
COLETTE DUMPS ALL OF HER ONCE CLOSE FRIENDS WHO REFUSE TO CONVERT.

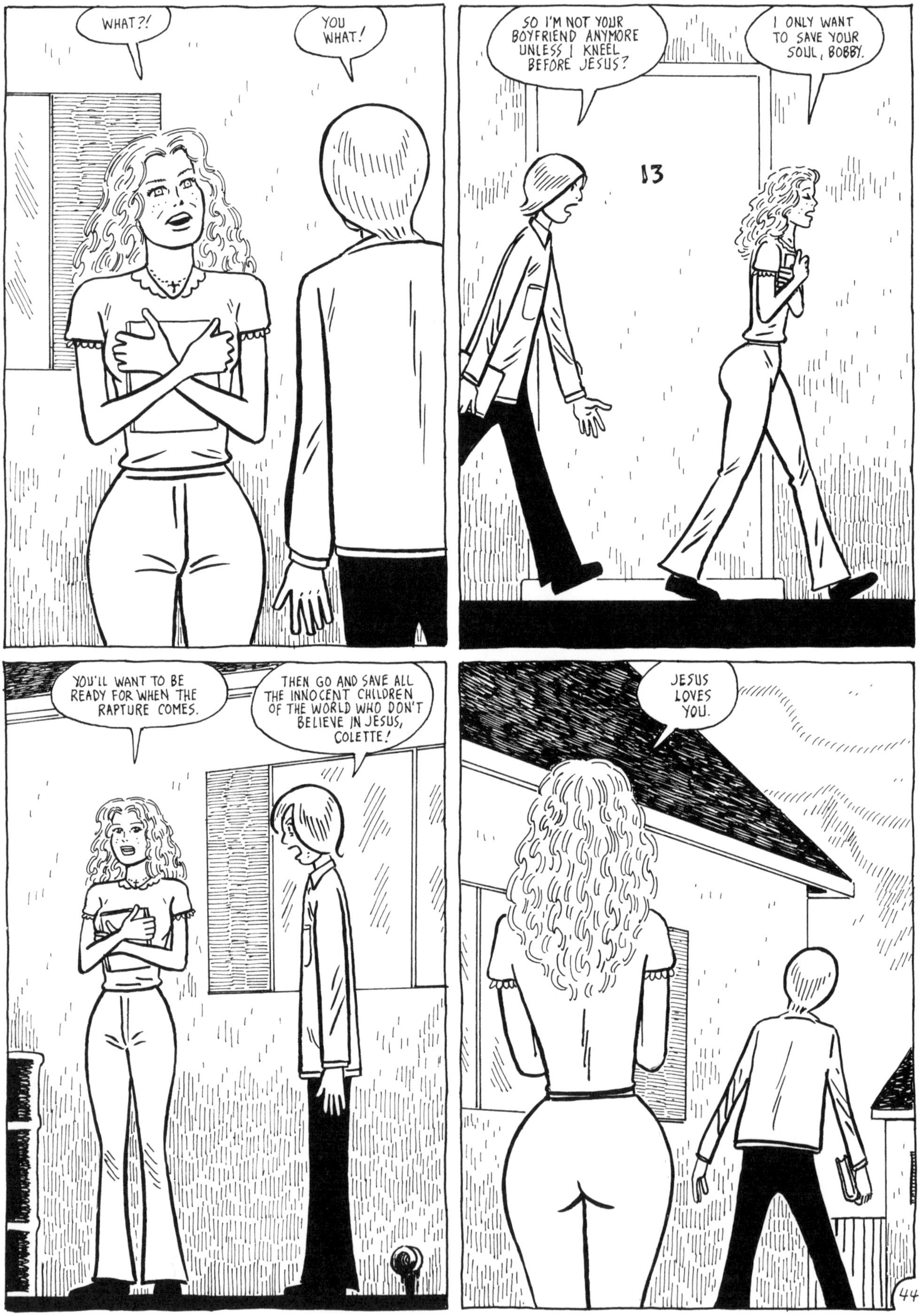
WHAT?!
YOU WHAT!
SO I'M NOT YOUR BOYFRIEND ANYMORE UNLESS I KNEEL BEFORE JESUS?
I ONLY WANT TO SAVE YOUR SOUL, BOBBY.
13
YOU'LL WANT TO BE READY FOR WHEN THE RAPTURE COMES.
THEN GO AND SAVE ALL THE INNOCENT CHILDREN OF THE WORLD WHO DON'T BELIEVE IN JESUS, COLETTE!
JESUS LOVES YOU.

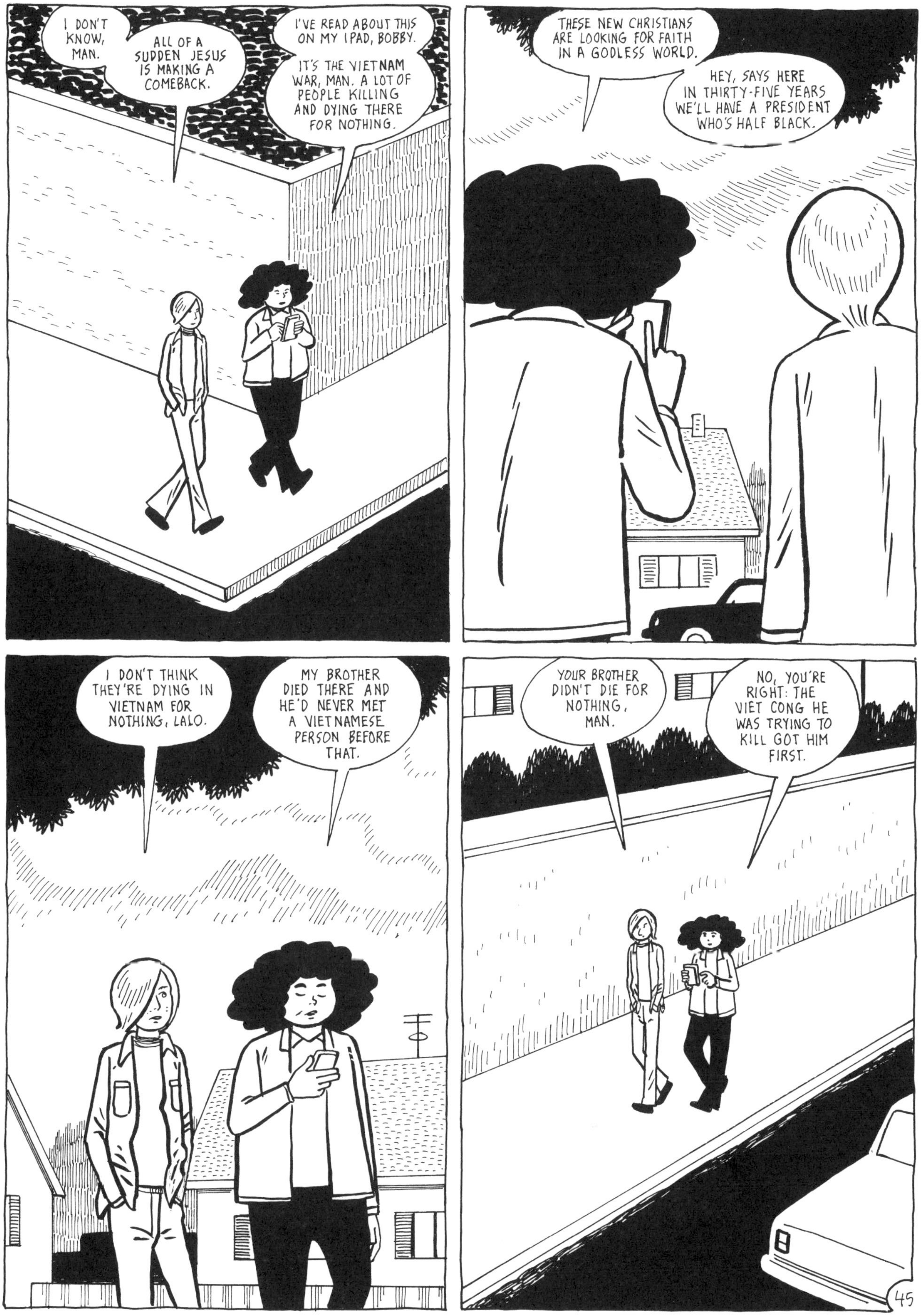

I DON'T KNOW, MAN.
ALL OF A SUDDEN JESUS IS MAKING A COMEBACK.
I'VE READ ABOUT THIS ON MY IPAD, BOBBY.
IT'S THE VIETNAM WAR, MAN. A LOT OF PEOPLE KILLING AND DYING THERE FOR NOTHING.
THESE NEW CHRISTIANS ARE LOOKING FOR FAITH IN A GODLESS WORLD.
HEY, SAYS HERE IN THIRTY-FIVE YEARS WE'LL HAVE A PRESIDENT WHO'S HALF BLACK.
I DON'T THINK THEY'RE DYING IN VIETNAM FOR NOTHING, LALO.
MY BROTHER DIED THERE AND HE'D NEVER MET A VIETNAMESE PERSON BEFORE THAT.
YOUR BROTHER DIDN'T DIE FOR NOTHING, MAN.
NO, YOU'RE RIGHT: THE VIET CONG HE WAS TRYING TO KILL GOT HIM FIRST.

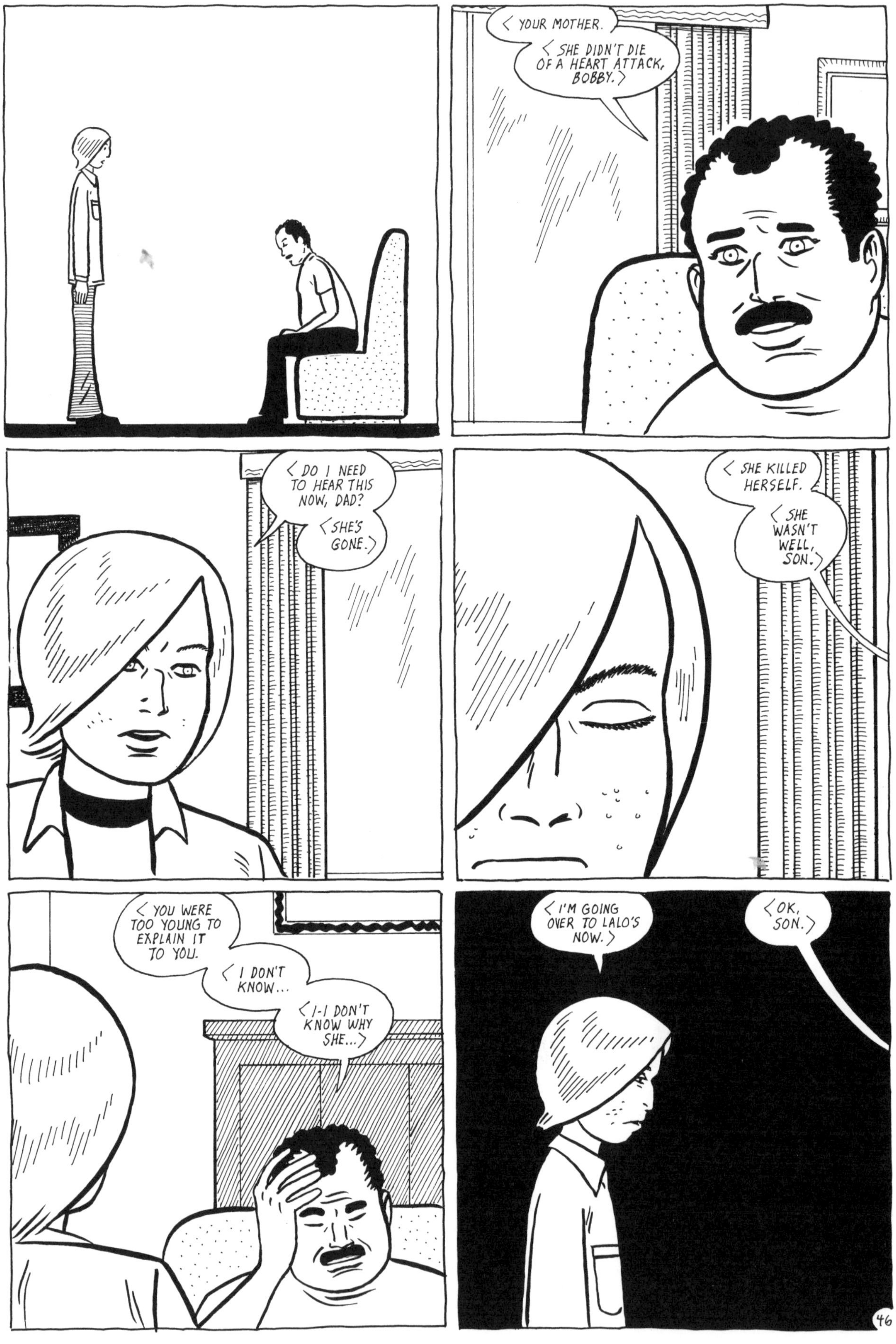
< YOUR MOTHER.
< SHE DIDN'T DIE OF A HEART ATTACK, BOBBY. >
< DO I NEED TO HEAR THIS NOW, DAD?
< SHE'S GONE. >
< SHE KILLED HERSELF.
< SHE WASN'T WELL, SON. >
< YOU WERE TOO YOUNG TO EXPLAIN IT TO YOU.
< I DON'T KNOW...
< I-I DON'T KNOW WHY SHE... >
< I'M GOING OVER TO LALO'S NOW. >
< OK, SON. >

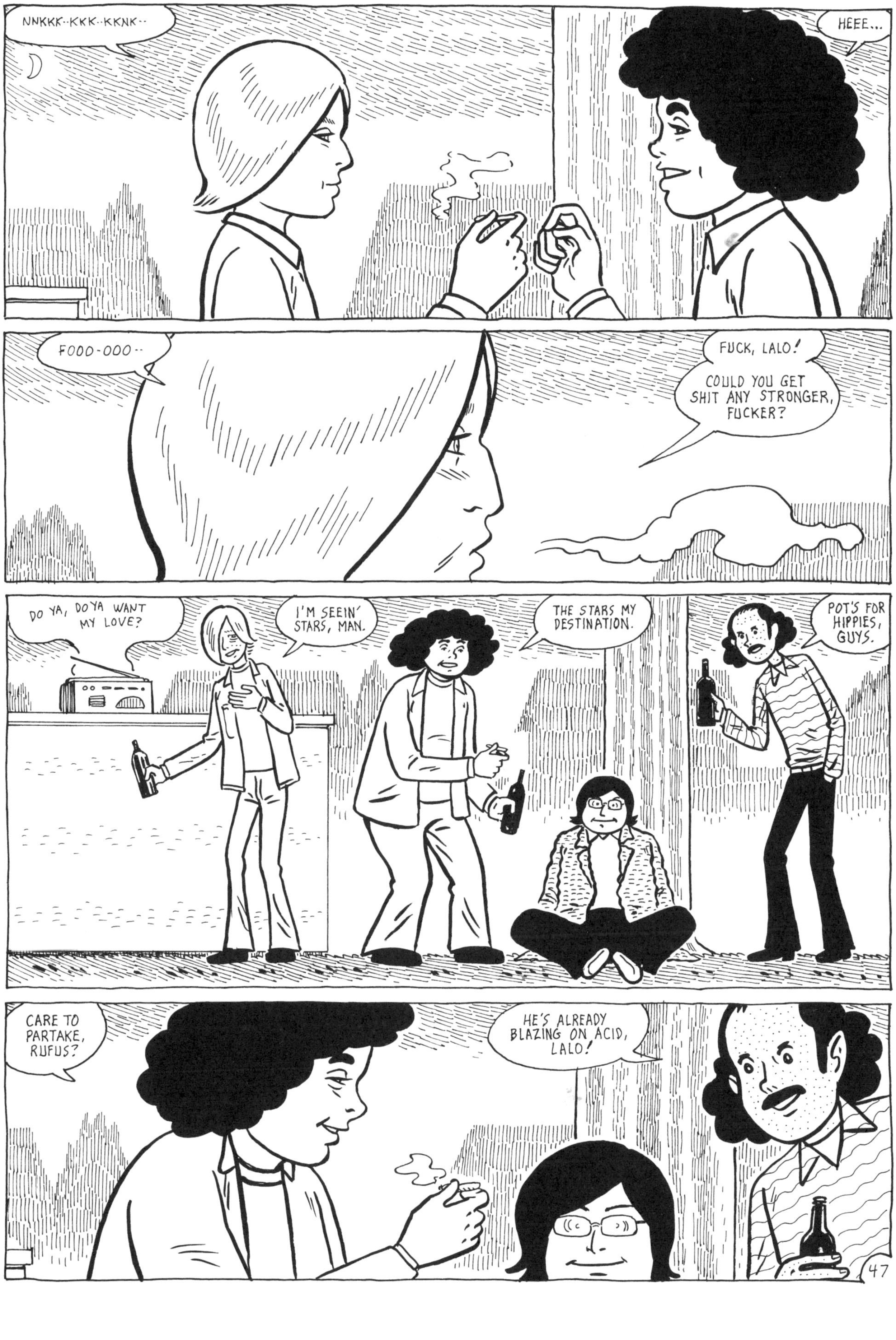
NNKKK··KKK··KKNK··
HEEE...
FOOO-OOO··
FUCK, LALO!
COULD YOU GET SHIT ANY STRONGER, FUCKER?
DO YA, DO YA WANT MY LOVE?
I'M SEEIN' STARS, MAN.
THE STARS MY DESTINATION.
POT'S FOR HIPPIES, GUYS.
CARE TO PARTAKE, RUFUS?
HE'S ALREADY BLAZING ON ACID, LALO!

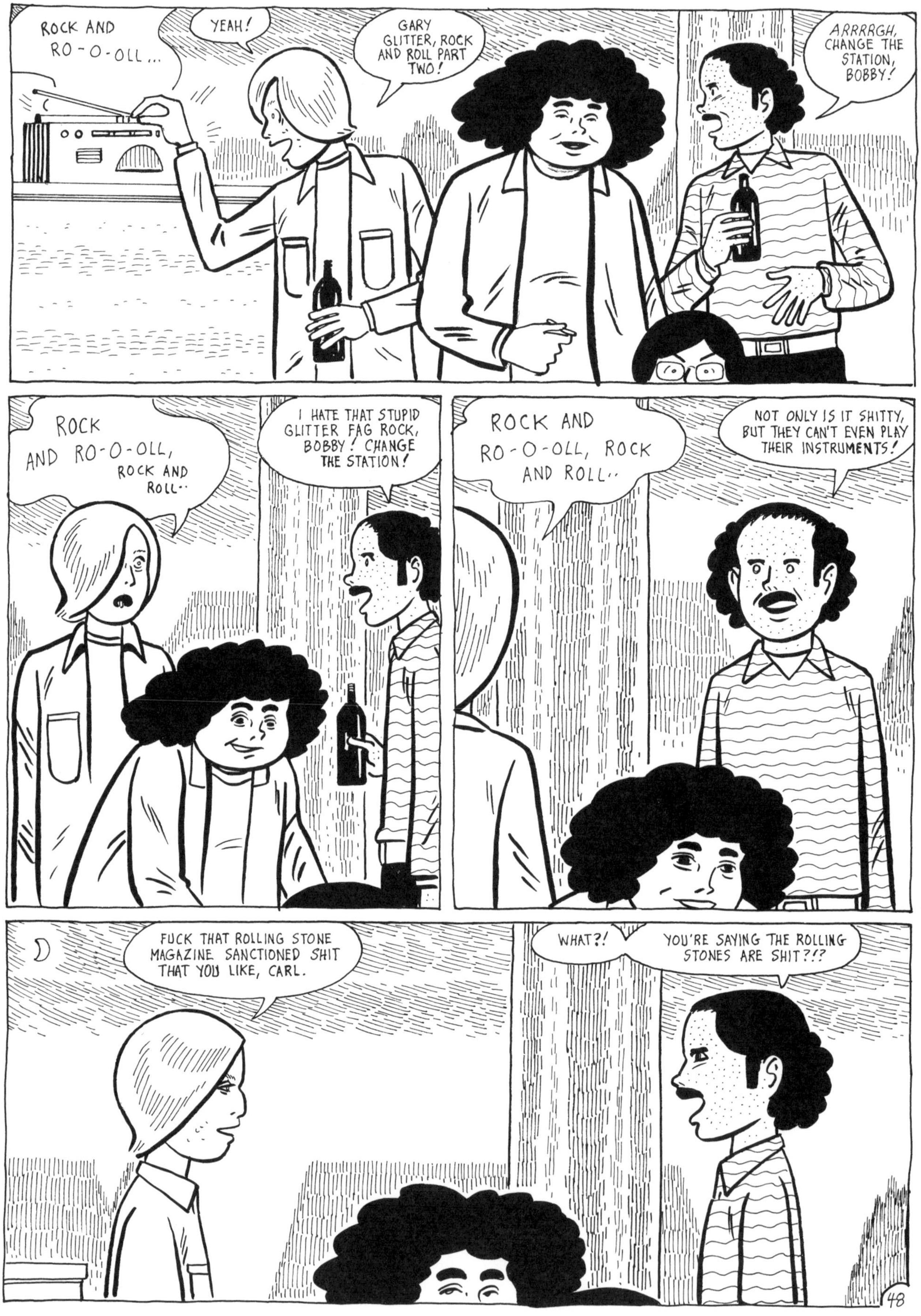
ROCK AND RO-O-OLL...
YEAH!
GARY GLITTER, ROCK AND ROLL PART TWO!
ARRRRGH, CHANGE THE STATION, BOBBY!
ROCK AND RO-O-OLL, ROCK AND ROLL..
I HATE THAT STUPID GLITTER FAG ROCK, BOBBY! CHANGE THE STATION!
ROCK AND RO-O-OLL, ROCK AND ROLL..
NOT ONLY IS IT SHITTY, BUT THEY CAN'T EVEN PLAY THEIR INSTRUMENTS!
FUCK THAT ROLLING STONE MAGAZINE SANCTIONED SHIT THAT YOU LIKE, CARL.
WHAT?!
YOU'RE SAYING THE ROLLING STONES ARE SHIT?!?

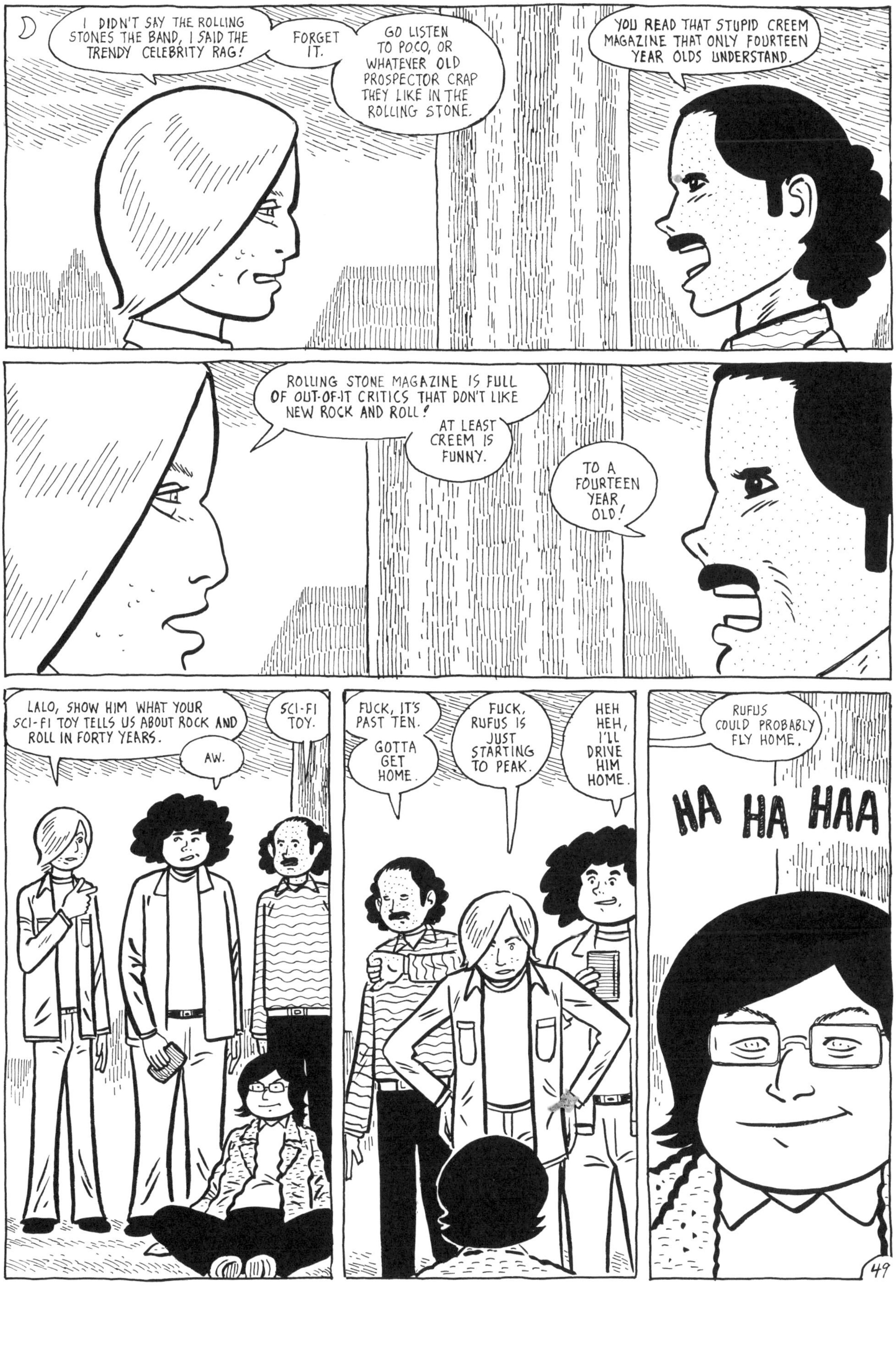

I DIDN'T SAY THE ROLLING STONES THE BAND, I SAID THE TRENDY CELEBRITY RAG!
FORGET IT.
GO LISTEN TO POCO, OR WHATEVER OLD PROSPECTOR CRAP THEY LIKE IN THE ROLLING STONE.
YOU READ THAT STUPID CREEM MAGAZINE THAT ONLY FOURTEEN YEAR OLDS UNDERSTAND.
ROLLING STONE MAGAZINE IS FULL OF OUT-OF-IT CRITICS THAT DON'T LIKE NEW ROCK AND ROLL!
AT LEAST CREEM IS FUNNY.
TO A FOURTEEN YEAR OLD!
LALO, SHOW HIM WHAT YOUR SCI-FI TOY TELLS US ABOUT ROCK AND ROLL IN FORTY YEARS.
AW.
SCI-FI TOY.
FUCK, IT'S PAST TEN.
GOTTA GET HOME.
FUCK, RUFUS IS JUST STARTING TO PEAK.
HEH HEH, I'LL DRIVE HIM HOME.
RUFUS COULD PROBABLY FLY HOME.
HA HA HAA

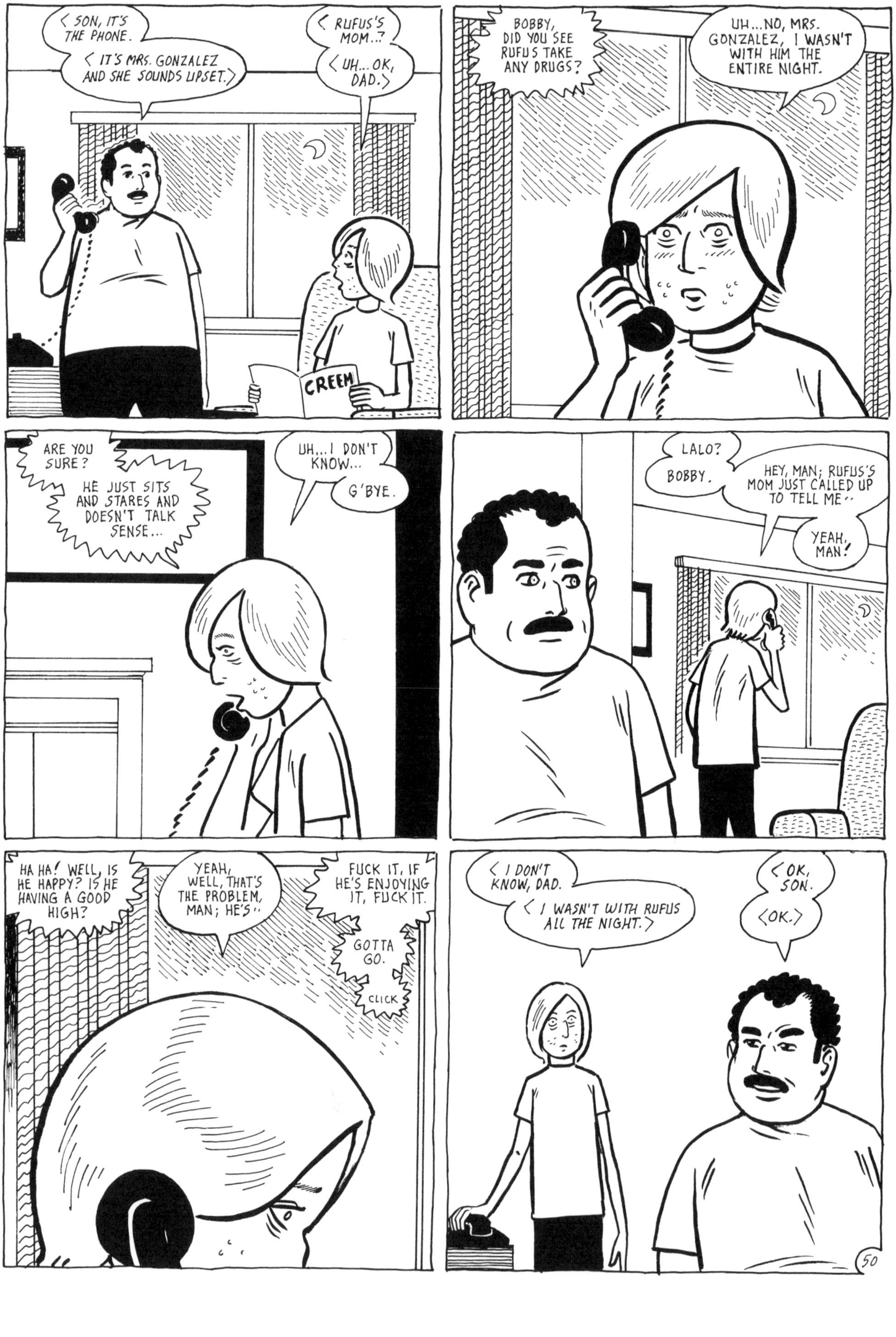
< SON, IT'S THE PHONE.
< IT'S MRS. GONZALEZ AND SHE SOUNDS UPSET.>
< RUFUS'S MOM...?
< UH... OK, DAD.>
CREEM
BOBBY, DID YOU SEE RUFUS TAKE ANY DRUGS?
UH... NO, MRS. GONZALEZ, I WASN'T WITH HIM THE ENTIRE NIGHT.
ARE YOU SURE?
HE JUST SITS AND STARES AND DOESN'T TALK SENSE...
UH... I DON'T KNOW...
G'BYE.
LALO?
BOBBY.
HEY, MAN; RUFUS'S MOM JUST CALLED UP TO TELL ME..
YEAH, MAN!
HA HA! WELL, IS HE HAPPY? IS HE HAVING A GOOD HIGH?
YEAH, WELL, THAT'S THE PROBLEM, MAN; HE'S..
FUCK IT. IF HE'S ENJOYING IT, FUCK IT.
GOTTA GO.
CLICK
< I DON'T KNOW, DAD.
< I WASN'T WITH RUFUS ALL THE NIGHT.>
< OK, SON.
<OK.>

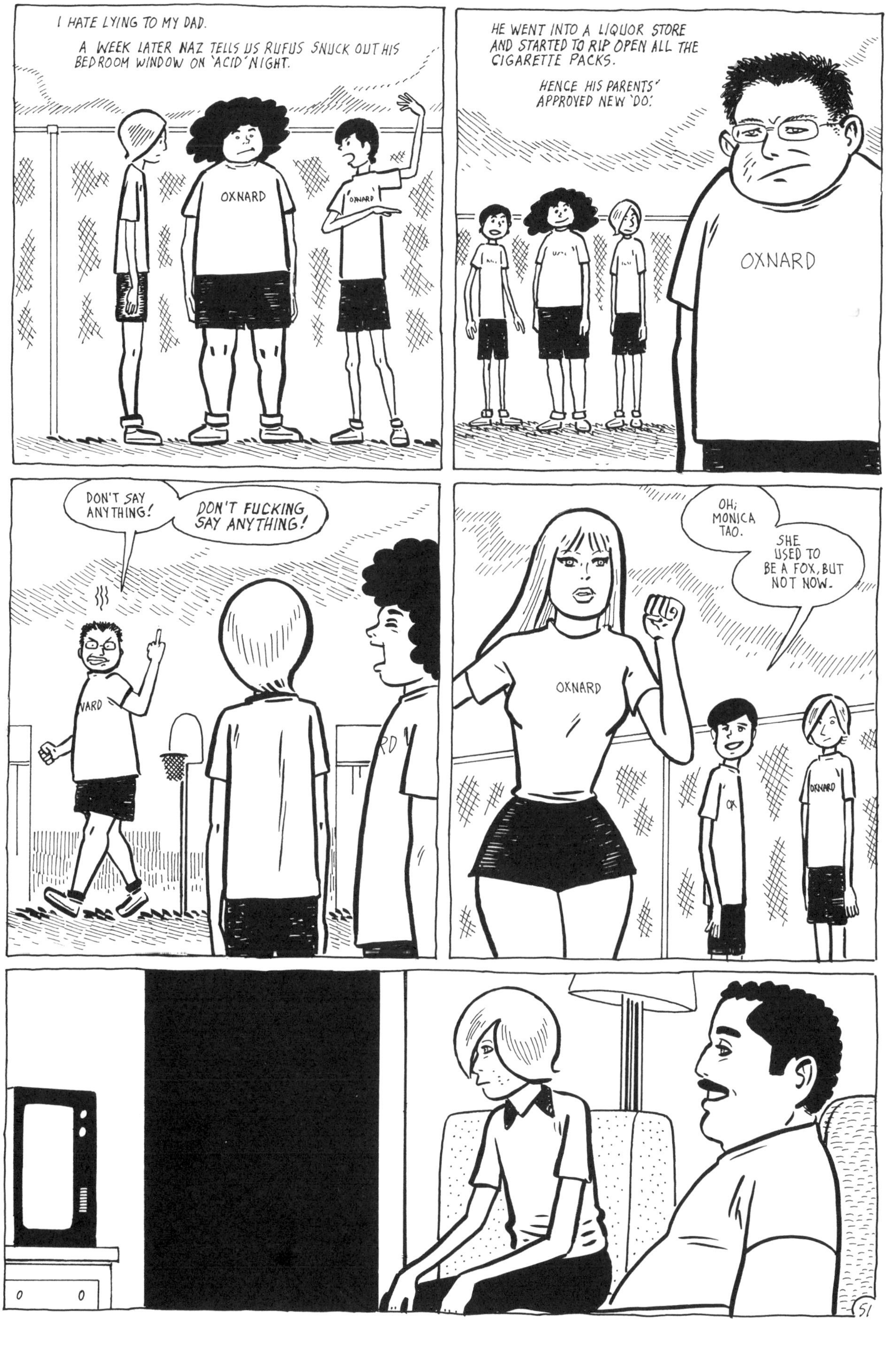
I HATE LYING TO MY DAD.
A WEEK LATER NAZ TELLS US RUFUS SNUCK OUT HIS BEDROOM WINDOW ON 'ACID' NIGHT.
OXNARD
HE WENT INTO A LIQUOR STORE AND STARTED TO RIP OPEN ALL THE CIGARETTE PACKS.
HENCE HIS PARENTS' APPROVED NEW 'DO.'
OXNARD
DON'T SAY ANYTHING!
DON'T FUCKING SAY ANYTHING!
OH, MONICA TAO.
SHE USED TO BE A FOX, BUT NOT NOW.
OXNARD

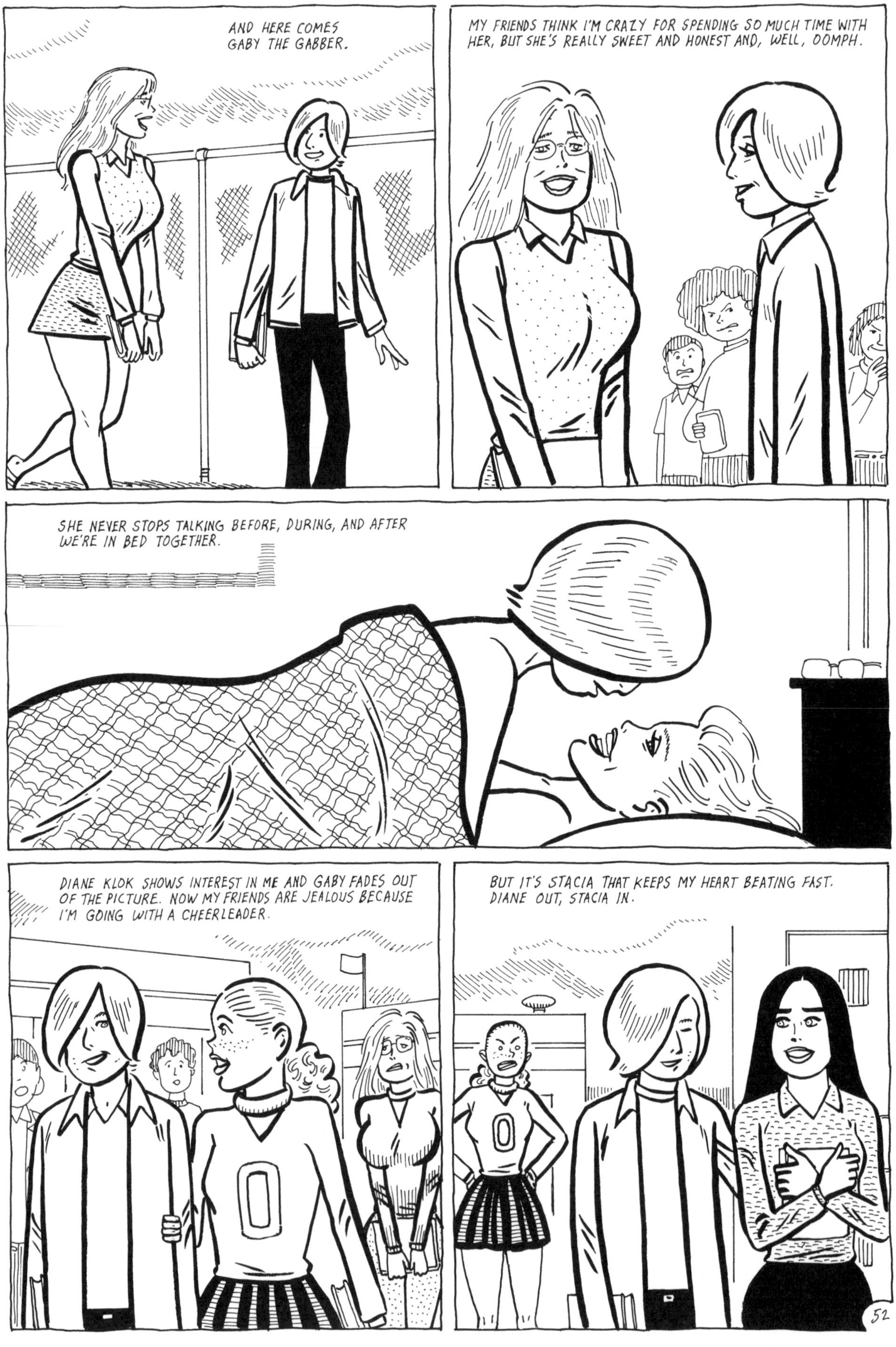
AND HERE COMES GABY THE GABBER.
MY FRIENDS THINK I'M CRAZY FOR SPENDING SO MUCH TIME WITH HER, BUT SHE'S REALLY SWEET AND HONEST AND, WELL, OOMPH.
SHE NEVER STOPS TALKING BEFORE, DURING, AND AFTER WE'RE IN BED TOGETHER.
DIANE KLOK SHOWS INTEREST IN ME AND GABY FADES OUT OF THE PICTURE. NOW MY FRIENDS ARE JEALOUS BECAUSE I'M GOING WITH A CHEERLEADER.
BUT IT'S STACIA THAT KEEPS MY HEART BEATING FAST. DIANE OUT, STACIA IN.

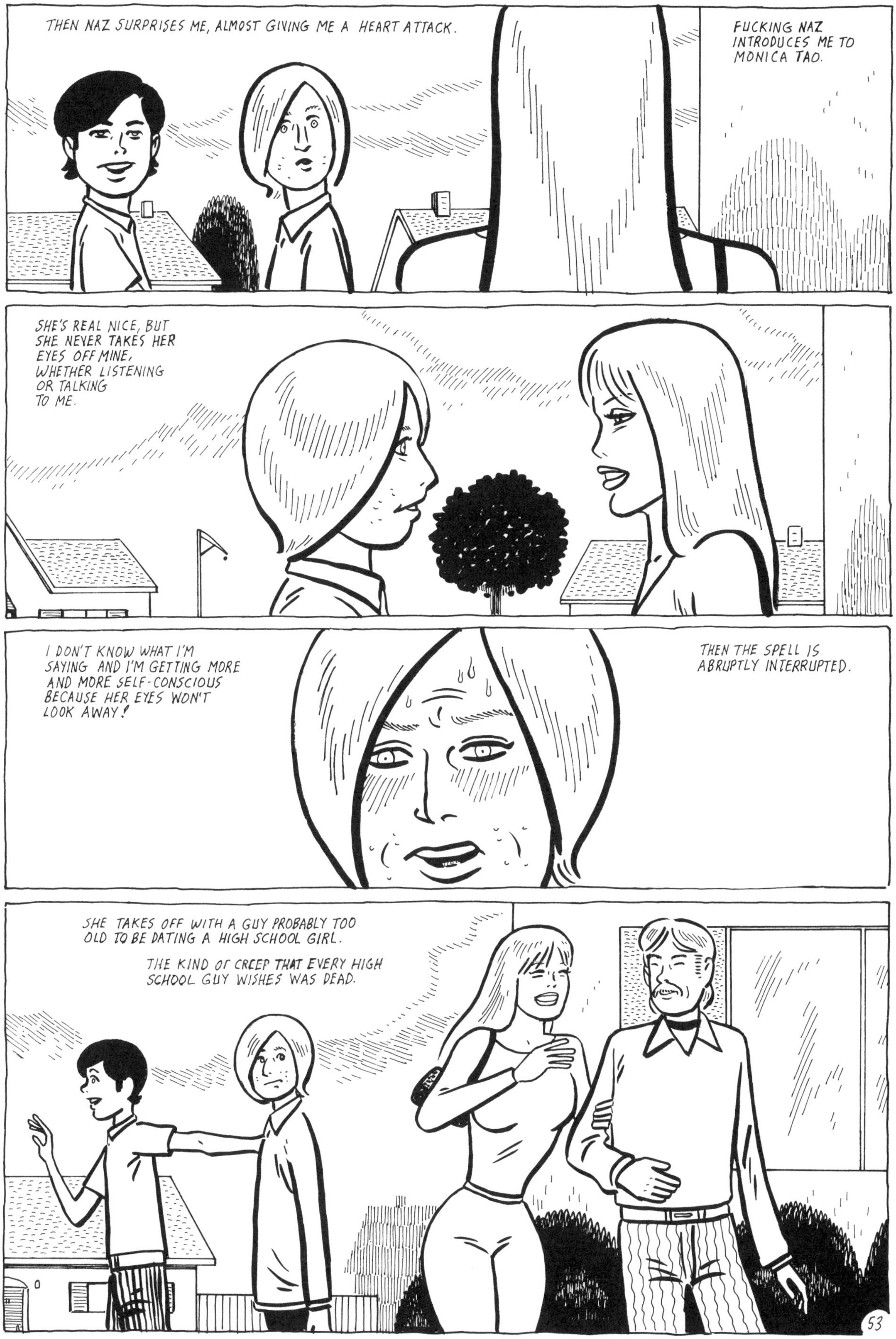
THEN NAZ SURPRISES ME, ALMOST GIVING ME A HEART ATTACK.
FUCKING NAZ INTRODUCES ME TO MONICA TAO.
SHE'S REAL NICE, BUT SHE NEVER TAKES HER EYES OFF MINE, WHETHER LISTENING OR TALKING TO ME.
I DON'T KNOW WHAT I'M SAYING AND I'M GETTING MORE AND MORE SELF-CONSCIOUS BECAUSE HER EYES WON'T LOOK AWAY!
THEN THE SPELL IS ABRUPTLY INTERRUPTED.
SHE TAKES OFF WITH A GUY PROBABLY TOO OLD TO BE DATING A HIGH SCHOOL GIRL.
THE KIND OF CREEP THAT EVERY HIGH SCHOOL GUY WISHES WAS DEAD.

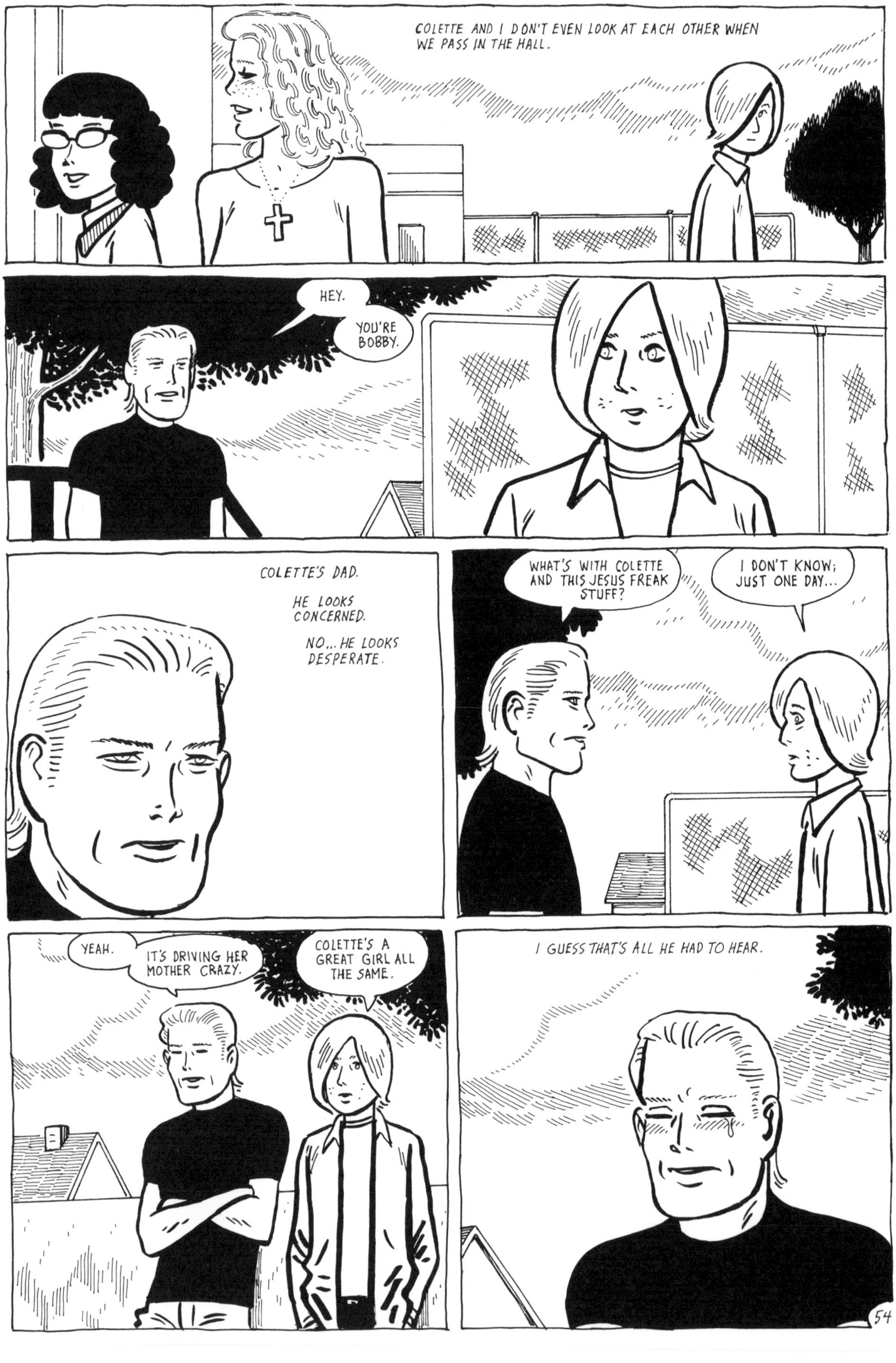
COLETTE AND I DON'T EVEN LOOK AT EACH OTHER WHEN WE PASS IN THE HALL.
HEY.
YOU'RE BOBBY.
COLETTE'S DAD.
HE LOOKS CONCERNED.
NO... HE LOOKS DESPERATE.
WHAT'S WITH COLETTE AND THIS JESUS FREAK STUFF?
I DON'T KNOW; JUST ONE DAY...
YEAH.
IT'S DRIVING HER MOTHER CRAZY.
COLETTE'S A GREAT GIRL ALL THE SAME.
I GUESS THAT'S ALL HE HAD TO HEAR.

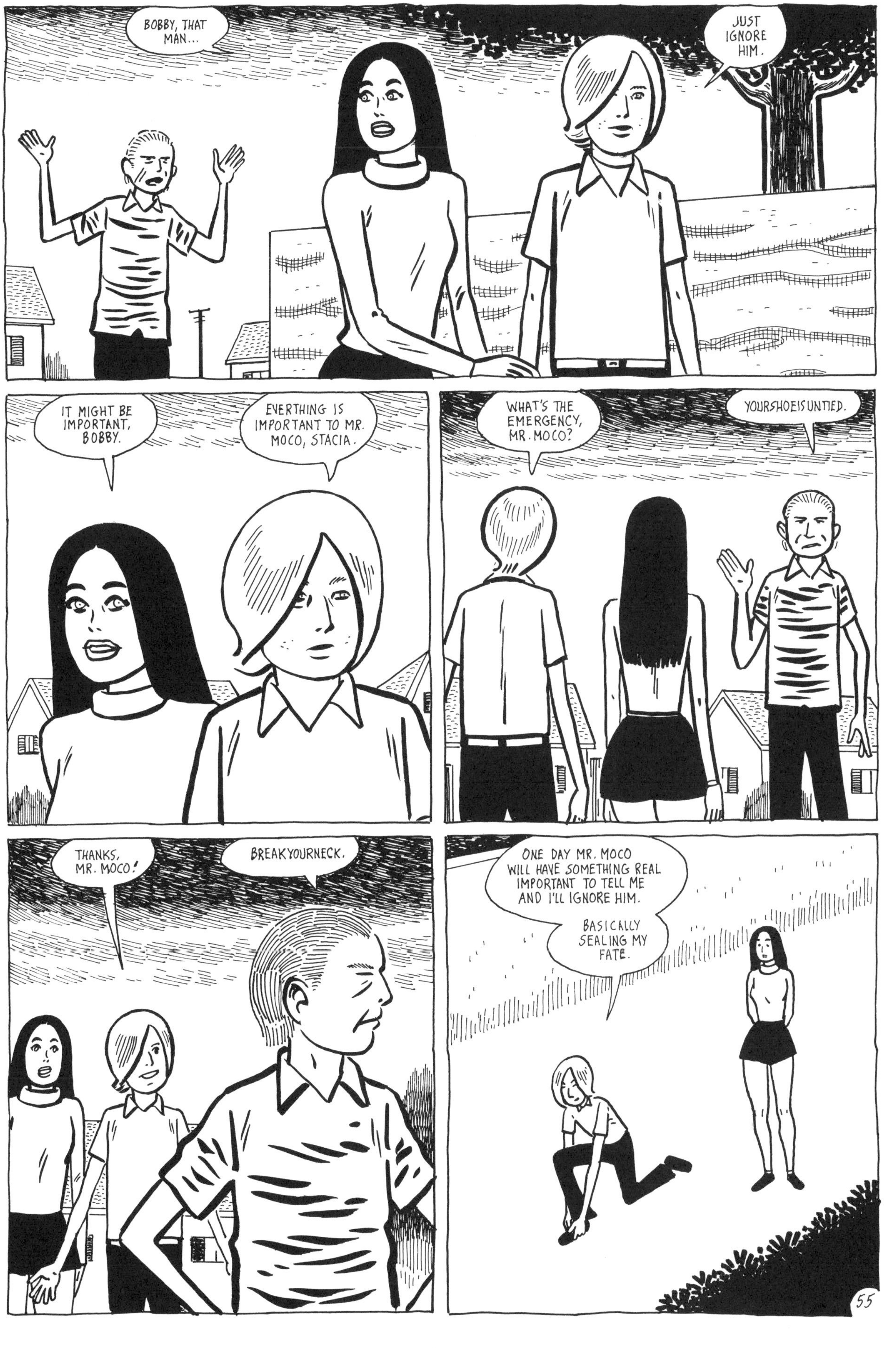
BOBBY, THAT MAN...
JUST IGNORE HIM.
IT MIGHT BE IMPORTANT, BOBBY.
EVERTHING IS IMPORTANT TO MR. MOCO, STACIA.
WHAT'S THE EMERGENCY, MR. MOCO?
YOURSHOEISUNTIED.
THANKS, MR. MOCO!
BREAKYOURNECK.
ONE DAY MR. MOCO WILL HAVE SOMETHING REAL IMPORTANT TO TELL ME AND I'LL IGNORE HIM.
BASICALLY SEALING MY FATE.

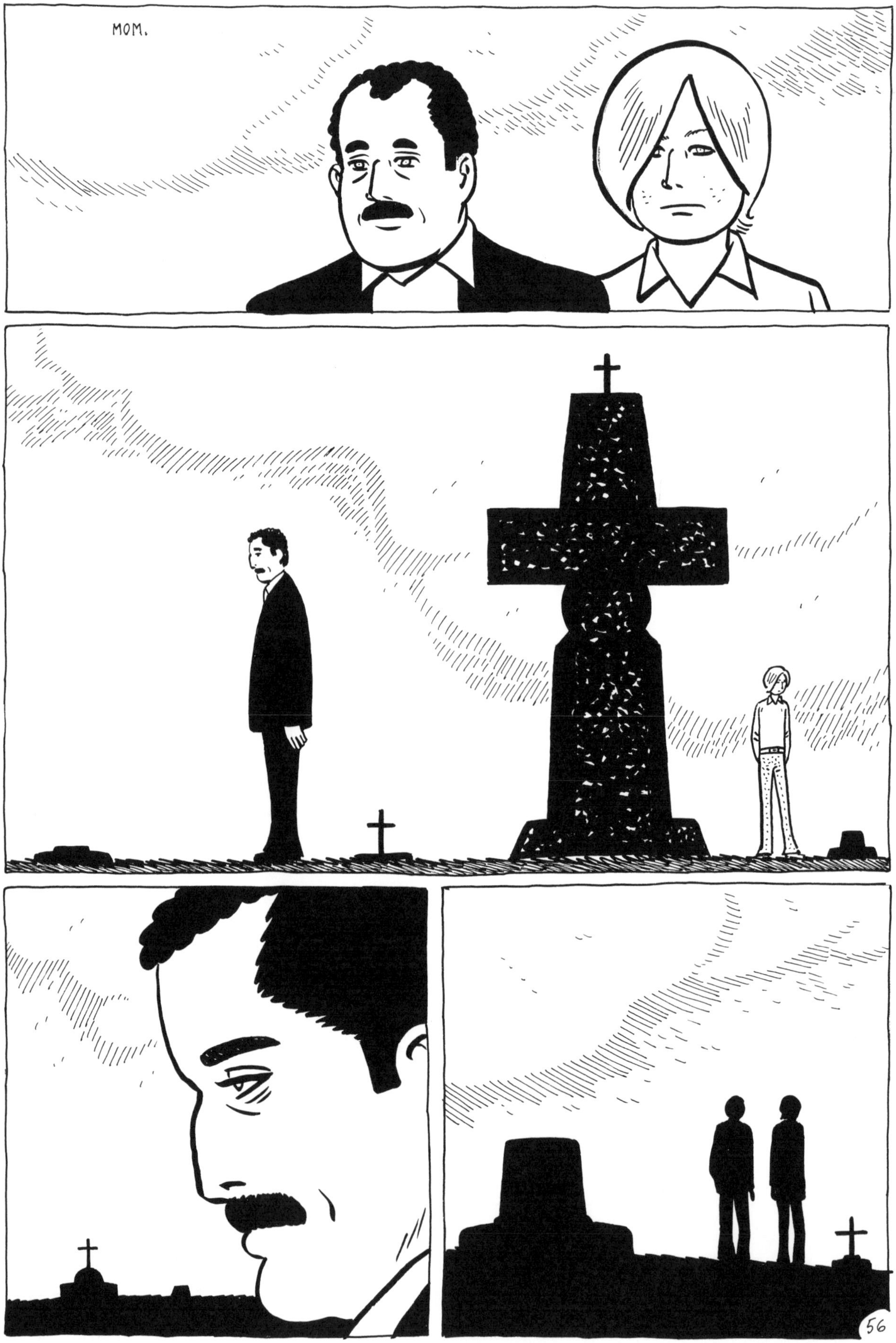
MOM.

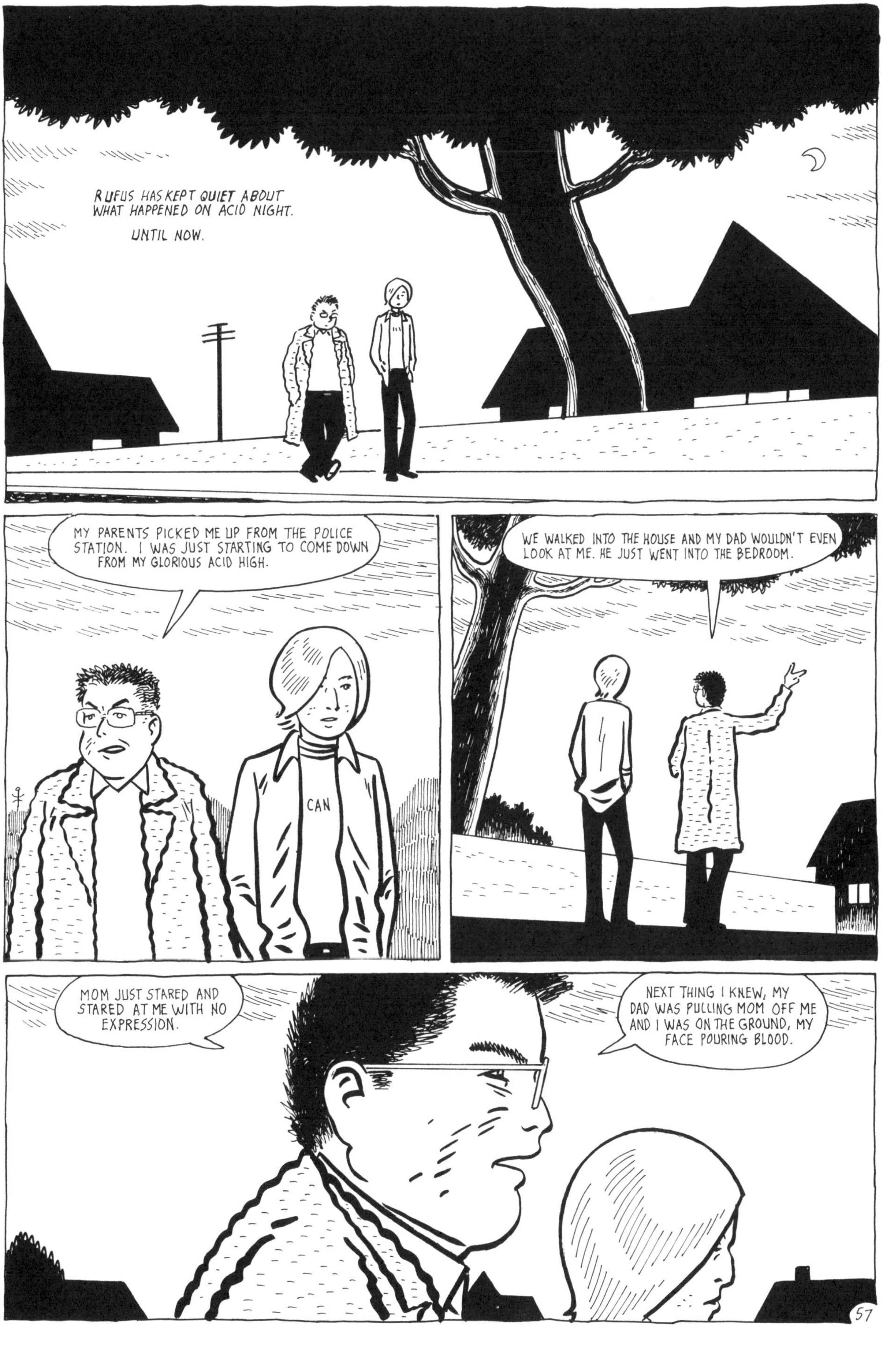
RUFUS HAS KEPT QUIET ABOUT WHAT HAPPENED ON ACID NIGHT.
UNTIL NOW.
MY PARENTS PICKED ME UP FROM THE POLICE STATION. I WAS JUST STARTING TO COME DOWN FROM MY GLORIOUS ACID HIGH.
CAN
WE WALKED INTO THE HOUSE AND MY DAD WOULDN'T EVEN LOOK AT ME. HE JUST WENT INTO THE BEDROOM.
MOM JUST STARED AND STARED AT ME WITH NO EXPRESSION.
NEXT THING I KNEW, MY DAD WAS PULLING MOM OFF ME AND I WAS ON THE GROUND, MY FACE POURING BLOOD.

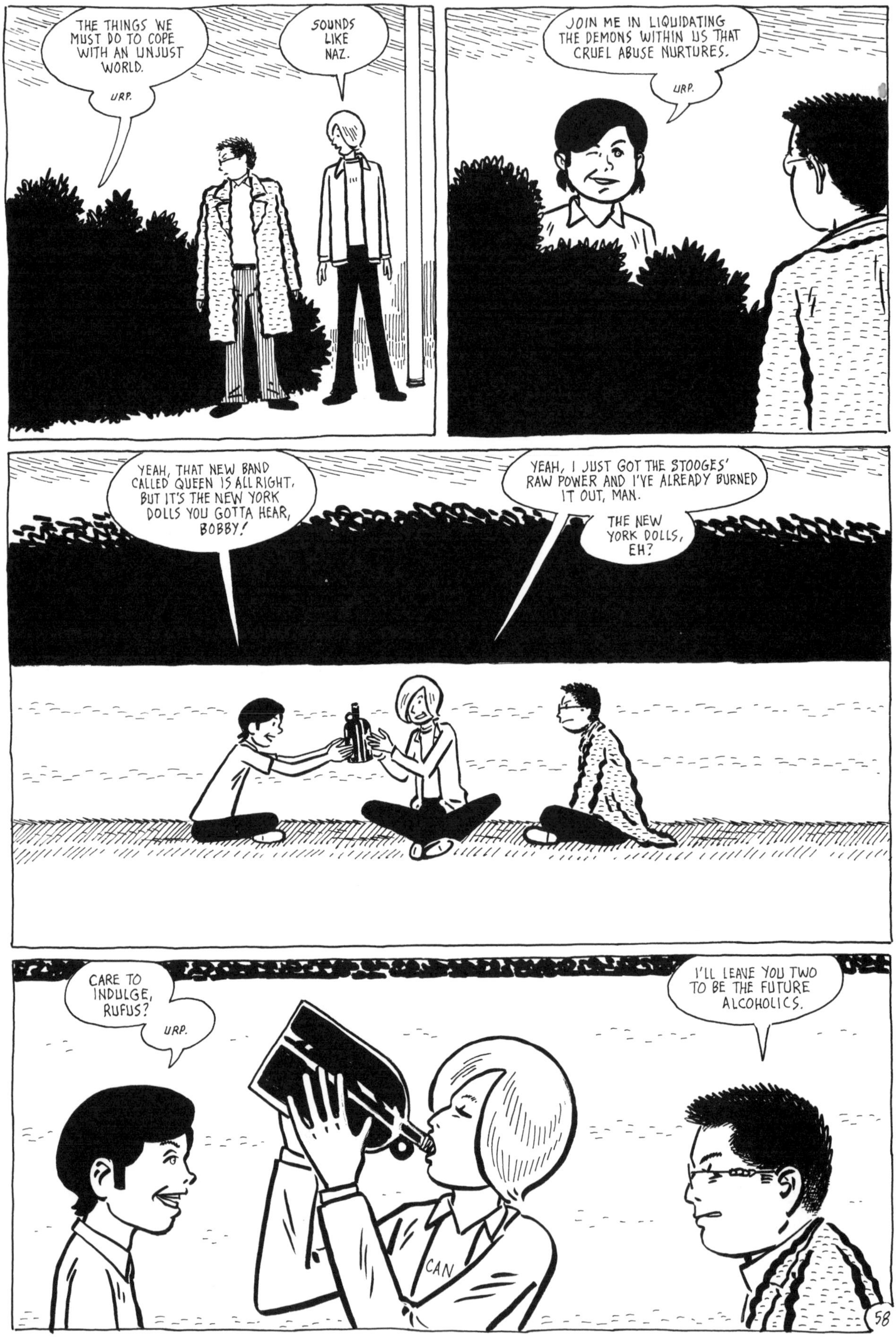

THE THINGS WE MUST DO TO COPE WITH AN UNJUST WORLD.
URP.
SOUNDS LIKE NAZ.
JOIN ME IN LIQUIDATING THE DEMONS WITHIN US THAT CRUEL ABUSE NURTURES.
URP.
YEAH, THAT NEW BAND CALLED QUEEN IS ALL RIGHT, BUT IT'S THE NEW YORK DOLLS YOU GOTTA HEAR, BOBBY!
YEAH, I JUST GOT THE STOOGES' RAW POWER AND I'VE ALREADY BURNED IT OUT, MAN.
THE NEW YORK DOLLS, EH?
CARE TO INDULGE, RUFUS?
URP.
I'LL LEAVE YOU TWO TO BE THE FUTURE ALCOHOLICS.
CAN

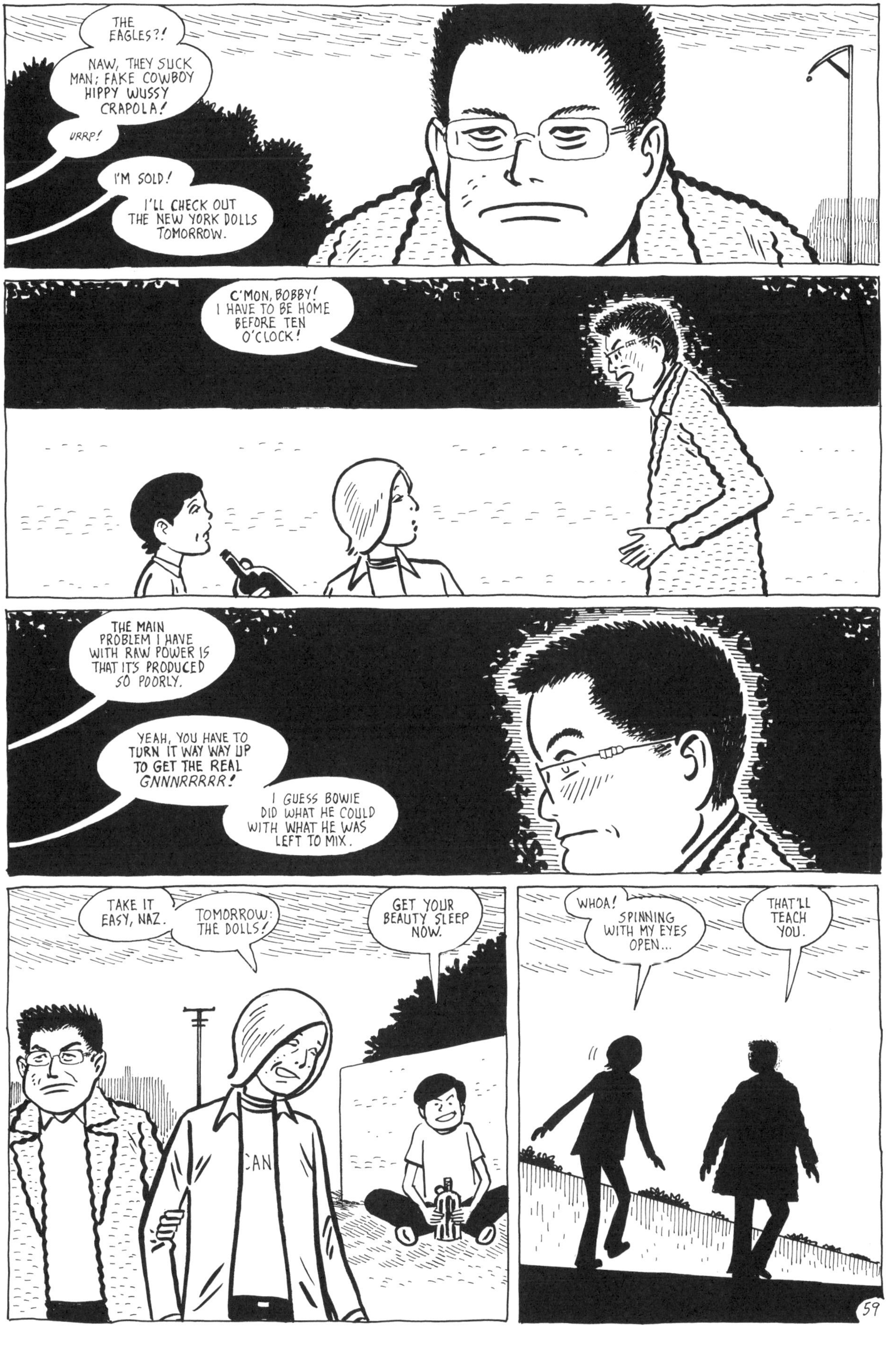
THE EAGLES?!
NAW, THEY SUCK MAN; FAKE COWBOY HIPPY WUSSY CRAPOLA!
URRP!
I'M SOLD!
I'LL CHECK OUT THE NEW YORK DOLLS TOMORROW.
C'MON, BOBBY! I HAVE TO BE HOME BEFORE TEN O'CLOCK!
THE MAIN PROBLEM I HAVE WITH RAW POWER IS THAT IT'S PRODUCED SO POORLY.
YEAH, YOU HAVE TO TURN IT WAY WAY UP TO GET THE REAL GNNNRRRRR!
I GUESS BOWIE DID WHAT HE COULD WITH WHAT HE WAS LEFT TO MIX.
TAKE IT EASY, NAZ.
TOMORROW: THE DOLLS!
GET YOUR BEAUTY SLEEP NOW.
CAN
WHOA!
SPINNING WITH MY EYES OPEN...
THAT'LL TEACH YOU.

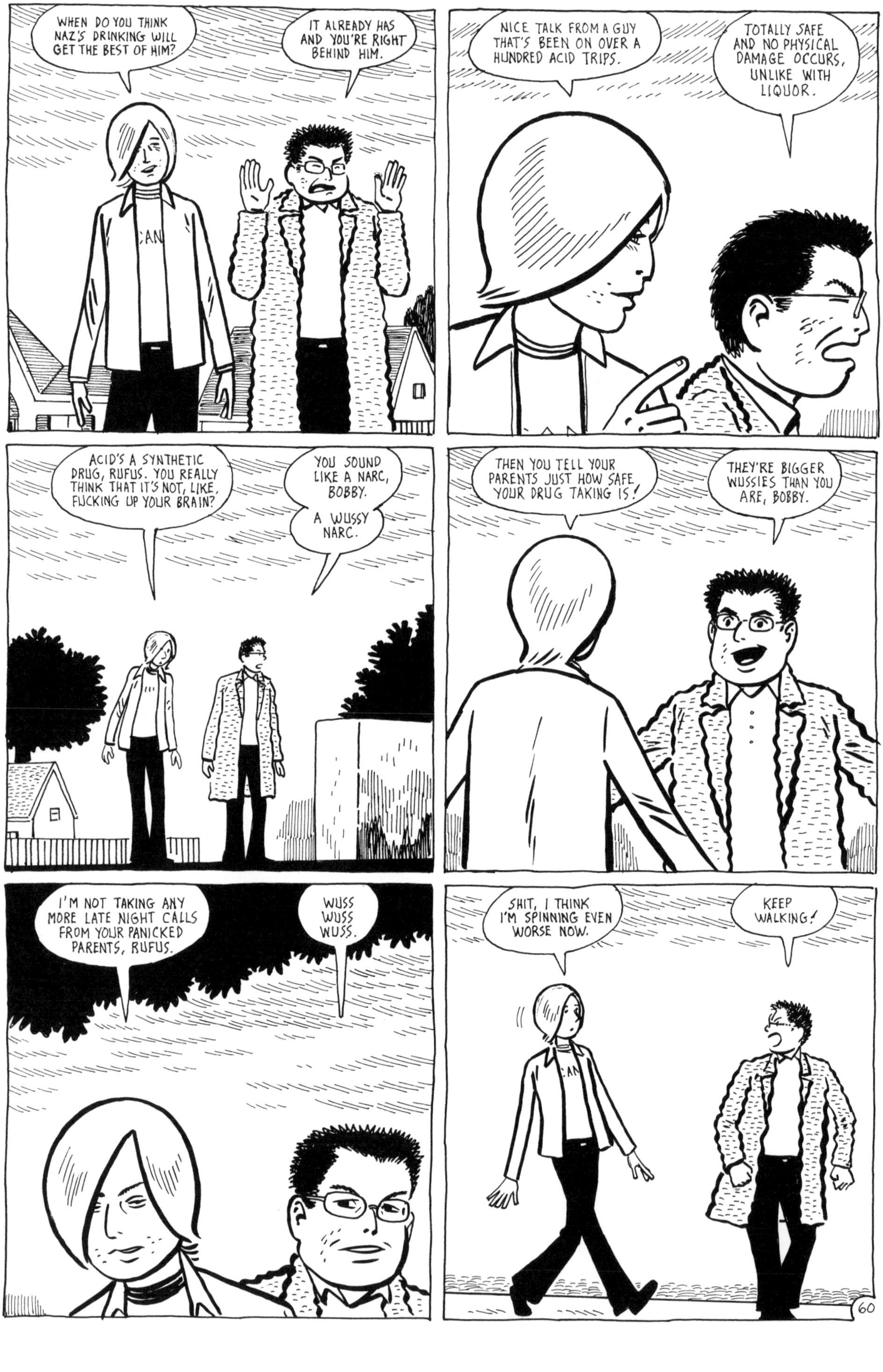
WHEN DO YOU THINK NAZ'S DRINKING WILL GET THE BEST OF HIM?
IT ALREADY HAS AND YOU'RE RIGHT BEHIND HIM.
NICE TALK FROM A GUY THAT'S BEEN ON OVER A HUNDRED ACID TRIPS.
TOTALLY SAFE AND NO PHYSICAL DAMAGE OCCURS, UNLIKE WITH LIQUOR.
ACID'S A SYNTHETIC DRUG, RUFUS. YOU REALLY THINK THAT IT'S NOT, LIKE, FUCKING UP YOUR BRAIN?
YOU SOUND LIKE A NARC, BOBBY.
A WUSSY NARC.
THEN YOU TELL YOUR PARENTS JUST HOW SAFE YOUR DRUG TAKING IS!
THEY'RE BIGGER WUSSIES THAN YOU ARE, BOBBY.
I'M NOT TAKING ANY MORE LATE NIGHT CALLS FROM YOUR PANICKED PARENTS, RUFUS.
WUSS WUSS WUSS.
SHIT, I THINK I'M SPINNING EVEN WORSE NOW.
KEEP WALKING!

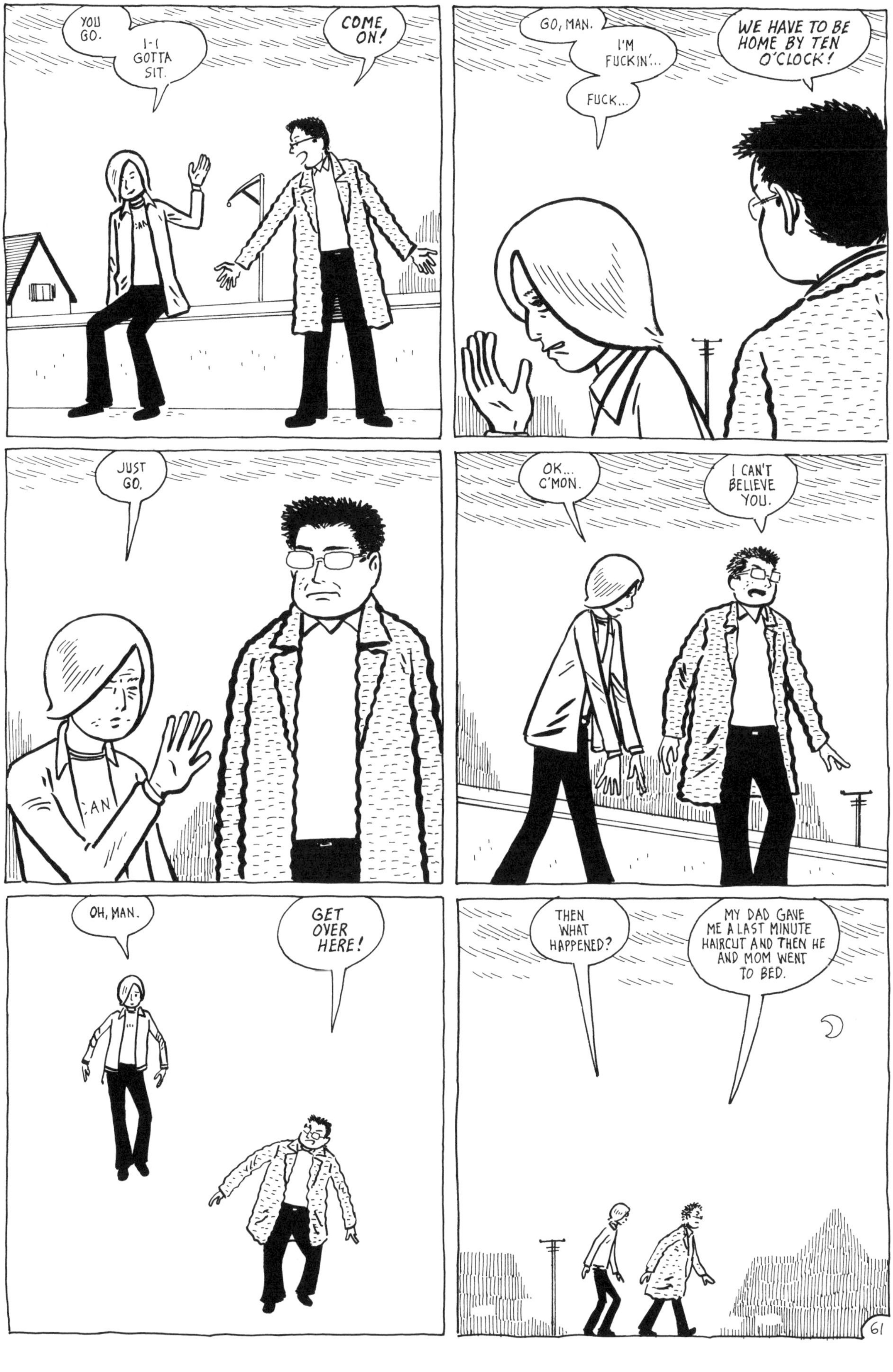
YOU GO.
I-I GOTTA SIT.
COME ON!
GO, MAN.
I'M FUCKIN'...
FUCK...
WE HAVE TO BE HOME BY TEN O'CLOCK!
JUST GO.
OK... C'MON.
I CAN'T BELIEVE YOU.
OH, MAN.
GET OVER HERE!
THEN WHAT HAPPENED?
MY DAD GAVE ME A LAST MINUTE HAIRCUT AND THEN HE AND MOM WENT TO BED.

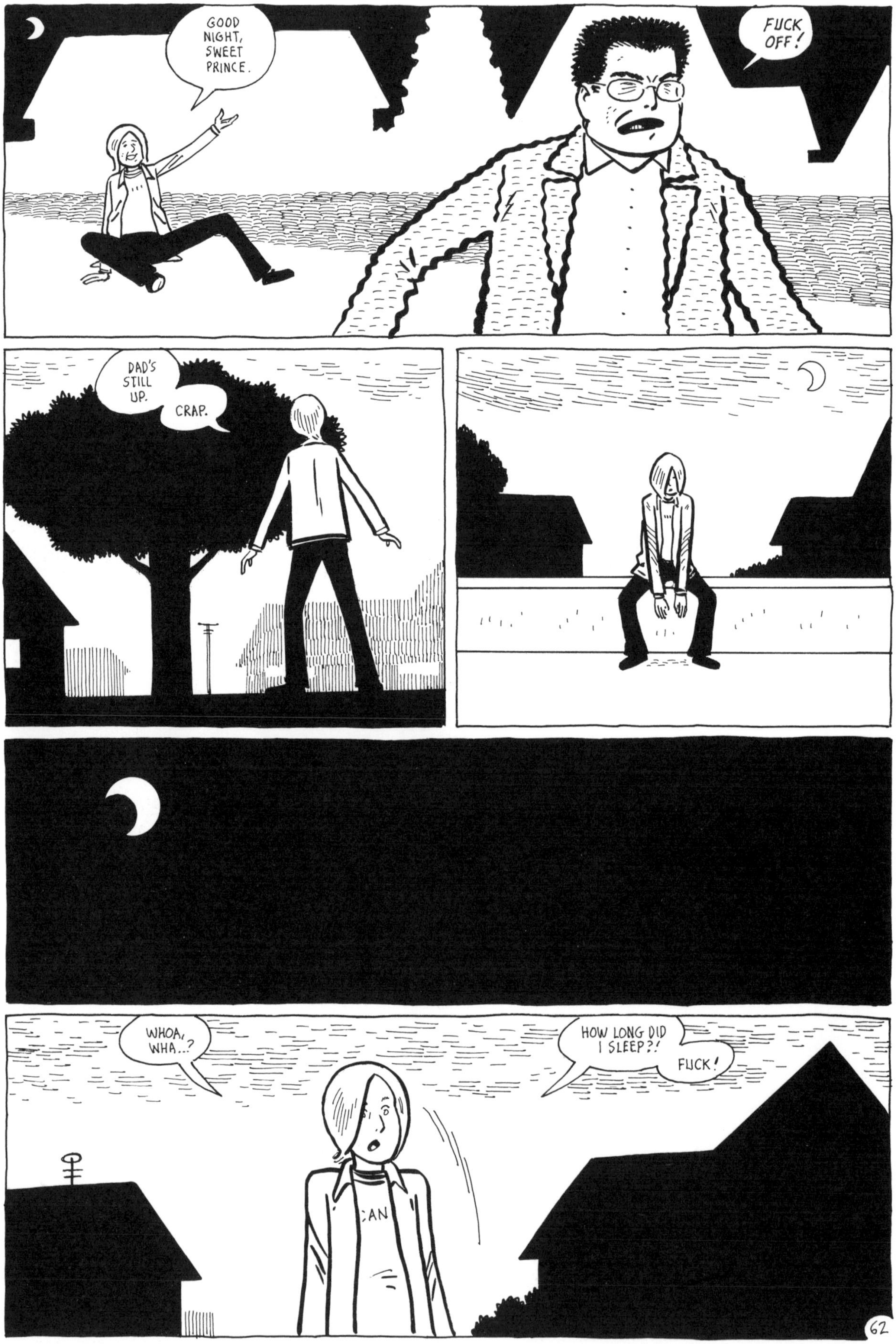
GOOD NIGHT, SWEET PRINCE.
FUCK OFF!
DAD'S STILL UP.
CRAP.
WHOA, WHA..?
HOW LONG DID I SLEEP?!
FUCK!
CAN

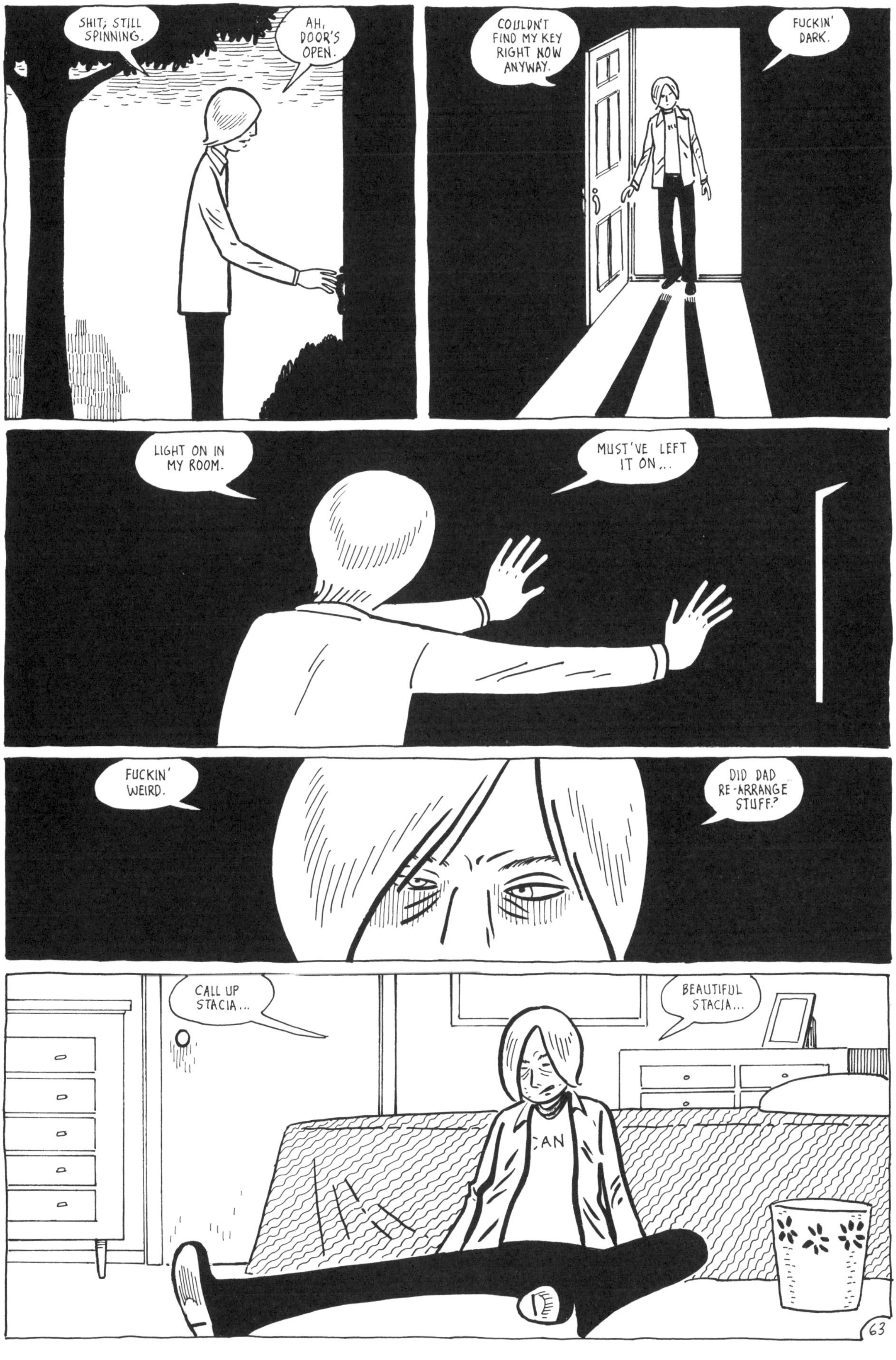
SHIT; STILL SPINNING.
AH, DOOR'S OPEN.
COULDN'T FIND MY KEY RIGHT NOW ANYWAY.
FUCKIN' DARK.
LIGHT ON IN MY ROOM.
MUST'VE LEFT IT ON...
FUCKIN' WEIRD.
DID DAD RE-ARRANGE STUFF?
CALL UP STACIA...
BEAUTIFUL STACIA...
CAN

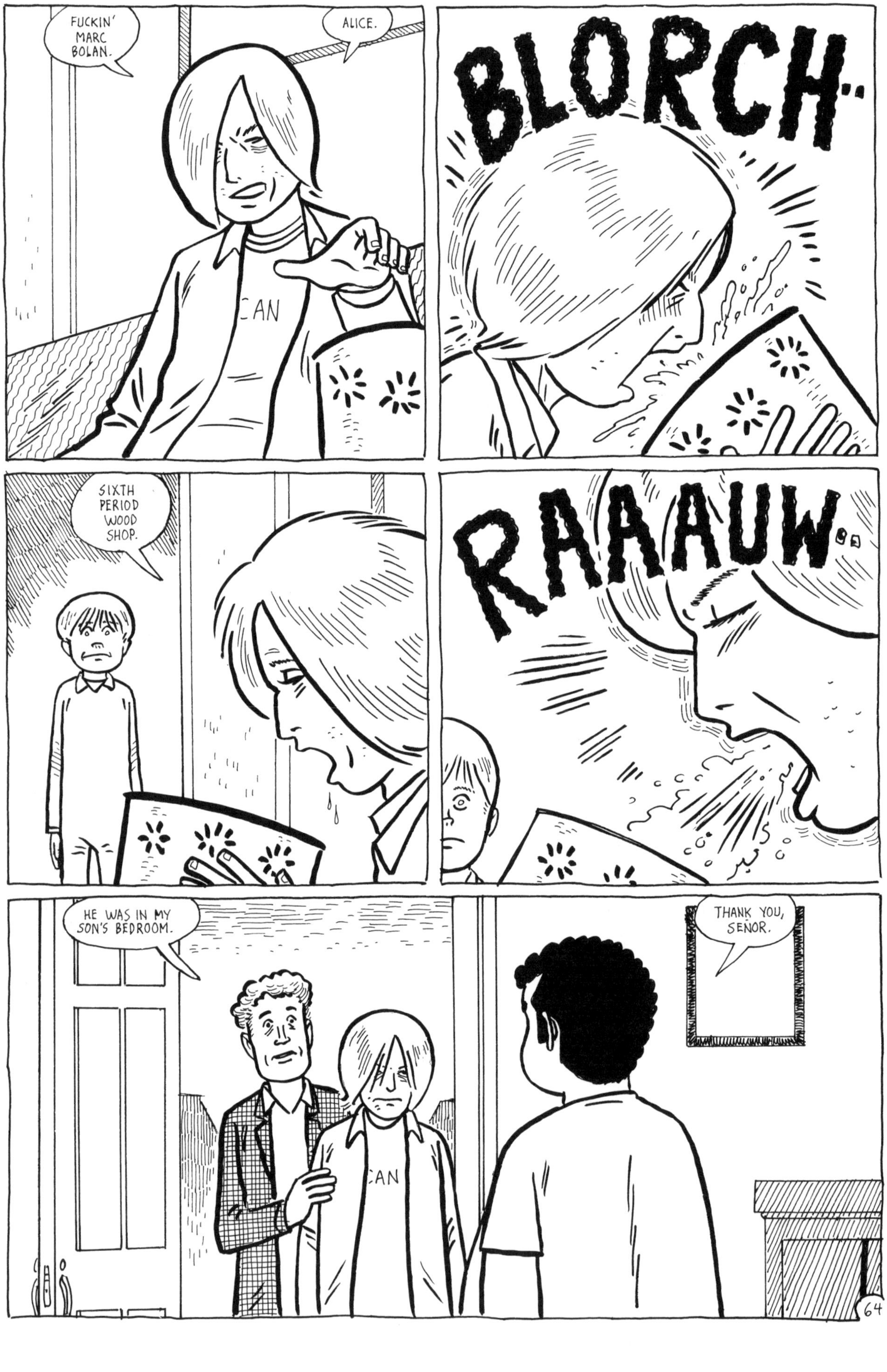
FUCKIN' MARC BOLAN.
ALICE.
BLORCH-
SIXTH PERIOD WOOD SHOP.
RAAAUW-
CAN
HE WAS IN MY SON'S BEDROOM.
THANK YOU, SEÑOR.

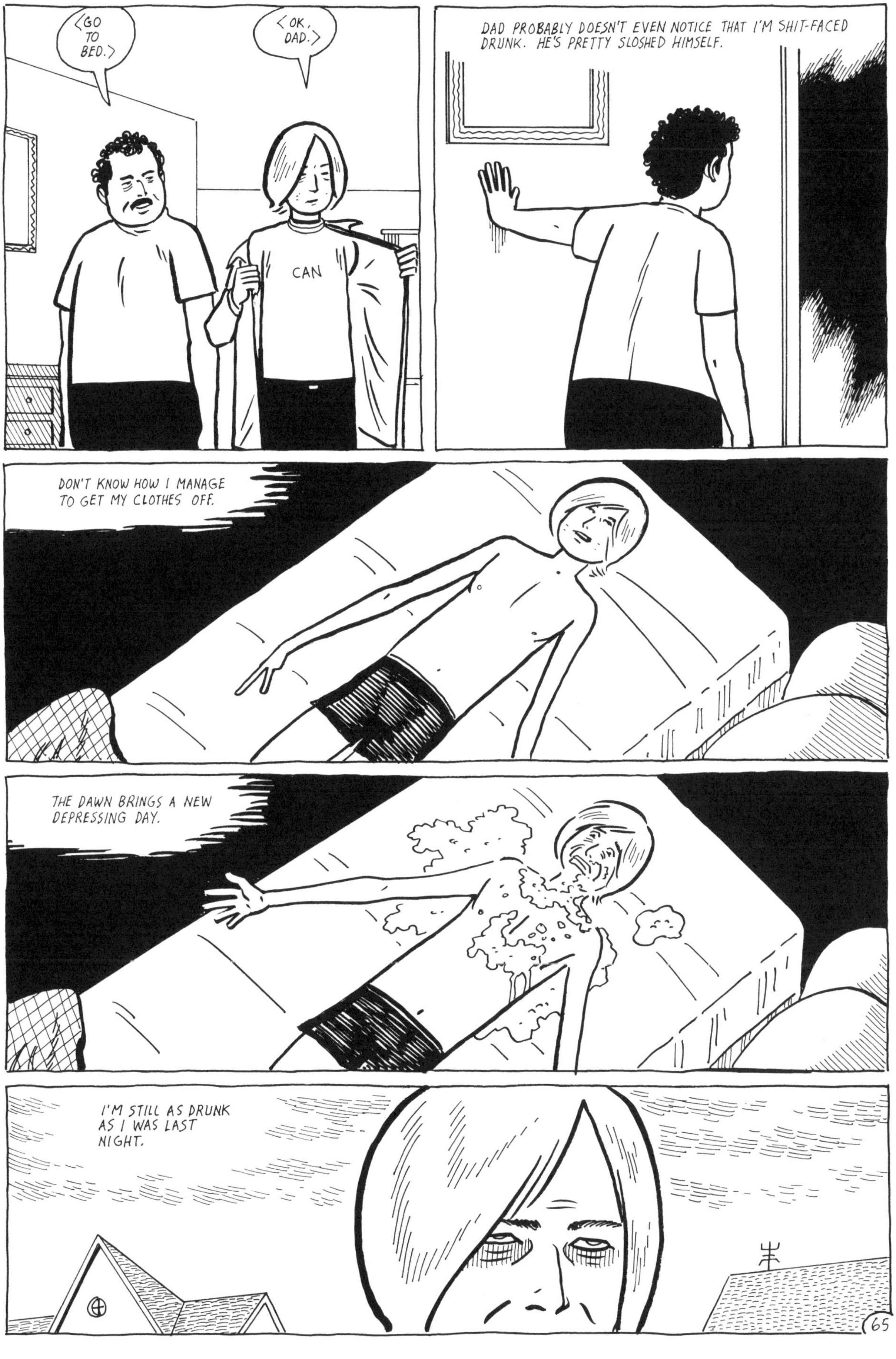

<GO TO BED.>
<OK, DAD.>
CAN
DAD PROBABLY DOESN'T EVEN NOTICE THAT I'M SHIT-FACED DRUNK. HE'S PRETTY SLOSHED HIMSELF.
DON'T KNOW HOW I MANAGE TO GET MY CLOTHES OFF.
THE DAWN BRINGS A NEW DEPRESSING DAY.
I'M STILL AS DRUNK AS I WAS LAST NIGHT.

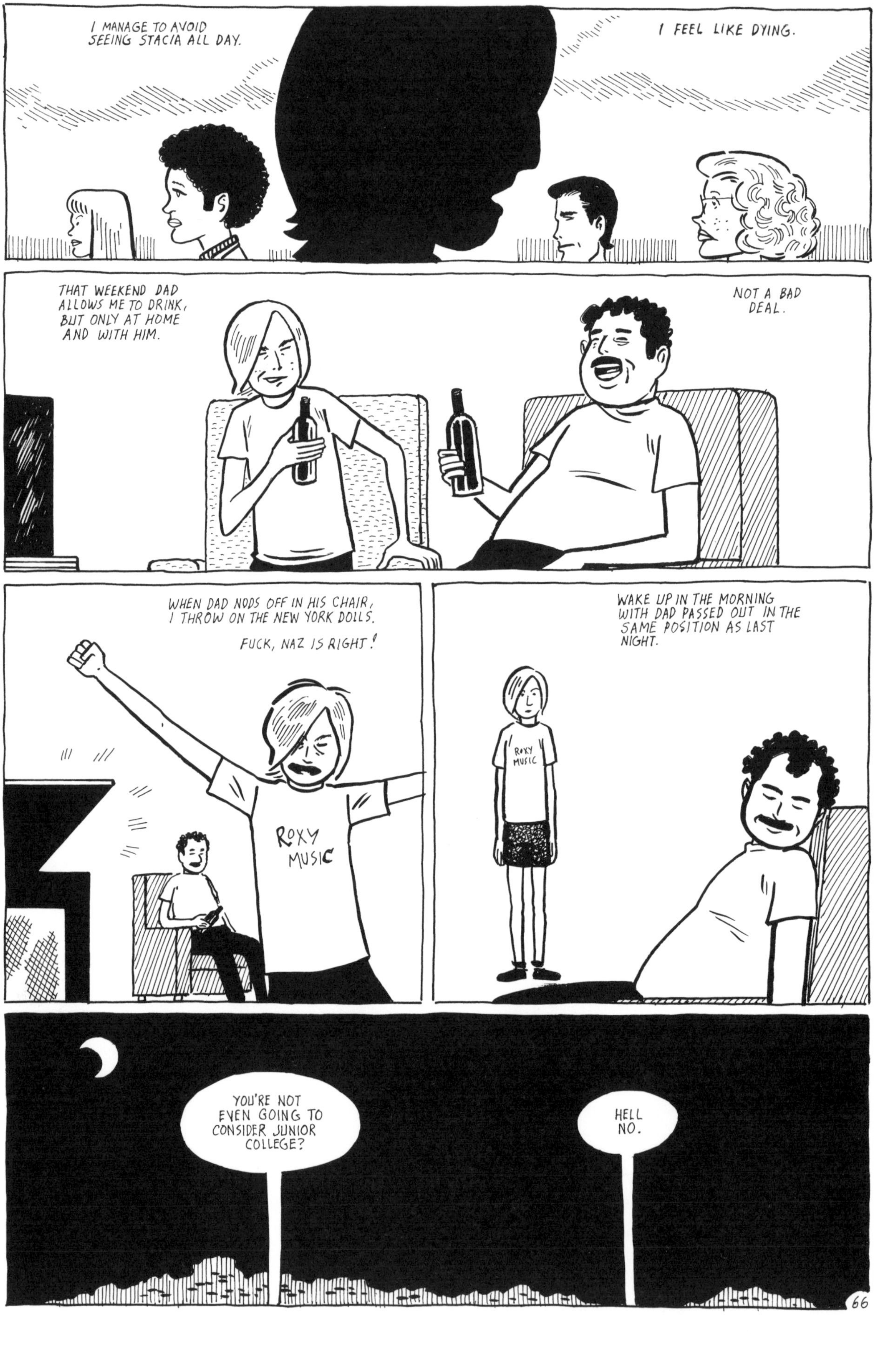
I MANAGE TO AVOID SEEING STACIA ALL DAY.
I FEEL LIKE DYING.
THAT WEEKEND DAD ALLOWS ME TO DRINK, BUT ONLY AT HOME AND WITH HIM.
NOT A BAD DEAL.
WHEN DAD NODS OFF IN HIS CHAIR, I THROW ON THE NEW YORK DOLLS.
FUCK, NAZ IS RIGHT!
ROXY MUSIC
WAKE UP IN THE MORNING WITH DAD PASSED OUT IN THE SAME POSITION AS LAST NIGHT.
ROXY MUSIC
YOU'RE NOT EVEN GOING TO CONSIDER JUNIOR COLLEGE?
HELL NO.

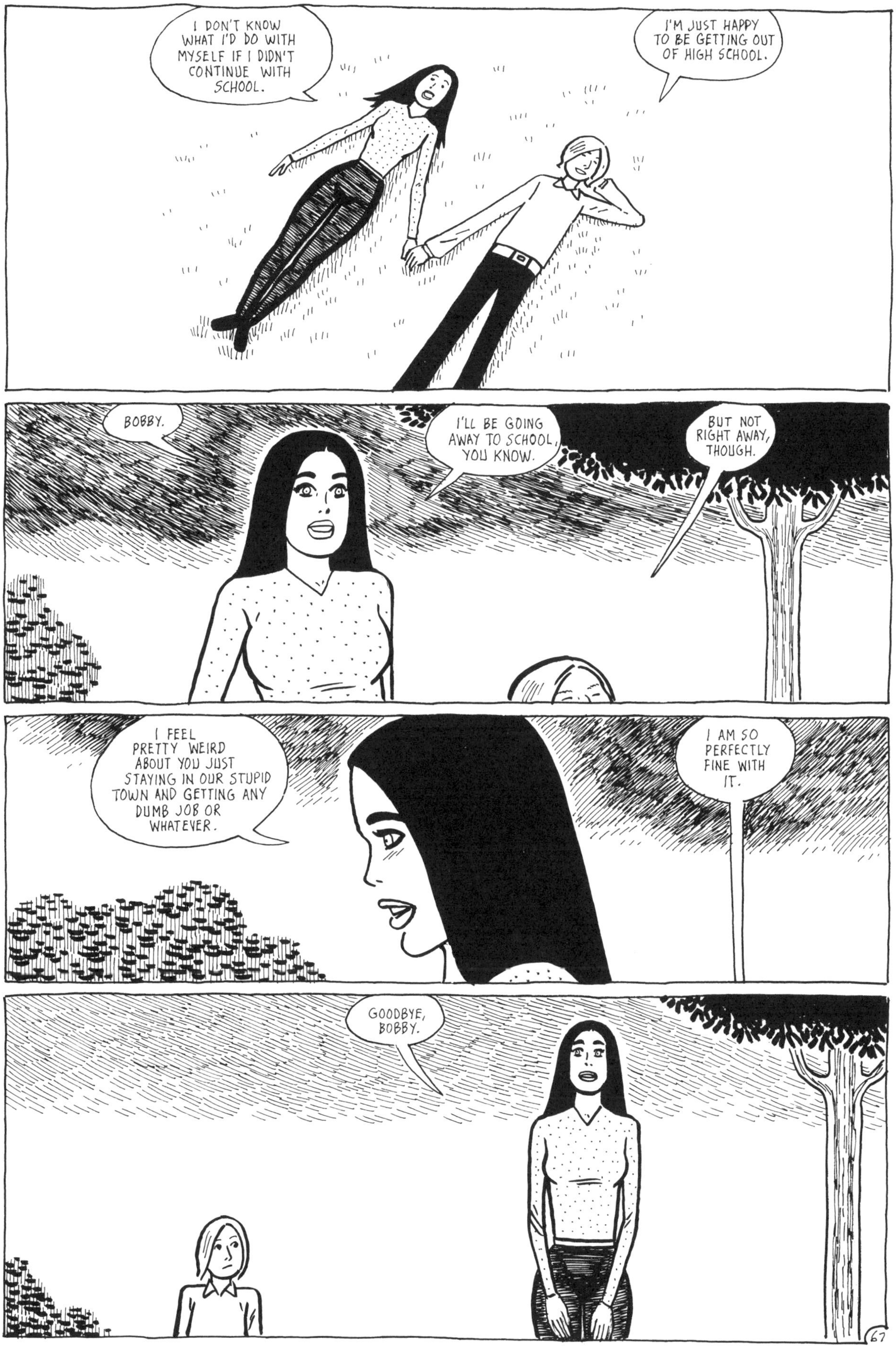

I DON'T KNOW WHAT I'D DO WITH MYSELF IF I DIDN'T CONTINUE WITH SCHOOL.
I'M JUST HAPPY TO BE GETTING OUT OF HIGH SCHOOL.
BOBBY.
I'LL BE GOING AWAY TO SCHOOL, YOU KNOW.
BUT NOT RIGHT AWAY, THOUGH.
I FEEL PRETTY WEIRD ABOUT YOU JUST STAYING IN OUR STUPID TOWN AND GETTING ANY DUMB JOB OR WHATEVER.
I AM SO PERFECTLY FINE WITH IT.
GOODBYE, BOBBY.

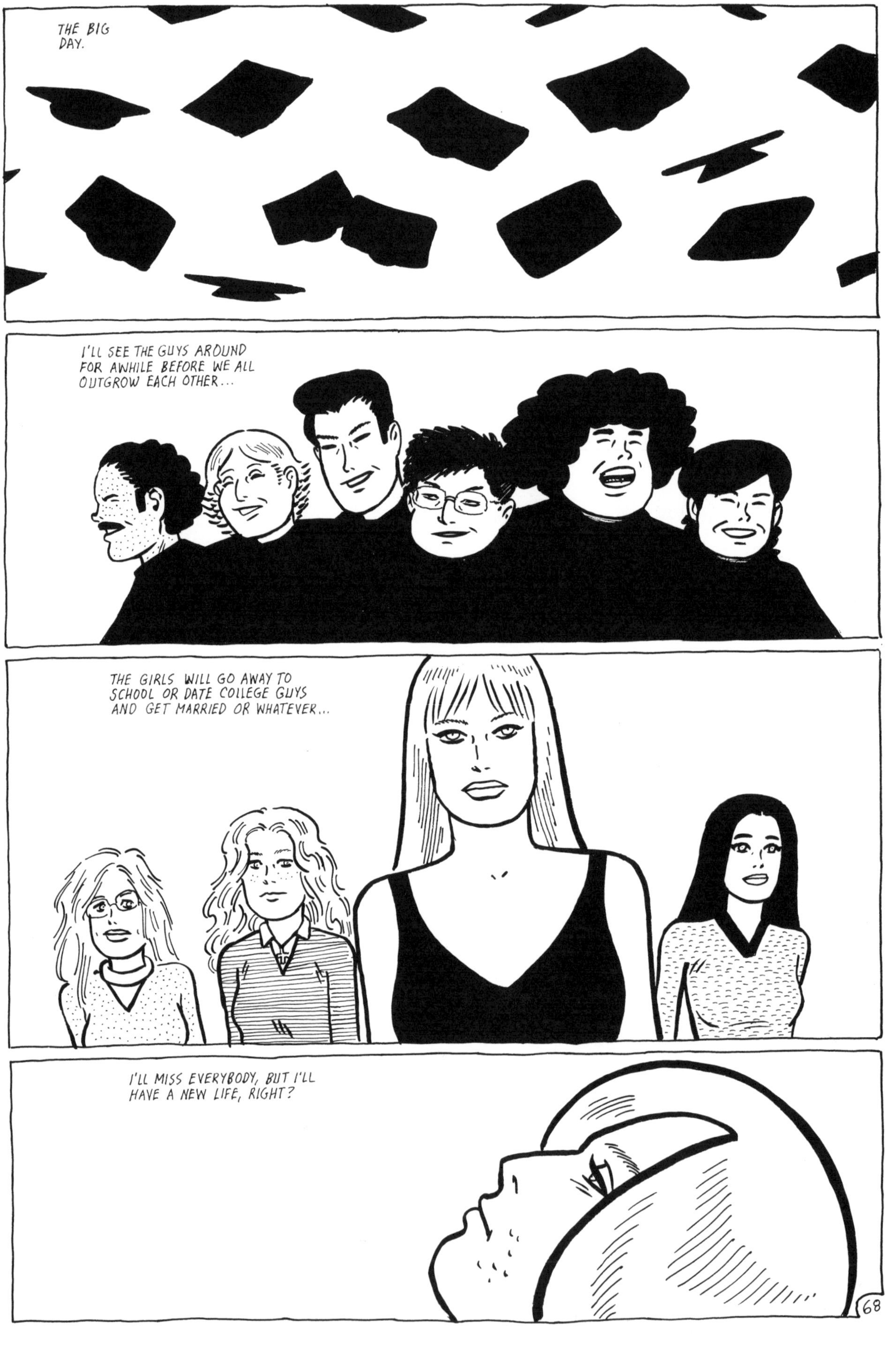

THE BIG DAY.
I'LL SEE THE GUYS AROUND FOR AWHILE BEFORE WE ALL OUTGROW EACH OTHER...
THE GIRLS WILL GO AWAY TO SCHOOL OR DATE COLLEGE GUYS AND GET MARRIED OR WHATEVER...
I'LL MISS EVERYBODY, BUT I'LL HAVE A NEW LIFE, RIGHT?

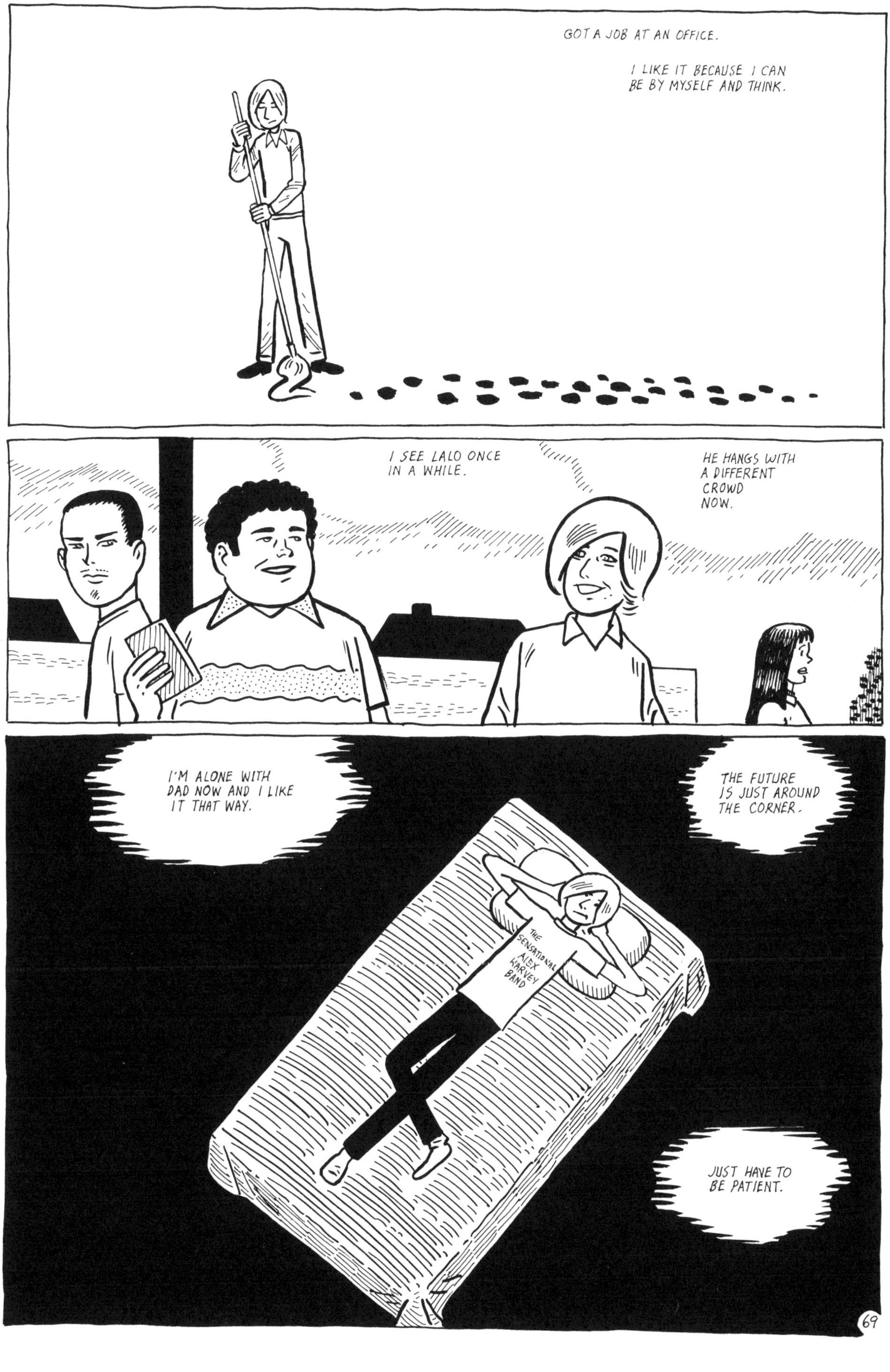
GOT A JOB AT AN OFFICE.
I LIKE IT BECAUSE I CAN BE BY MYSELF AND THINK.
I SEE LALO ONCE IN A WHILE.
HE HANGS WITH A DIFFERENT CROWD NOW.
I'M ALONE WITH DAD NOW AND I LIKE IT THAT WAY.
THE SENSATIONAL ALEX HARVEY BAND
THE FUTURE IS JUST AROUND THE CORNER.
JUST HAVE TO BE PATIENT.

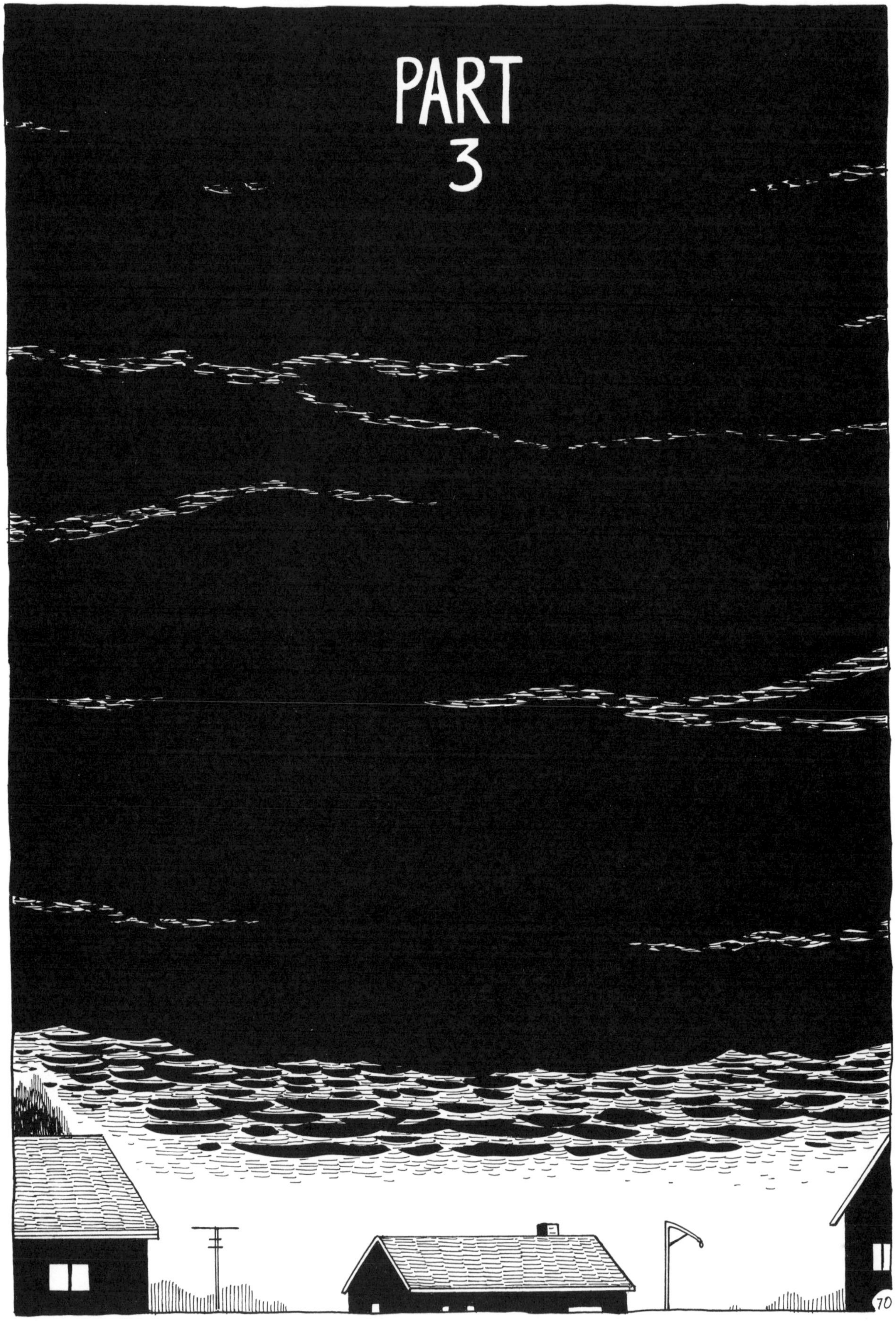
PART
3

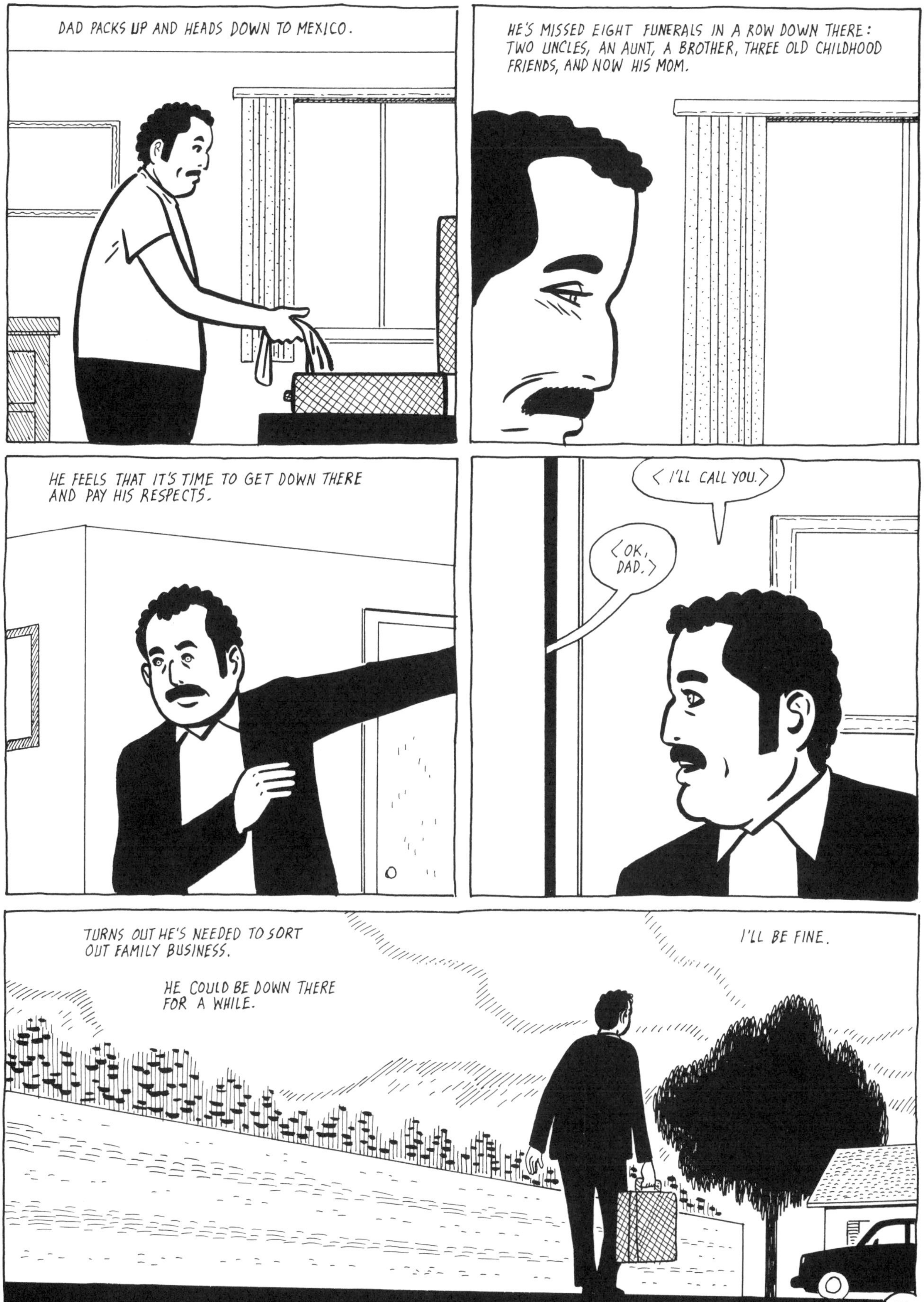

DAD PACKS UP AND HEADS DOWN TO MEXICO.
HE'S MISSED EIGHT FUNERALS IN A ROW DOWN THERE: TWO UNCLES, AN AUNT, A BROTHER, THREE OLD CHILDHOOD FRIENDS, AND NOW HIS MOM.
HE FEELS THAT IT'S TIME TO GET DOWN THERE AND PAY HIS RESPECTS.
< I'LL CALL YOU. >
< OK, DAD. >
TURNS OUT HE'S NEEDED TO SORT OUT FAMILY BUSINESS.
HE COULD BE DOWN THERE FOR A WHILE.
I'LL BE FINE.

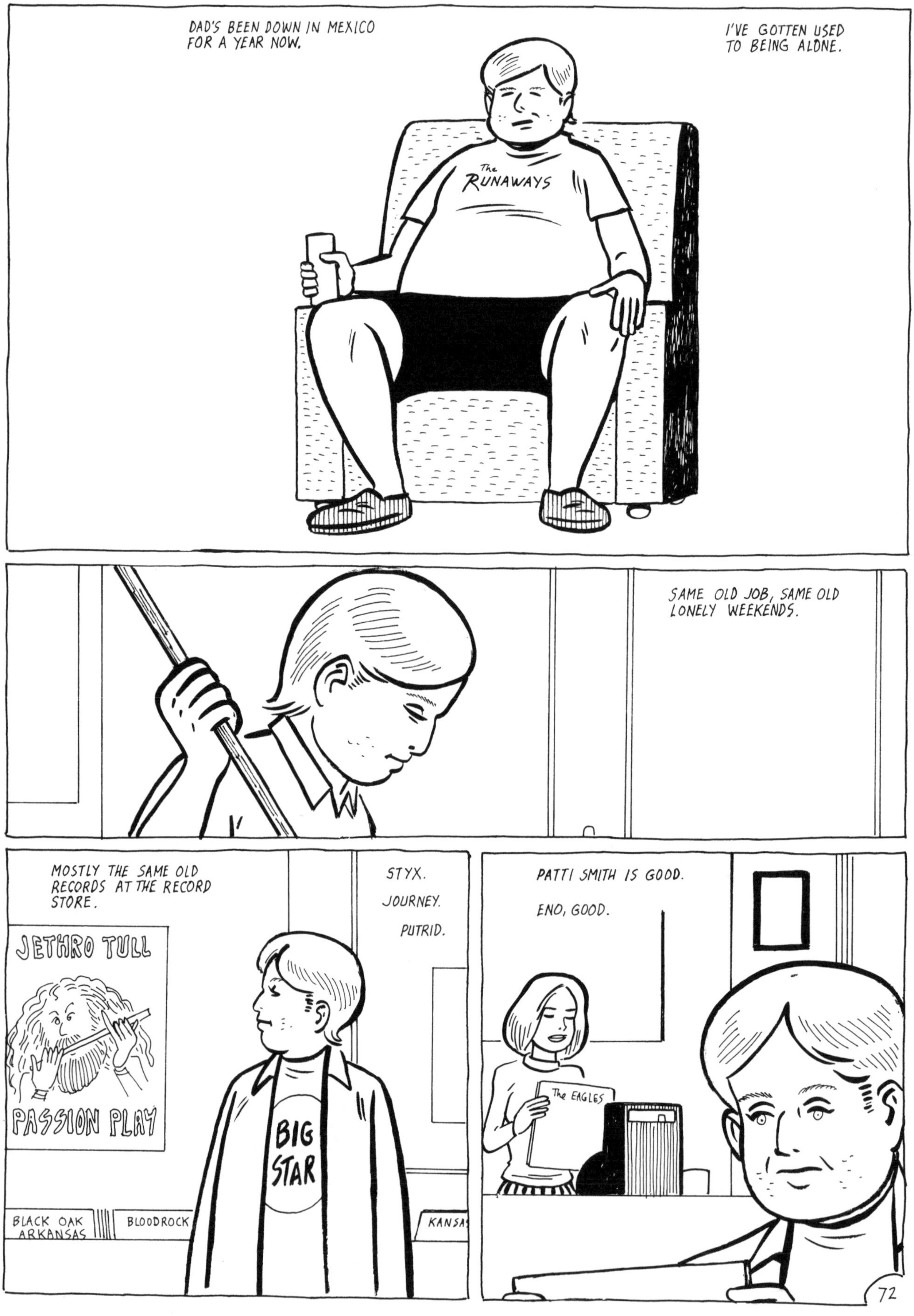
DAD'S BEEN DOWN IN MEXICO FOR A YEAR NOW.
I'VE GOTTEN USED TO BEING ALONE.
The RUNAWAYS
SAME OLD JOB, SAME OLD LONELY WEEKENDS.
MOSTLY THE SAME OLD RECORDS AT THE RECORD STORE.
JETHRO TULL
PASSION PLAY
BIG STAR
BLACK OAK ARKANSAS
BLOODROCK
STYX.
JOURNEY.
PUTRID.
PATTI SMITH IS GOOD.
ENO, GOOD.
The EAGLES

KISS ALIVE:
IT'LL DO.

HEY.

HEY, BOY.

LORENA MADRID!

MY CHILDHOOD SECRET LOVE!

I DON'T EVEN HEAR WHAT SHE'S SAYING TO ME, I JUST STARE INTO HER FACE, HER EYES.

I DON'T REMEMBER WHEN I SAW HER LAST. I DON'T REMEMBER IF SHE KNEW ME OR NOT.

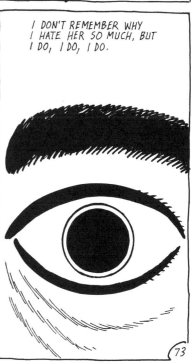

I DON'T REMEMBER WHY I HATE HER SO MUCH, BUT I DO, I DO, I DO.

73

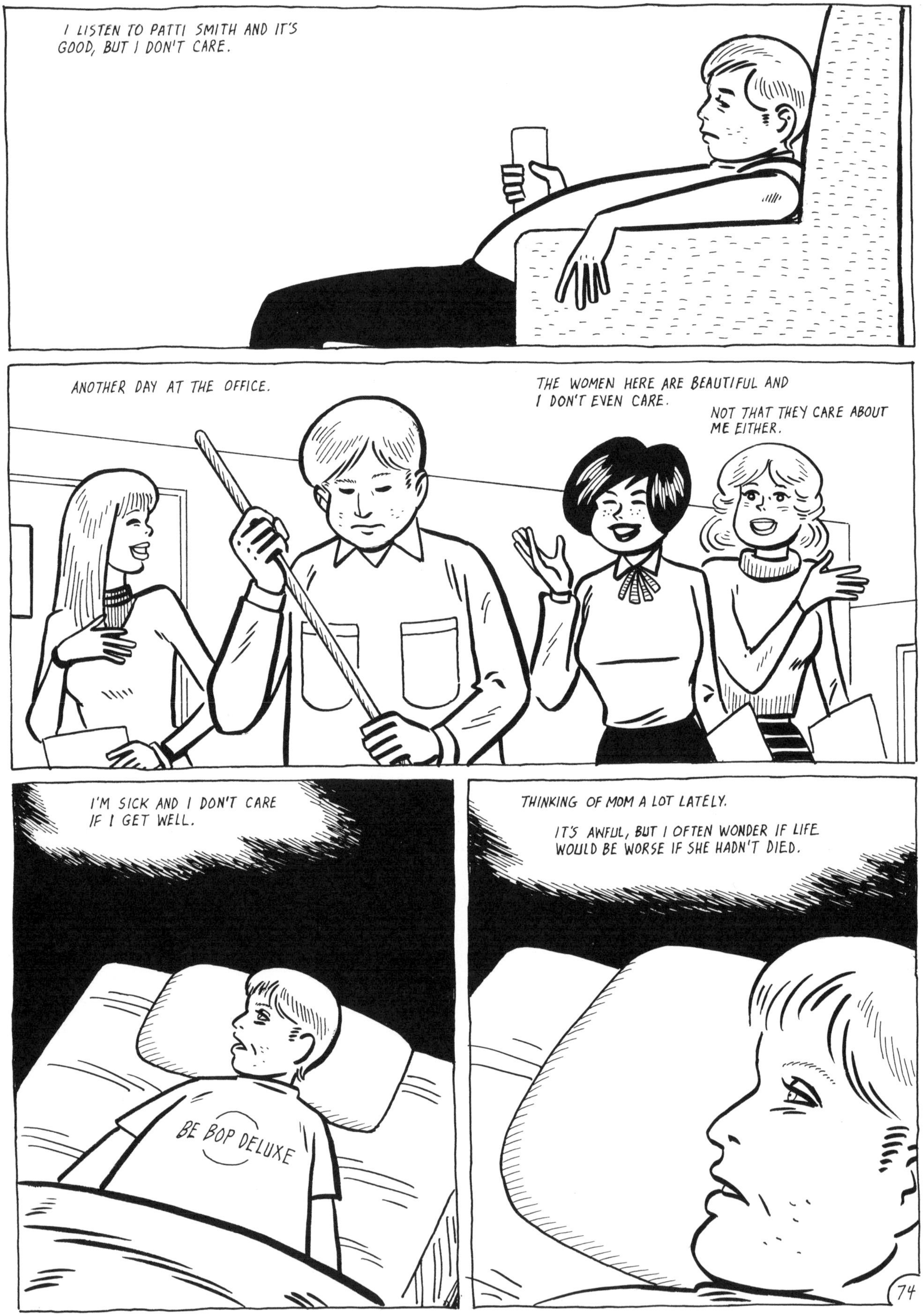
I LISTEN TO PATTI SMITH AND IT'S GOOD, BUT I DON'T CARE.
ANOTHER DAY AT THE OFFICE.
THE WOMEN HERE ARE BEAUTIFUL AND I DON'T EVEN CARE.
NOT THAT THEY CARE ABOUT ME EITHER.
I'M SICK AND I DON'T CARE IF I GET WELL.
BE BOP DELUXE
THINKING OF MOM A LOT LATELY.
IT'S AWFUL, BUT I OFTEN WONDER IF LIFE WOULD BE WORSE IF SHE HADN'T DIED.

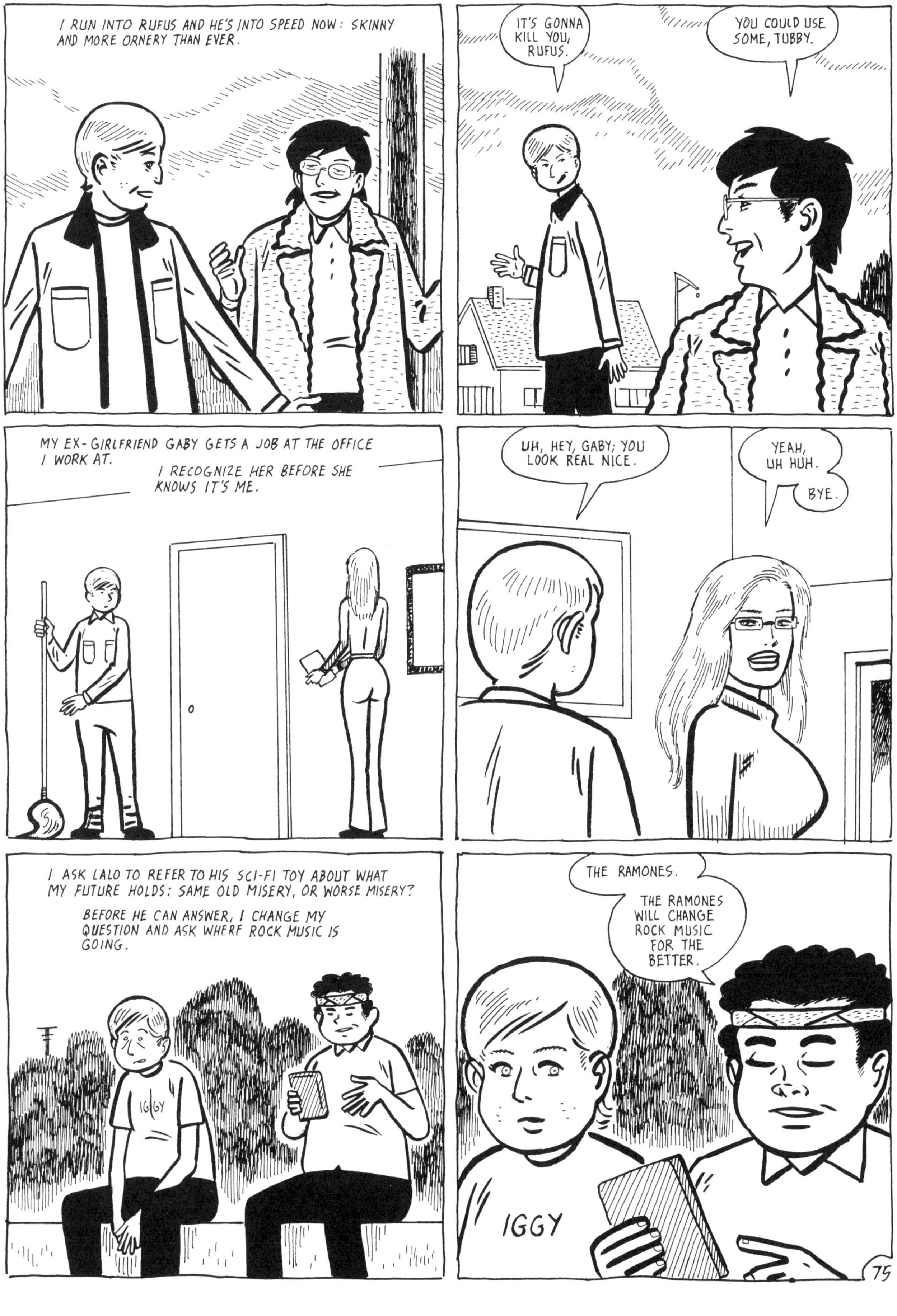

I RUN INTO RUFUS AND HE'S INTO SPEED NOW: SKINNY AND MORE ORNERY THAN EVER.
IT'S GONNA KILL YOU, RUFUS.
YOU COULD USE SOME, TUBBY.
MY EX-GIRLFRIEND GABY GETS A JOB AT THE OFFICE I WORK AT.
I RECOGNIZE HER BEFORE SHE KNOWS IT'S ME.
UH, HEY, GABY; YOU LOOK REAL NICE.
YEAH, UH HUH.
BYE.
I ASK LALO TO REFER TO HIS SCI-FI TOY ABOUT WHAT MY FUTURE HOLDS: SAME OLD MISERY, OR WORSE MISERY?
BEFORE HE CAN ANSWER, I CHANGE MY QUESTION AND ASK WHERE ROCK MUSIC IS GOING.
IGGY
THE RAMONES.
THE RAMONES WILL CHANGE ROCK MUSIC FOR THE BETTER.
IGGY

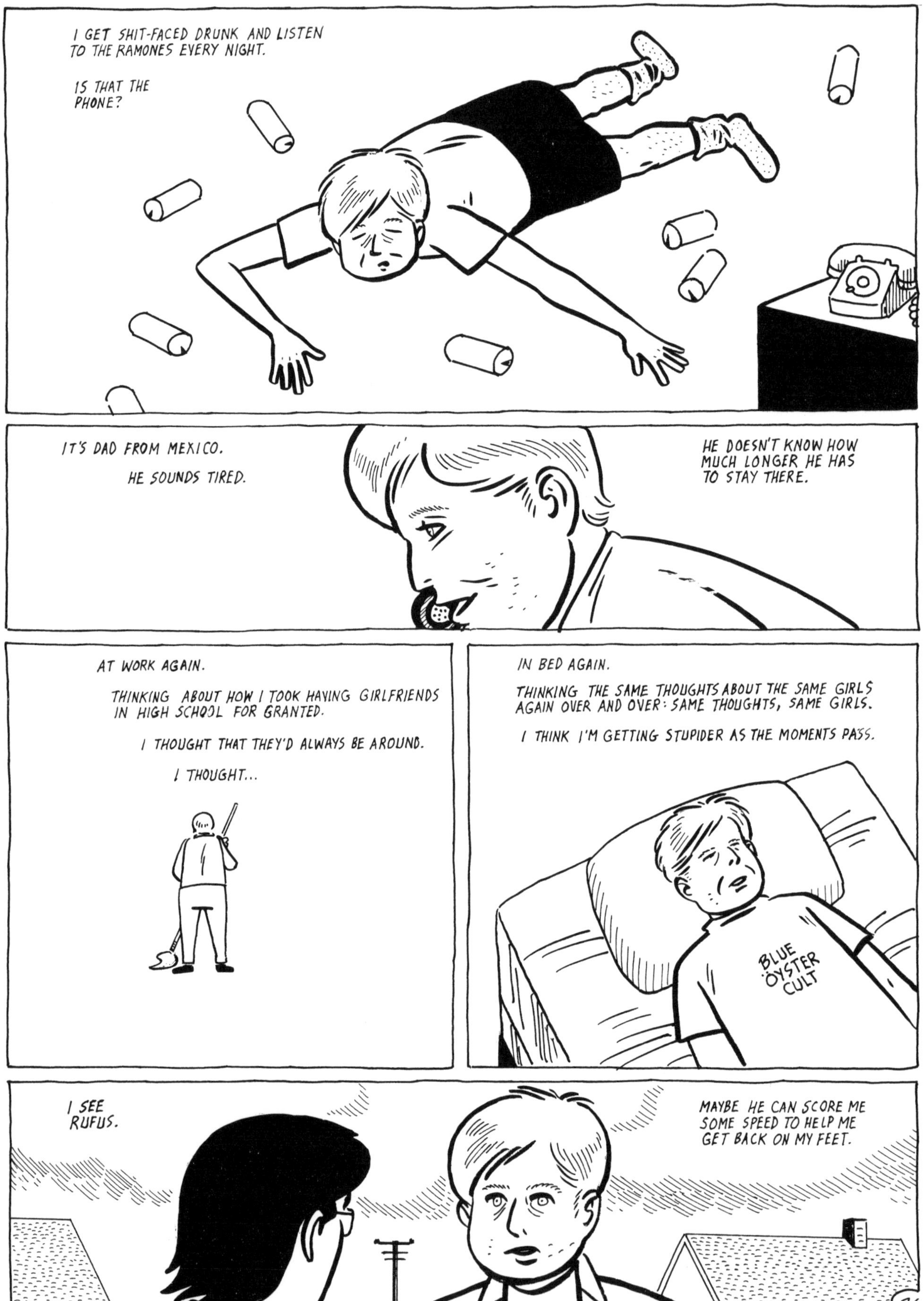
I GET SHIT-FACED DRUNK AND LISTEN TO THE RAMONES EVERY NIGHT.
IS THAT THE PHONE?
IT'S DAD FROM MEXICO.
HE SOUNDS TIRED.
HE DOESN'T KNOW HOW MUCH LONGER HE HAS TO STAY THERE.
AT WORK AGAIN.
THINKING ABOUT HOW I TOOK HAVING GIRLFRIENDS IN HIGH SCHOOL FOR GRANTED.
I THOUGHT THAT THEY'D ALWAYS BE AROUND.
I THOUGHT...
IN BED AGAIN.
THINKING THE SAME THOUGHTS ABOUT THE SAME GIRLS AGAIN OVER AND OVER: SAME THOUGHTS, SAME GIRLS.
I THINK I'M GETTING STUPIDER AS THE MOMENTS PASS.
BLUE ÖYSTER CULT
I SEE RUFUS.
MAYBE HE CAN SCORE ME SOME SPEED TO HELP ME GET BACK ON MY FEET.

I'M DOING SPEED A LOT AND I END UP AT A CHEAP TRICK CONCERT BY MYSELF.
STYX
The RAMONES
I MAKE THE MISTAKE OF WEARING A RAMONES T-SHIRT AND GET THE MOST SHIT I'VE EVER GOTTEN IN MY LIFE.
CHEAP TRICK COME ON AND THEY'RE REAL GOOD!
I GIVE 'EM ALL I'VE GOT!
The RAMONES
THE UNPLEASANT CROWD PUSHES ME FARTHER AND FARTHER BACK INTO THE HALL.
I DISAPPEAR INTO THE VOID.
TO THE POINT OF NO RETURN.

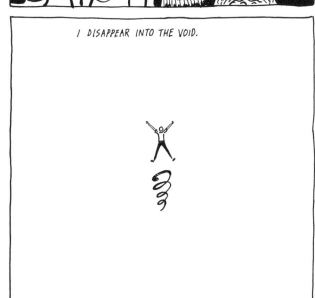

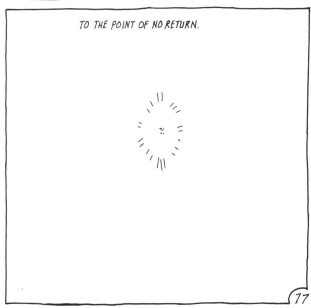

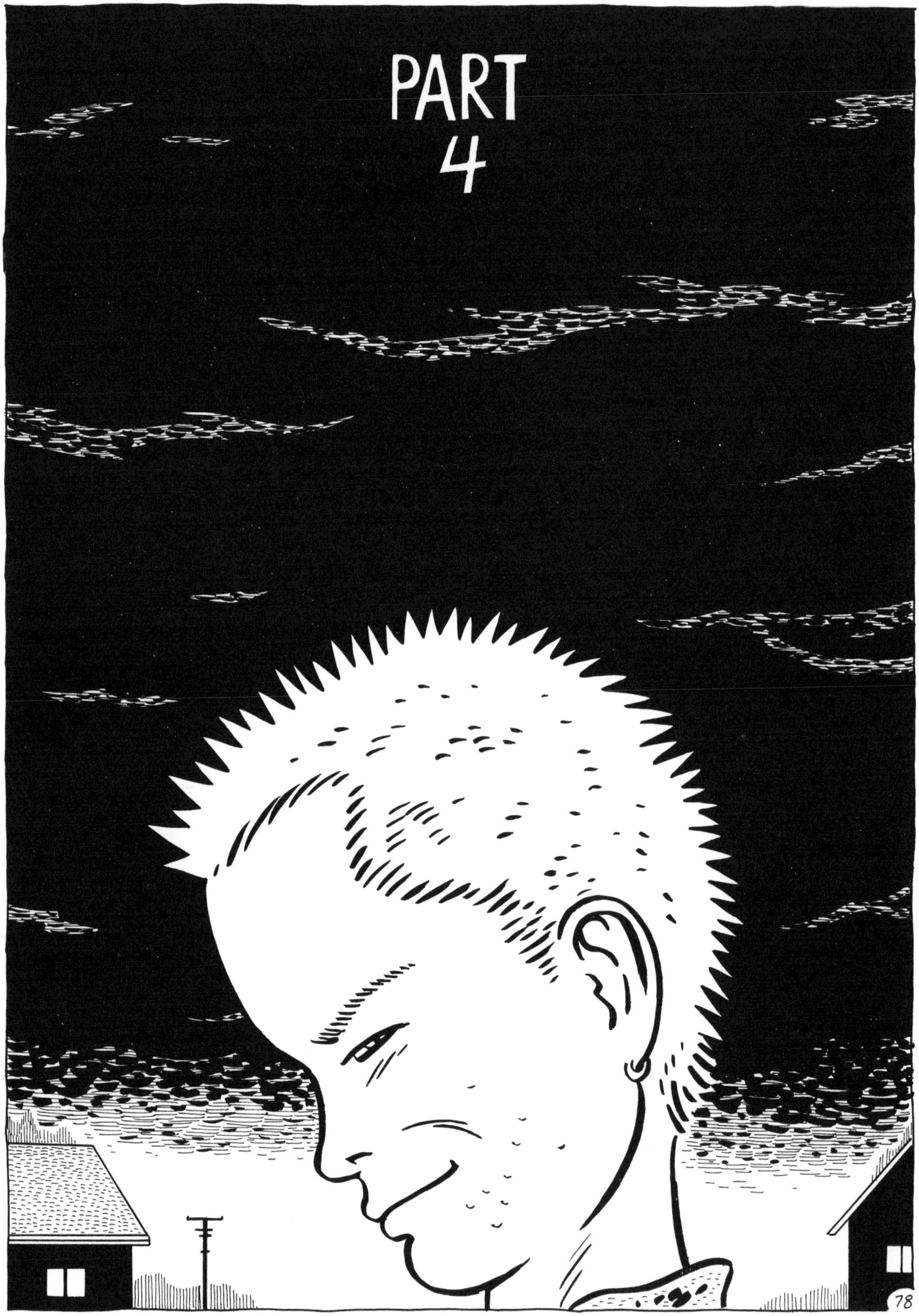
PART
4

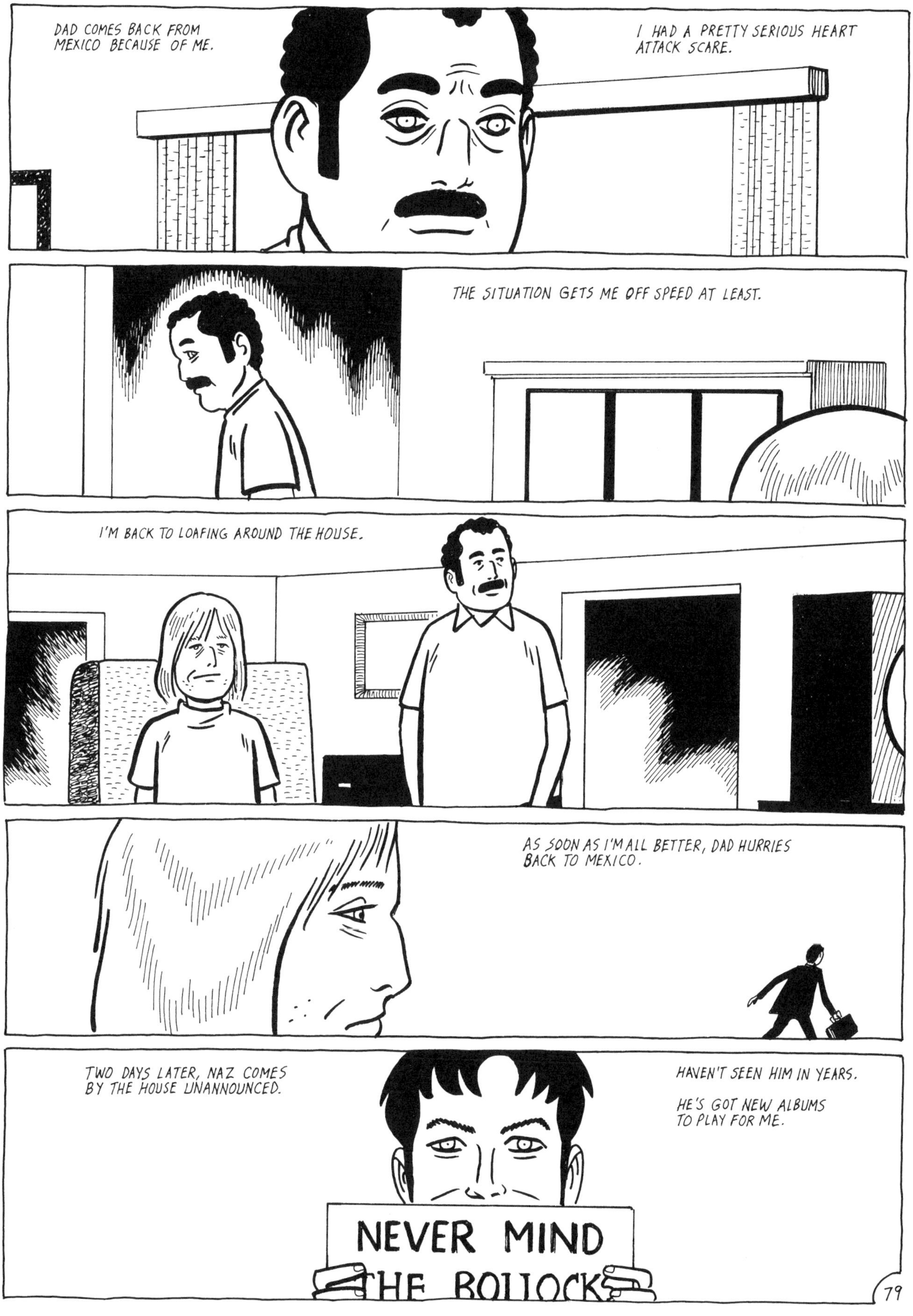
DAD COMES BACK FROM MEXICO BECAUSE OF ME.
I HAD A PRETTY SERIOUS HEART ATTACK SCARE.
THE SITUATION GETS ME OFF SPEED AT LEAST.
I'M BACK TO LOAFING AROUND THE HOUSE.
AS SOON AS I'M ALL BETTER, DAD HURRIES BACK TO MEXICO.
TWO DAYS LATER, NAZ COMES BY THE HOUSE UNANNOUNCED.
HAVEN'T SEEN HIM IN YEARS.
HE'S GOT NEW ALBUMS TO PLAY FOR ME.
NEVER MIND

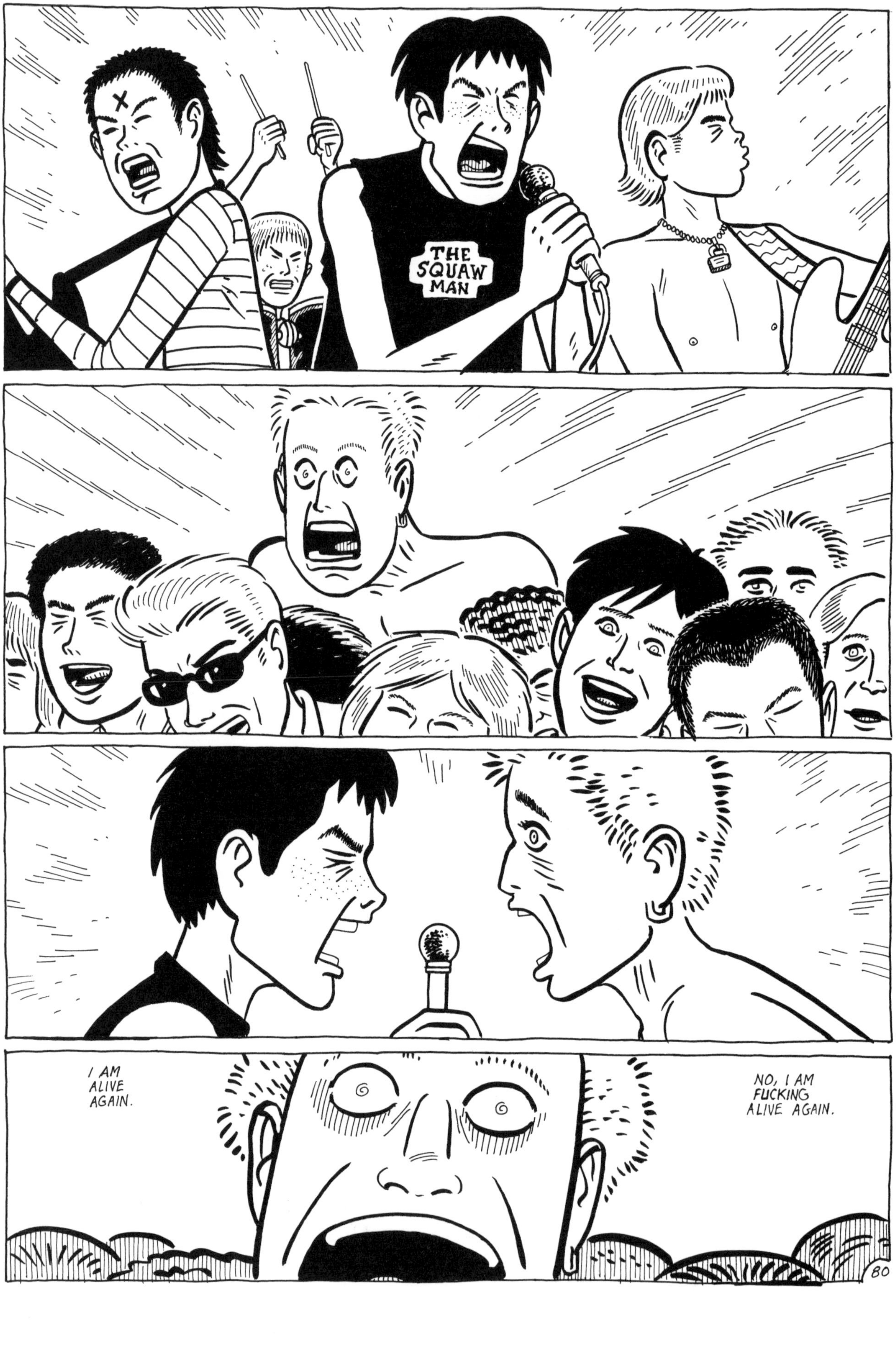
THE SQUAW MAN
I AM ALIVE AGAIN.
NO, I AM FUCKING ALIVE AGAIN.

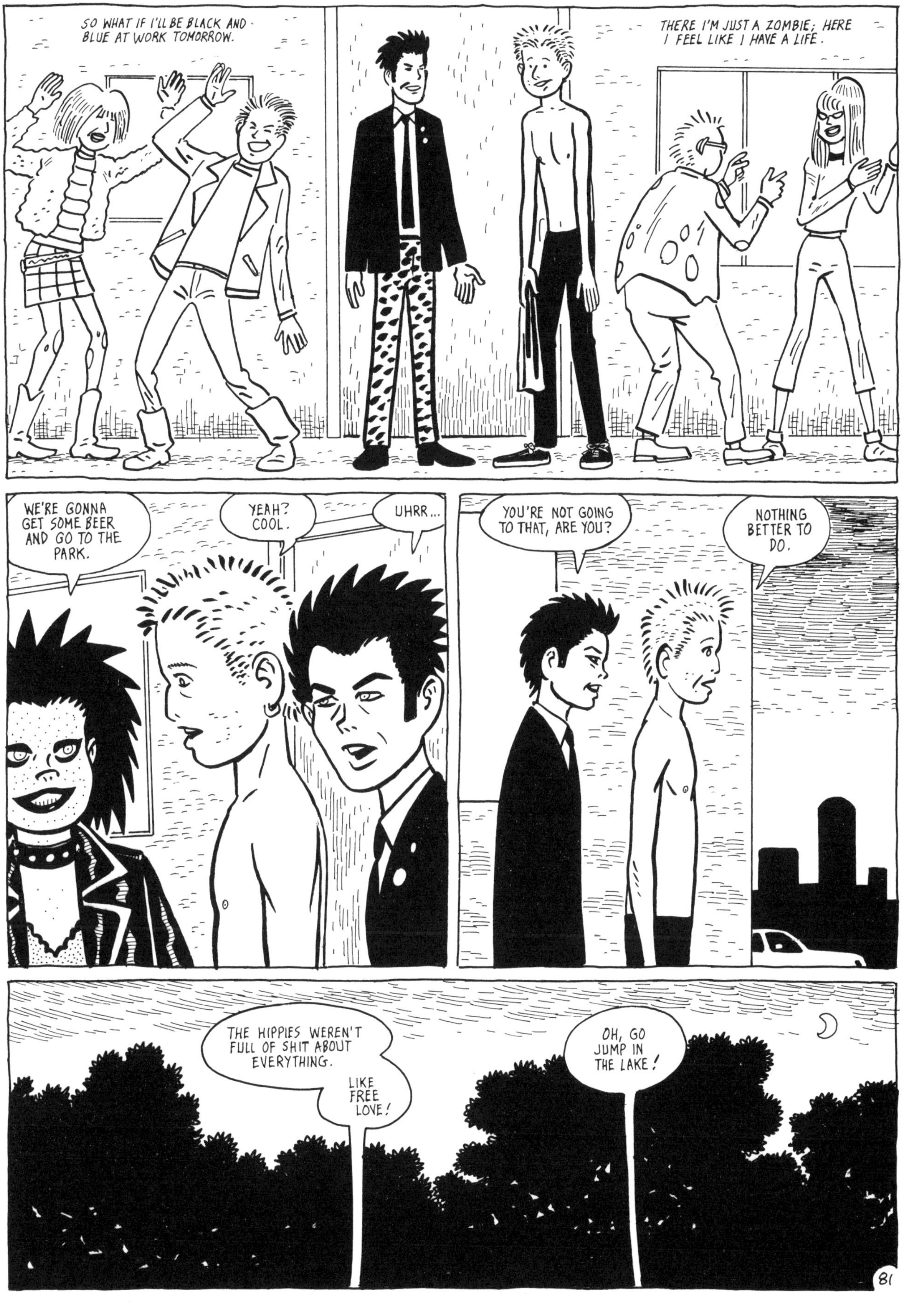

SO WHAT IF I'LL BE BLACK AND BLUE AT WORK TOMORROW.
THERE I'M JUST A ZOMBIE; HERE I FEEL LIKE I HAVE A LIFE.
WE'RE GONNA GET SOME BEER AND GO TO THE PARK.
YEAH? COOL.
UHRR...
YOU'RE NOT GOING TO THAT, ARE YOU?
NOTHING BETTER TO DO.
THE HIPPIES WEREN'T FULL OF SHIT ABOUT EVERYTHING.
LIKE FREE LOVE!
OH, GO JUMP IN THE LAKE!

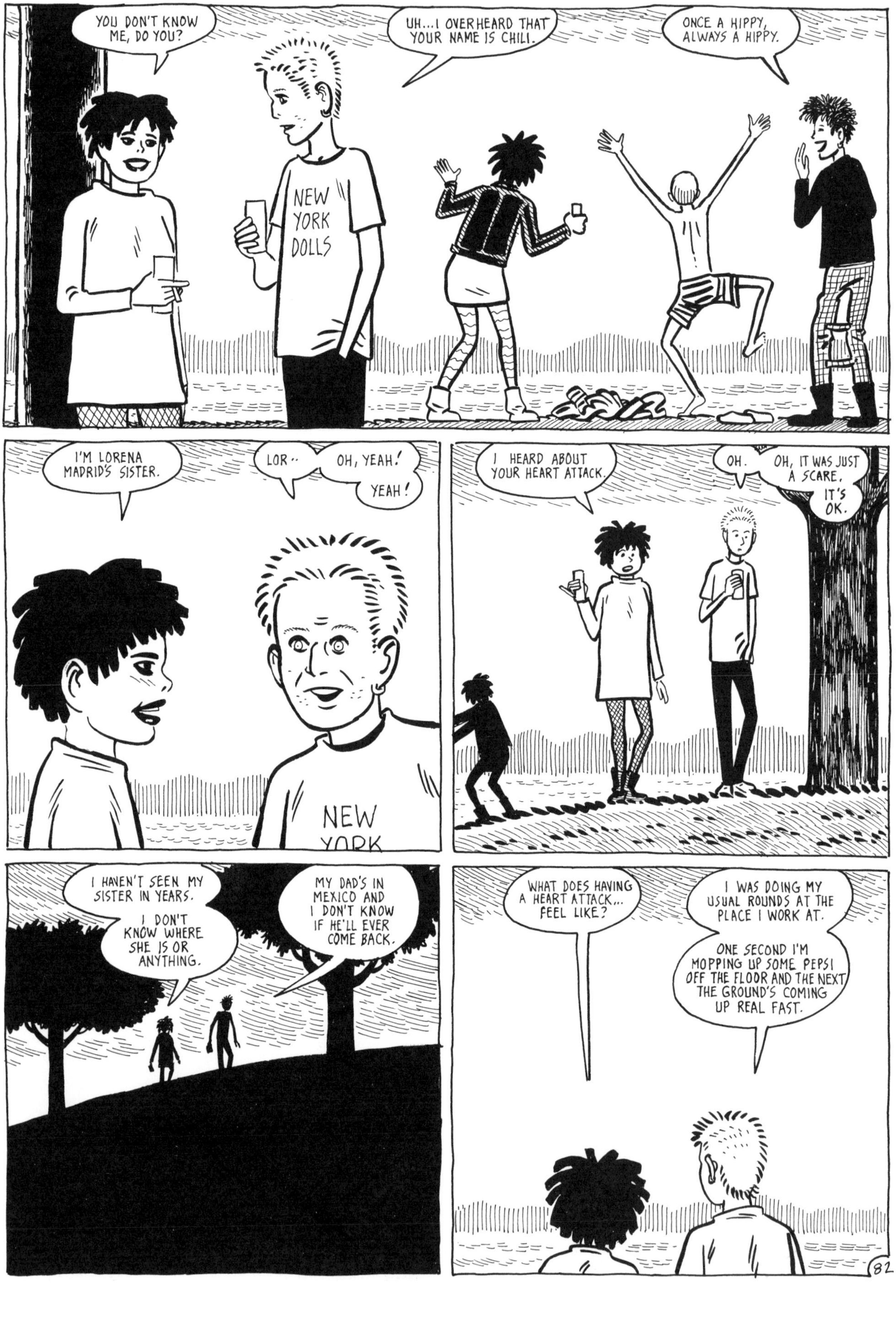

YOU DON'T KNOW ME, DO YOU?
UH... I OVERHEARD THAT YOUR NAME IS CHILI.
ONCE A HIPPY, ALWAYS A HIPPY.
NEW YORK DOLLS
I'M LORENA MADRID'S SISTER.
LOR··
OH, YEAH!
YEAH!
NEW YORK
I HEARD ABOUT YOUR HEART ATTACK.
OH.
OH, IT WAS JUST A SCARE.
IT'S OK.
I HAVEN'T SEEN MY SISTER IN YEARS.
I DON'T KNOW WHERE SHE IS OR ANYTHING.
MY DAD'S IN MEXICO AND I DON'T KNOW IF HE'LL EVER COME BACK.
WHAT DOES HAVING A HEART ATTACK... FEEL LIKE?
I WAS DOING MY USUAL ROUNDS AT THE PLACE I WORK AT.
ONE SECOND I'M MOPPING UP SOME PEPSI OFF THE FLOOR AND THE NEXT THE GROUND'S COMING UP REAL FAST.

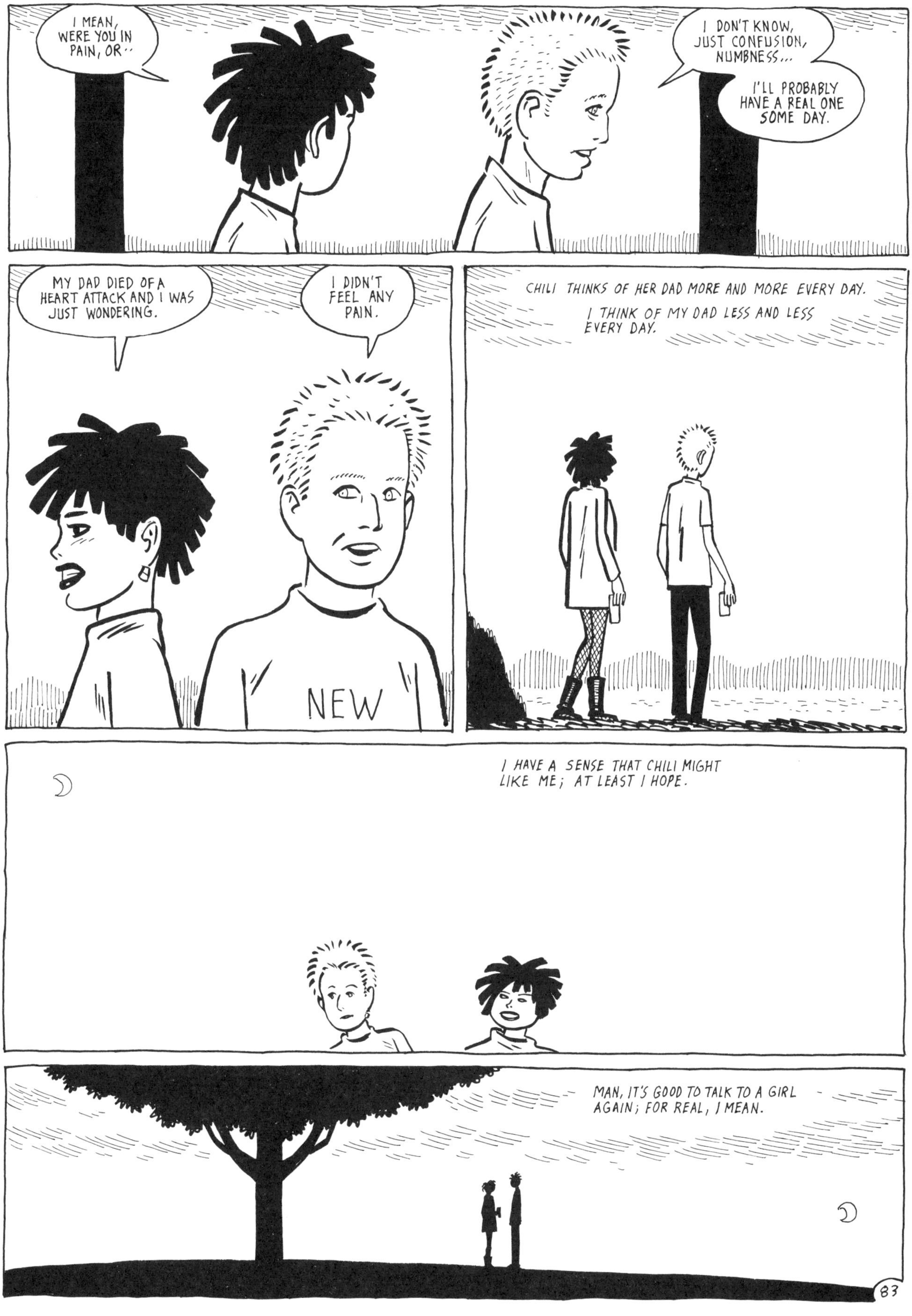

I MEAN, WERE YOU IN PAIN, OR··
I DON'T KNOW, JUST CONFUSION, NUMBNESS...
I'LL PROBABLY HAVE A REAL ONE SOME DAY.
MY DAD DIED OF A HEART ATTACK AND I WAS JUST WONDERING.
I DIDN'T FEEL ANY PAIN.
NEW
CHILI THINKS OF HER DAD MORE AND MORE EVERY DAY.
I THINK OF MY DAD LESS AND LESS EVERY DAY.
I HAVE A SENSE THAT CHILI MIGHT LIKE ME; AT LEAST I HOPE.
MAN, IT'S GOOD TO TALK TO A GIRL AGAIN; FOR REAL, I MEAN.

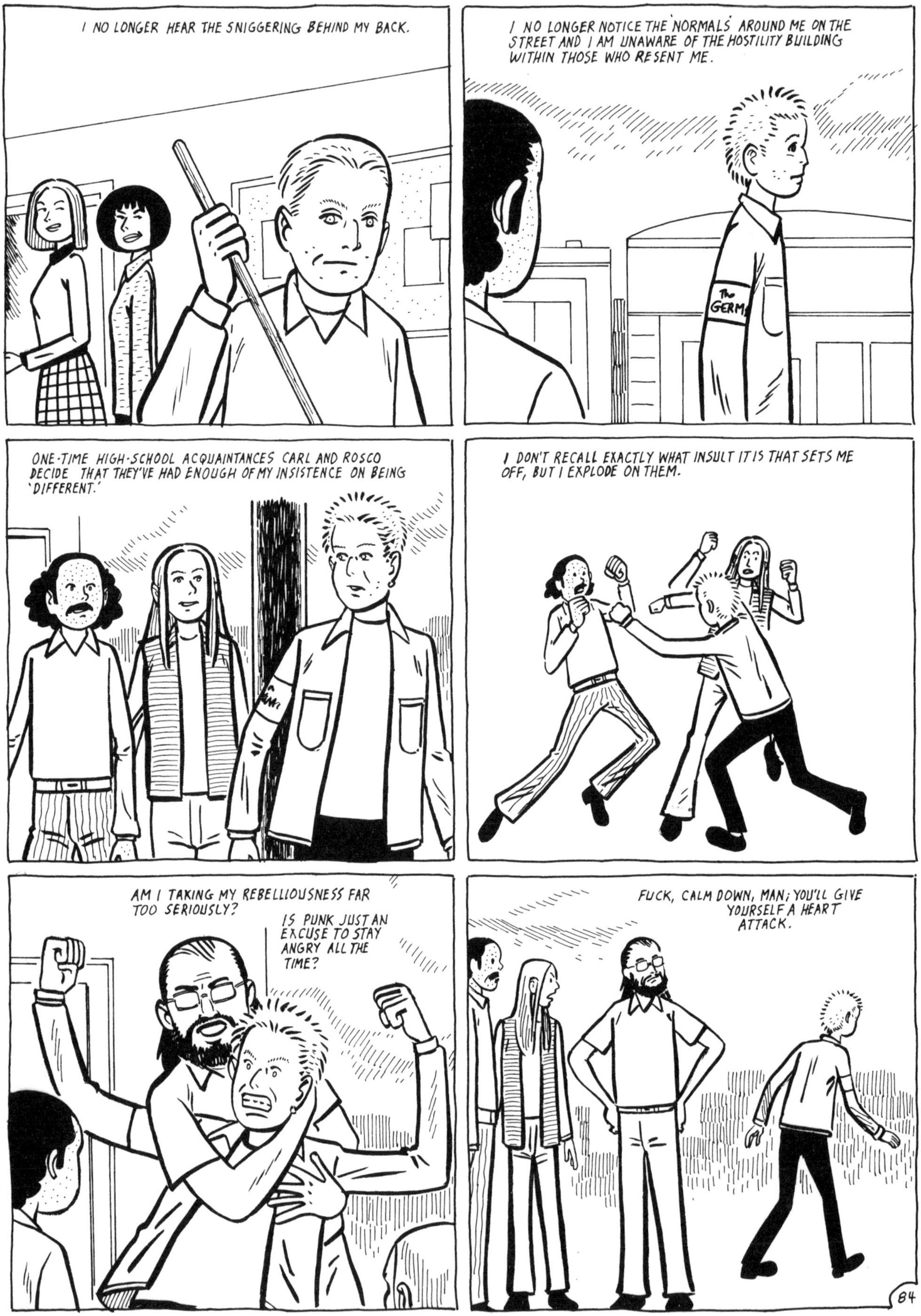
I NO LONGER HEAR THE SNIGGERING BEHIND MY BACK.
I NO LONGER NOTICE THE 'NORMALS' AROUND ME ON THE STREET AND I AM UNAWARE OF THE HOSTILITY BUILDING WITHIN THOSE WHO RESENT ME.
The GERMS
ONE-TIME HIGH-SCHOOL ACQUAINTANCES CARL AND ROSCO DECIDE THAT THEY'VE HAD ENOUGH OF MY INSISTENCE ON BEING 'DIFFERENT.'
I DON'T RECALL EXACTLY WHAT INSULT IT IS THAT SETS ME OFF, BUT I EXPLODE ON THEM.
AM I TAKING MY REBELLIOUSNESS FAR TOO SERIOUSLY?
IS PUNK JUST AN EXCUSE TO STAY ANGRY ALL THE TIME?
FUCK, CALM DOWN, MAN; YOU'LL GIVE YOURSELF A HEART ATTACK.

NAZ IS ACQUAINTED WITH LOCAL GENIUS GARAGE JAZZ MUSICIAN BARTON.

NAZ WANTS TO BRING HIM WITH US TO THE X GIG ON SATURDAY.

GOD, WHY?

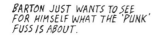

BARTON JUST WANTS TO SEE FOR HIMSELF WHAT THE 'PUNK' FUSS IS ABOUT.

BARTON KEEPS HIS JUDGING TO HIMSELF.

AS I SUSPECTED, BARTON HATES EVERYTHING ABOUT THE GIG, THE PEOPLE, THE MUSIC, THE ATTITUDE...

85

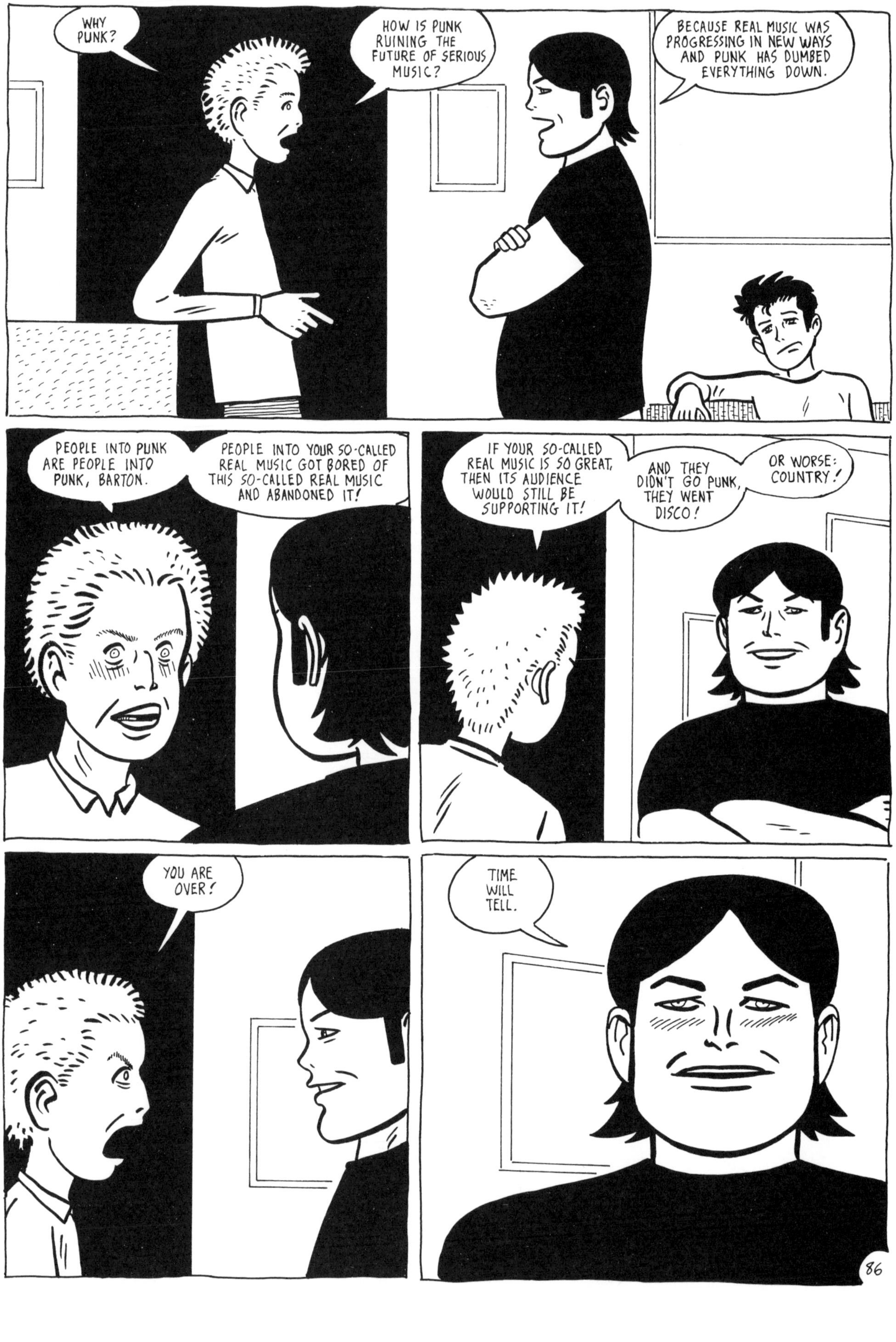
WHY PUNK?
HOW IS PUNK RUINING THE FUTURE OF SERIOUS MUSIC?
BECAUSE REAL MUSIC WAS PROGRESSING IN NEW WAYS AND PUNK HAS DUMBED EVERYTHING DOWN.
PEOPLE INTO PUNK ARE PEOPLE INTO PUNK, BARTON.
PEOPLE INTO YOUR SO-CALLED REAL MUSIC GOT BORED OF THIS SO-CALLED REAL MUSIC AND ABANDONED IT!
IF YOUR SO-CALLED REAL MUSIC IS SO GREAT, THEN ITS AUDIENCE WOULD STILL BE SUPPORTING IT!
AND THEY DIDN'T GO PUNK, THEY WENT DISCO!
OR WORSE: COUNTRY!
YOU ARE OVER!
TIME WILL TELL.

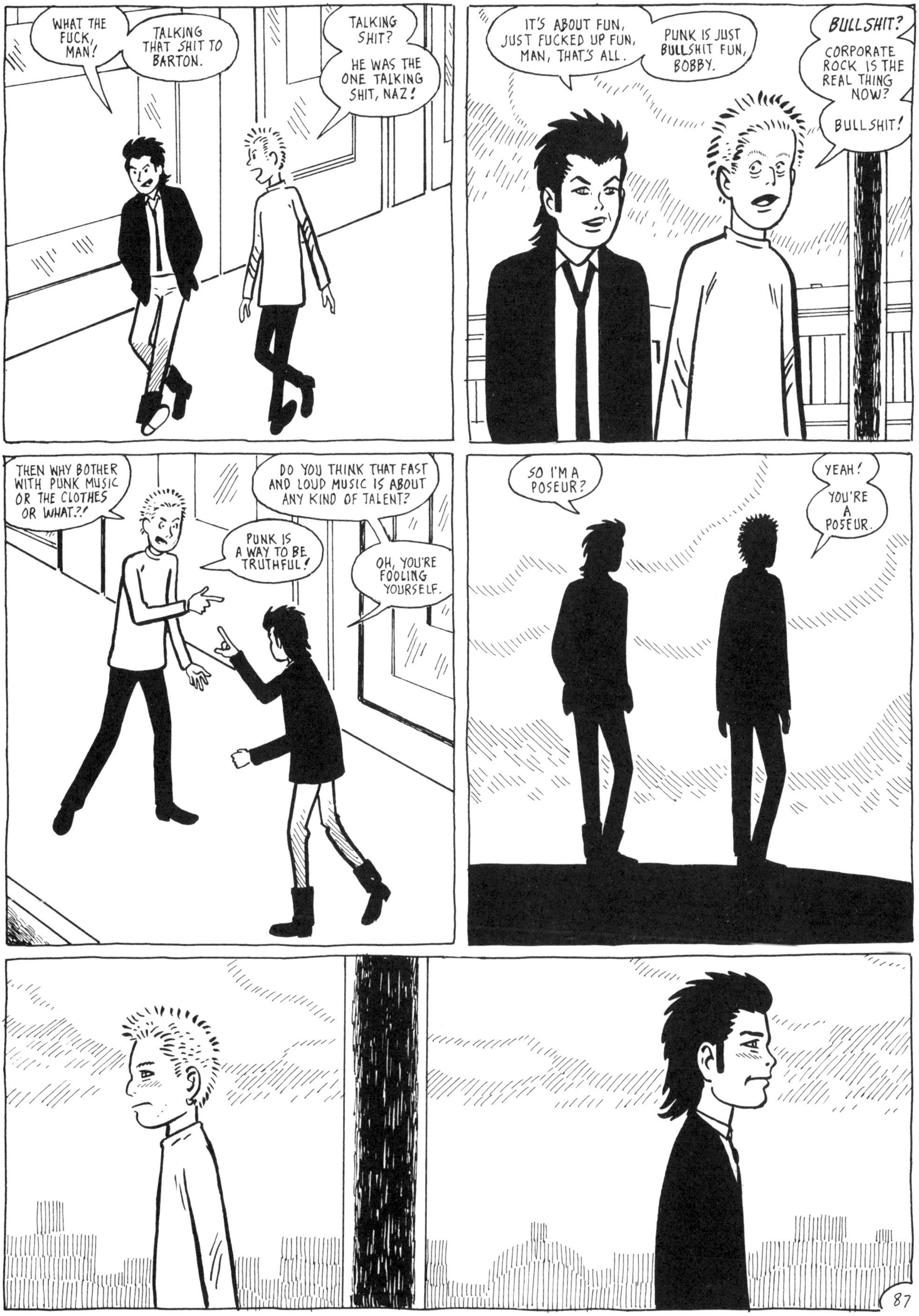
WHAT THE FUCK, MAN!
TALKING THAT SHIT TO BARTON.
TALKING SHIT?
HE WAS THE ONE TALKING SHIT, NAZ!
IT'S ABOUT FUN, JUST FUCKED UP FUN, MAN, THAT'S ALL.
PUNK IS JUST BULLSHIT FUN, BOBBY.
BULLSHIT?
CORPORATE ROCK IS THE REAL THING NOW?
BULLSHIT!
THEN WHY BOTHER WITH PUNK MUSIC OR THE CLOTHES OR WHAT?!
DO YOU THINK THAT FAST AND LOUD MUSIC IS ABOUT ANY KIND OF TALENT?
PUNK IS A WAY TO BE TRUTHFUL!
OH, YOU'RE FOOLING YOURSELF.
SO I'M A POSEUR?
YEAH!
YOU'RE A POSEUR.

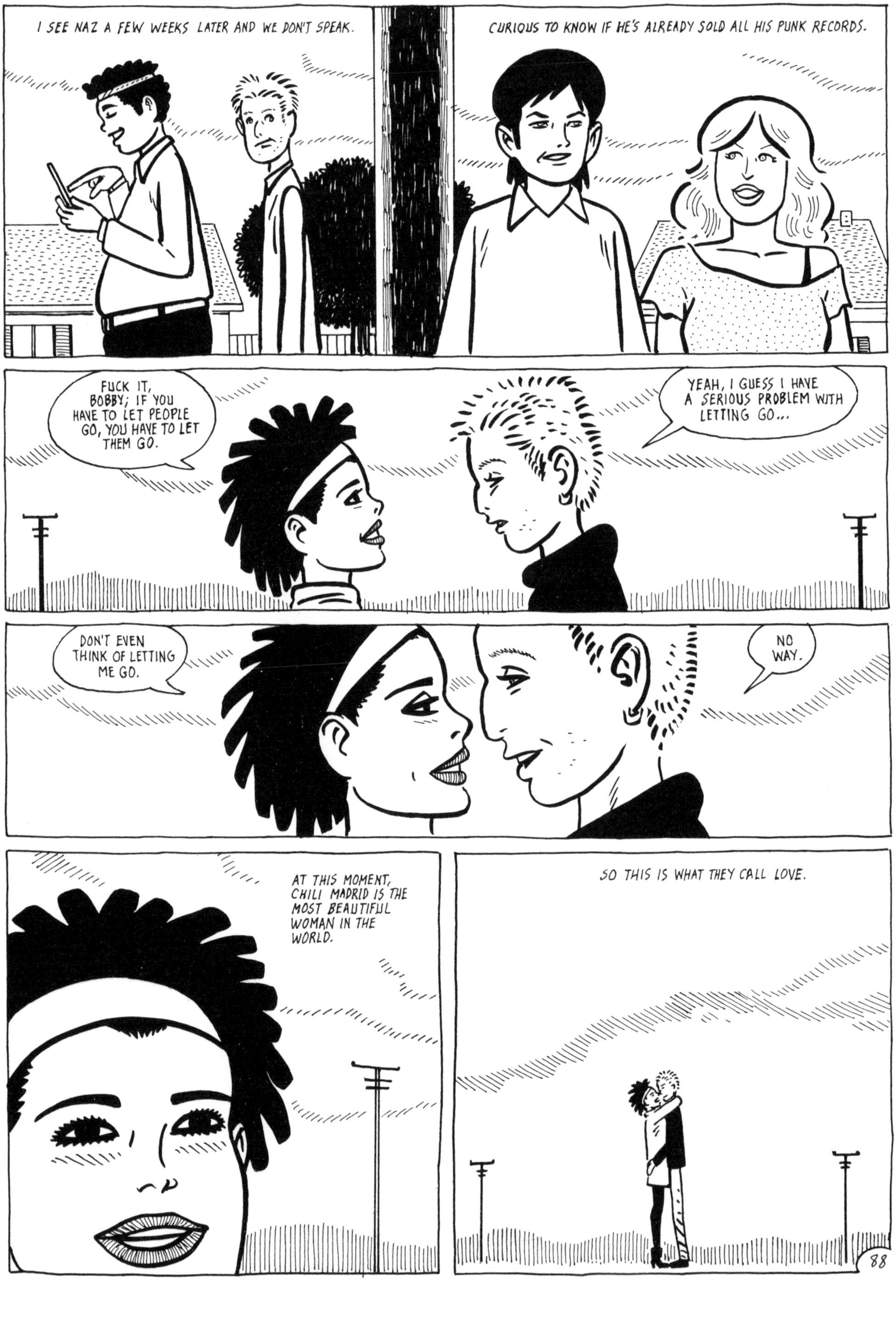
I SEE NAZ A FEW WEEKS LATER AND WE DON'T SPEAK.
CURIOUS TO KNOW IF HE'S ALREADY SOLD ALL HIS PUNK RECORDS.
FUCK IT, BOBBY; IF YOU HAVE TO LET PEOPLE GO, YOU HAVE TO LET THEM GO.
YEAH, I GUESS I HAVE A SERIOUS PROBLEM WITH LETTING GO...
DON'T EVEN THINK OF LETTING ME GO.
NO WAY.
AT THIS MOMENT, CHILI MADRID IS THE MOST BEAUTIFUL WOMAN IN THE WORLD.
SO THIS IS WHAT THEY CALL LOVE.

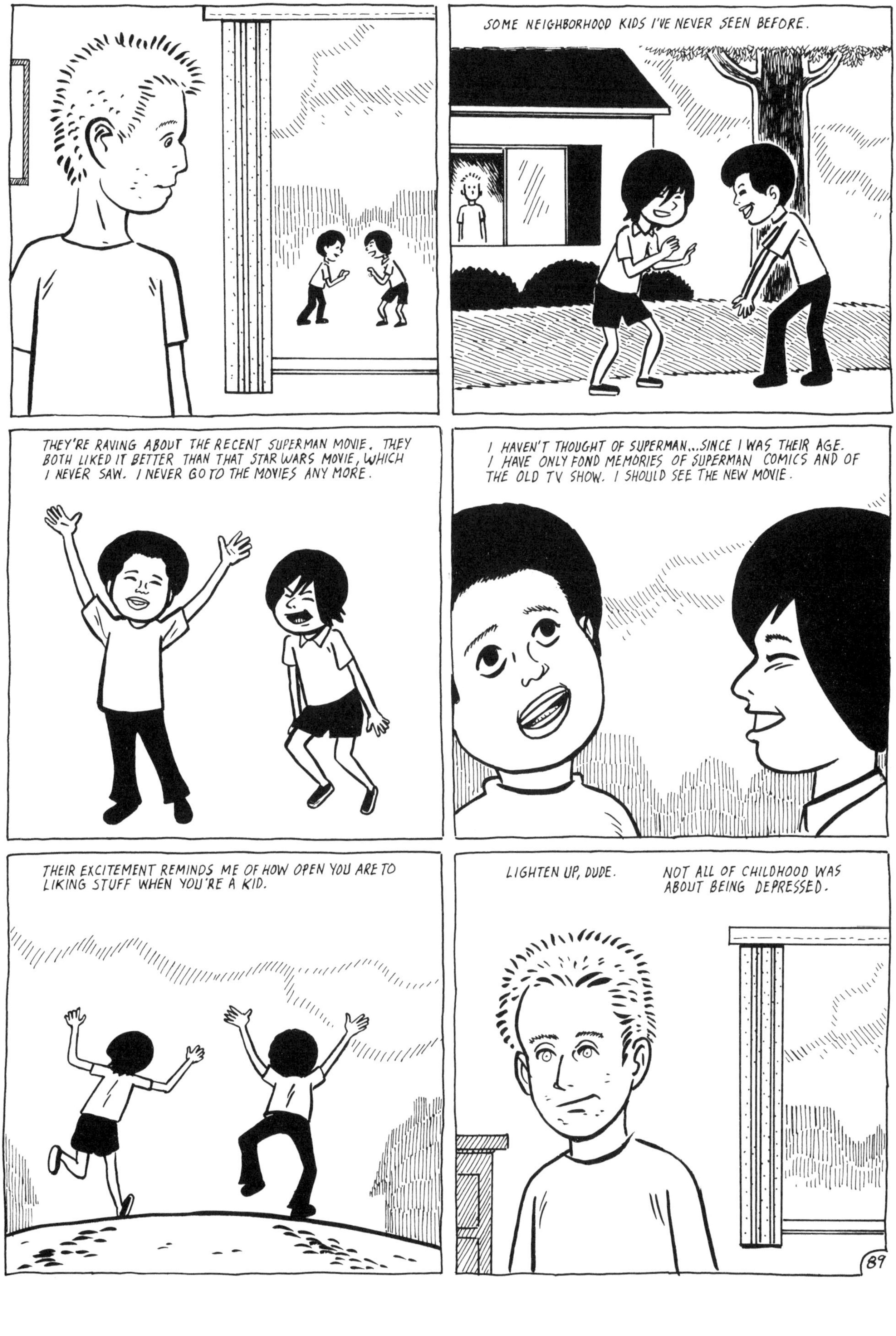
SOME NEIGHBORHOOD KIDS I'VE NEVER SEEN BEFORE.
THEY'RE RAVING ABOUT THE RECENT SUPERMAN MOVIE. THEY BOTH LIKED IT BETTER THAN THAT STAR WARS MOVIE, WHICH I NEVER SAW. I NEVER GO TO THE MOVIES ANY MORE.
I HAVEN'T THOUGHT OF SUPERMAN...SINCE I WAS THEIR AGE. I HAVE ONLY FOND MEMORIES OF SUPERMAN COMICS AND OF THE OLD TV SHOW. I SHOULD SEE THE NEW MOVIE.
THEIR EXCITEMENT REMINDS ME OF HOW OPEN YOU ARE TO LIKING STUFF WHEN YOU'RE A KID.
LIGHTEN UP, DUDE.
NOT ALL OF CHILDHOOD WAS ABOUT BEING DEPRESSED.
89

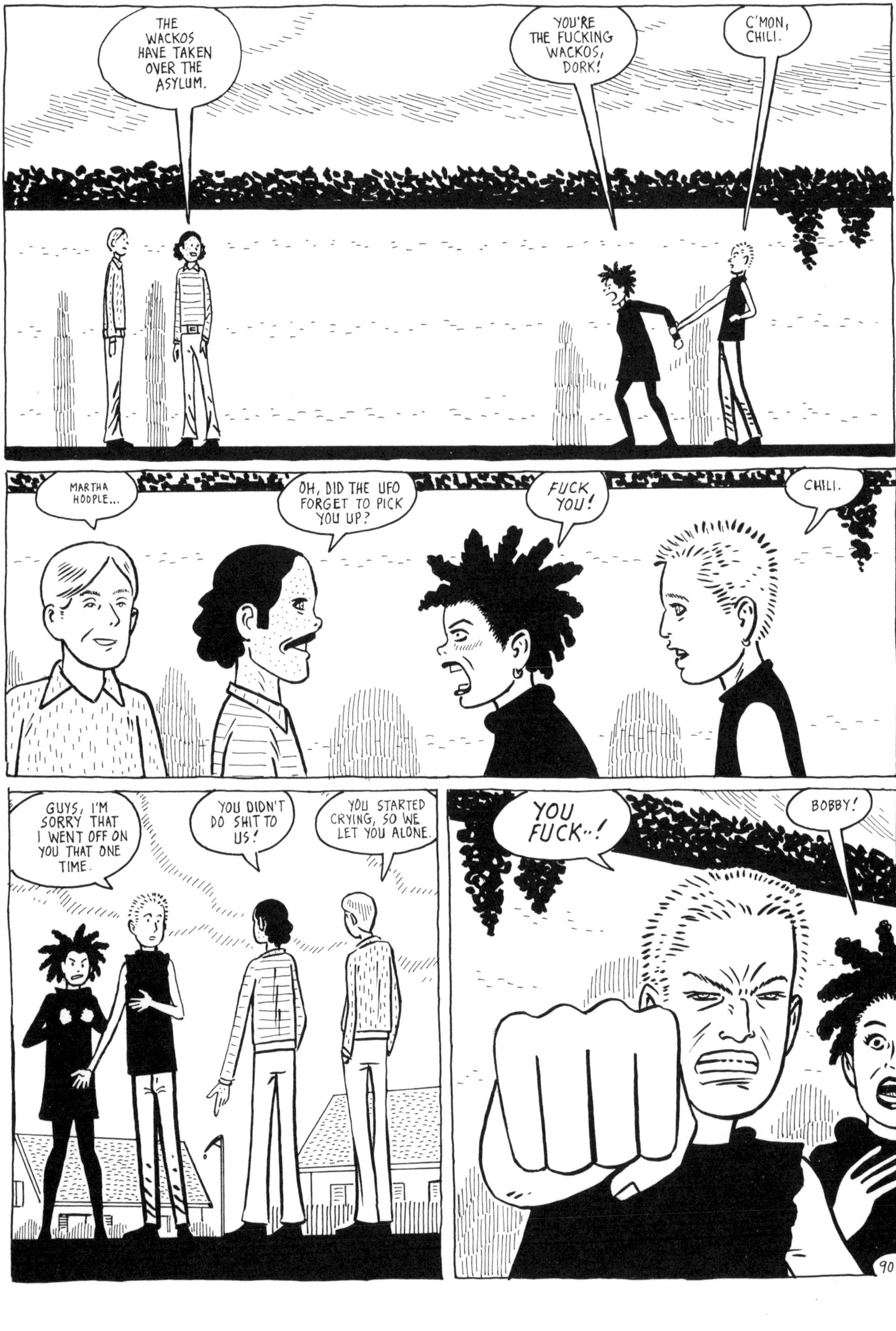
THE WACKOS HAVE TAKEN OVER THE ASYLUM.
YOU'RE THE FUCKING WACKOS, DORK!
C'MON, CHILI.
MARTHA HOOPLE...
OH, DID THE UFO FORGET TO PICK YOU UP?
FUCK YOU!
CHILI.
GUYS, I'M SORRY THAT I WENT OFF ON YOU THAT ONE TIME.
YOU DIDN'T DO SHIT TO US!
YOU STARTED CRYING, SO WE LET YOU ALONE.
YOU FUCK..!
BOBBY!

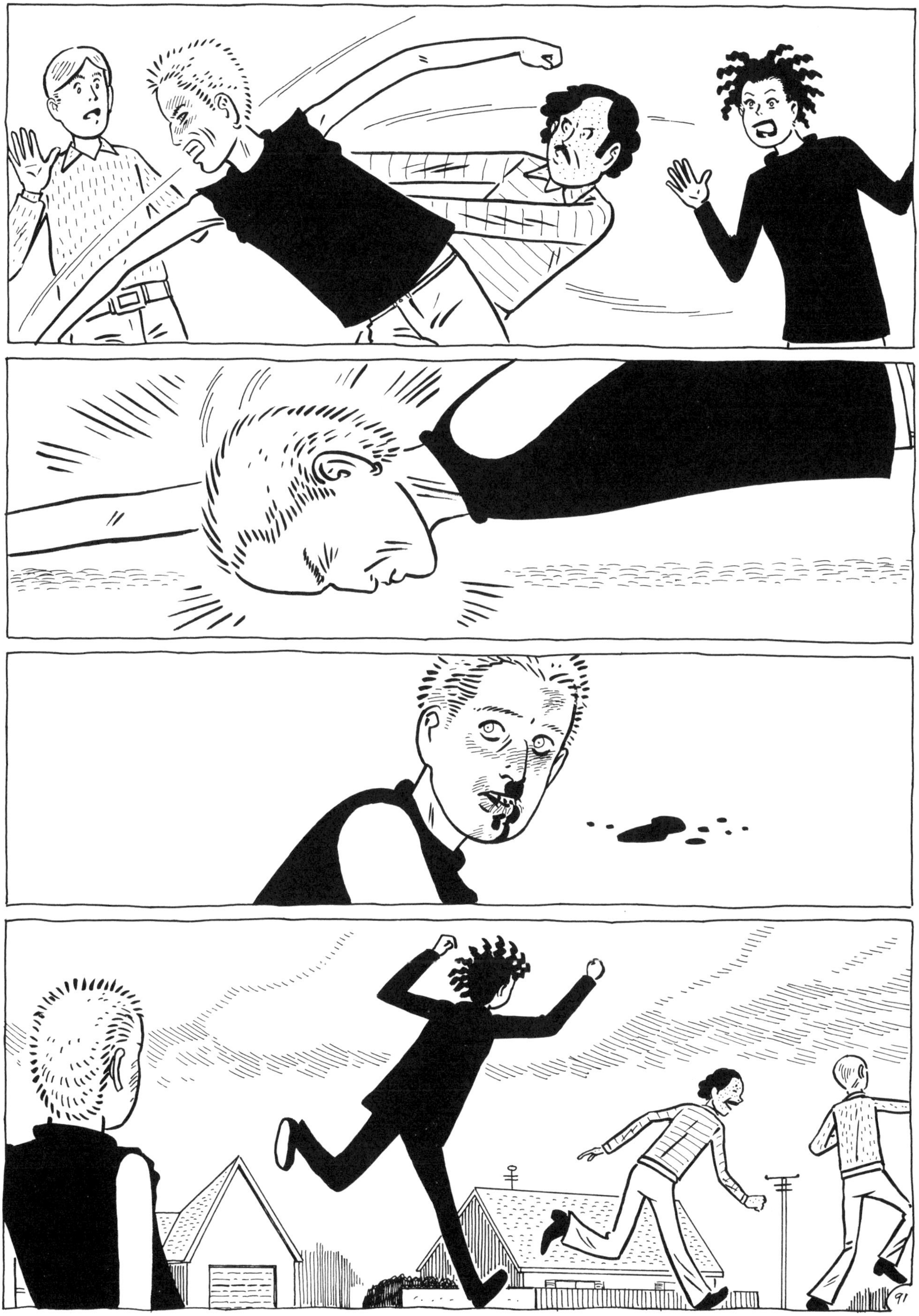

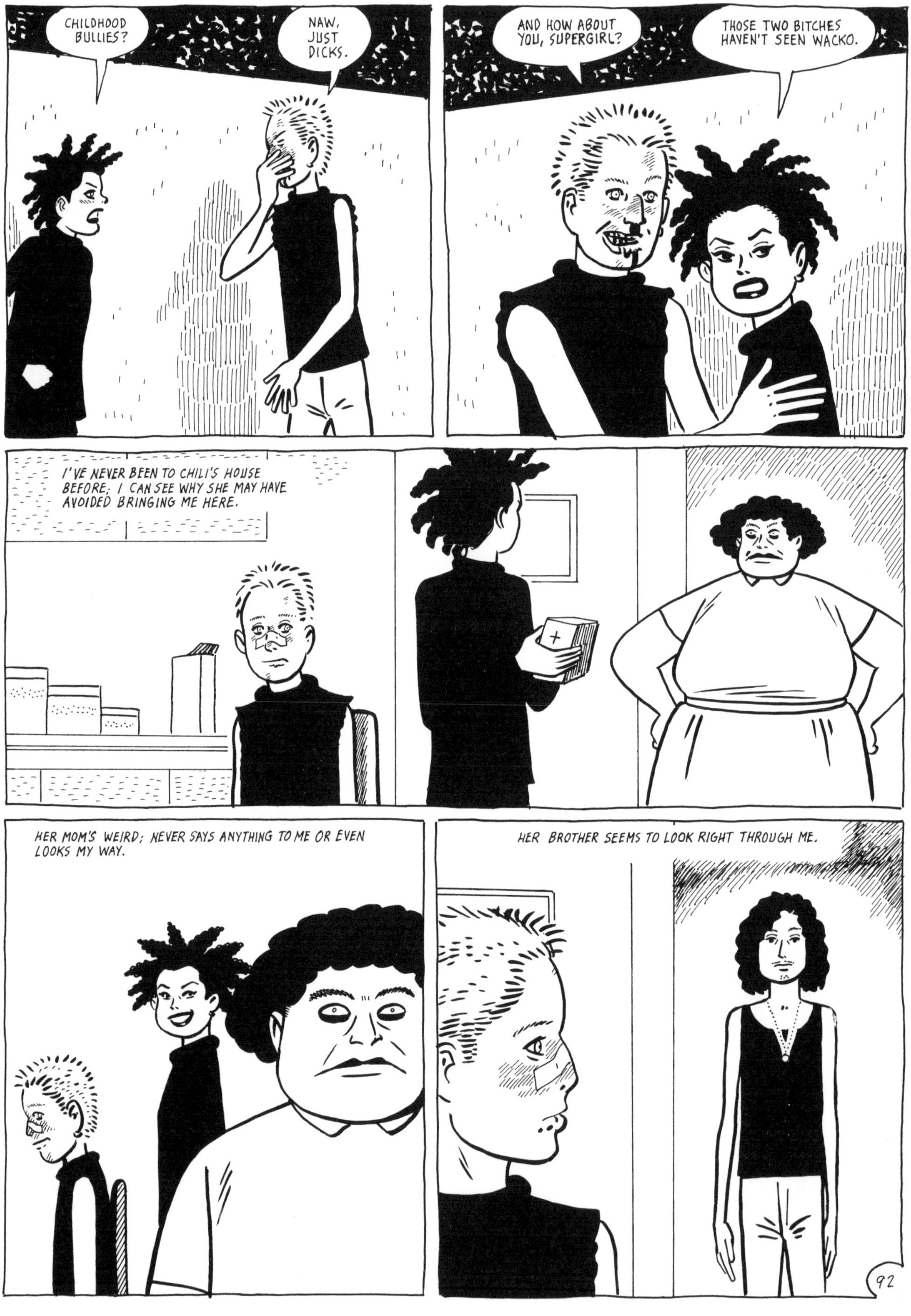

CHILDHOOD BULLIES?
NAW, JUST DICKS.
AND HOW ABOUT YOU, SUPERGIRL?
THOSE TWO BITCHES HAVEN'T SEEN WACKO.
I'VE NEVER BEEN TO CHILI'S HOUSE BEFORE; I CAN SEE WHY SHE MAY HAVE AVOIDED BRINGING ME HERE.
HER MOM'S WEIRD; NEVER SAYS ANYTHING TO ME OR EVEN LOOKS MY WAY.
HER BROTHER SEEMS TO LOOK RIGHT THROUGH ME.

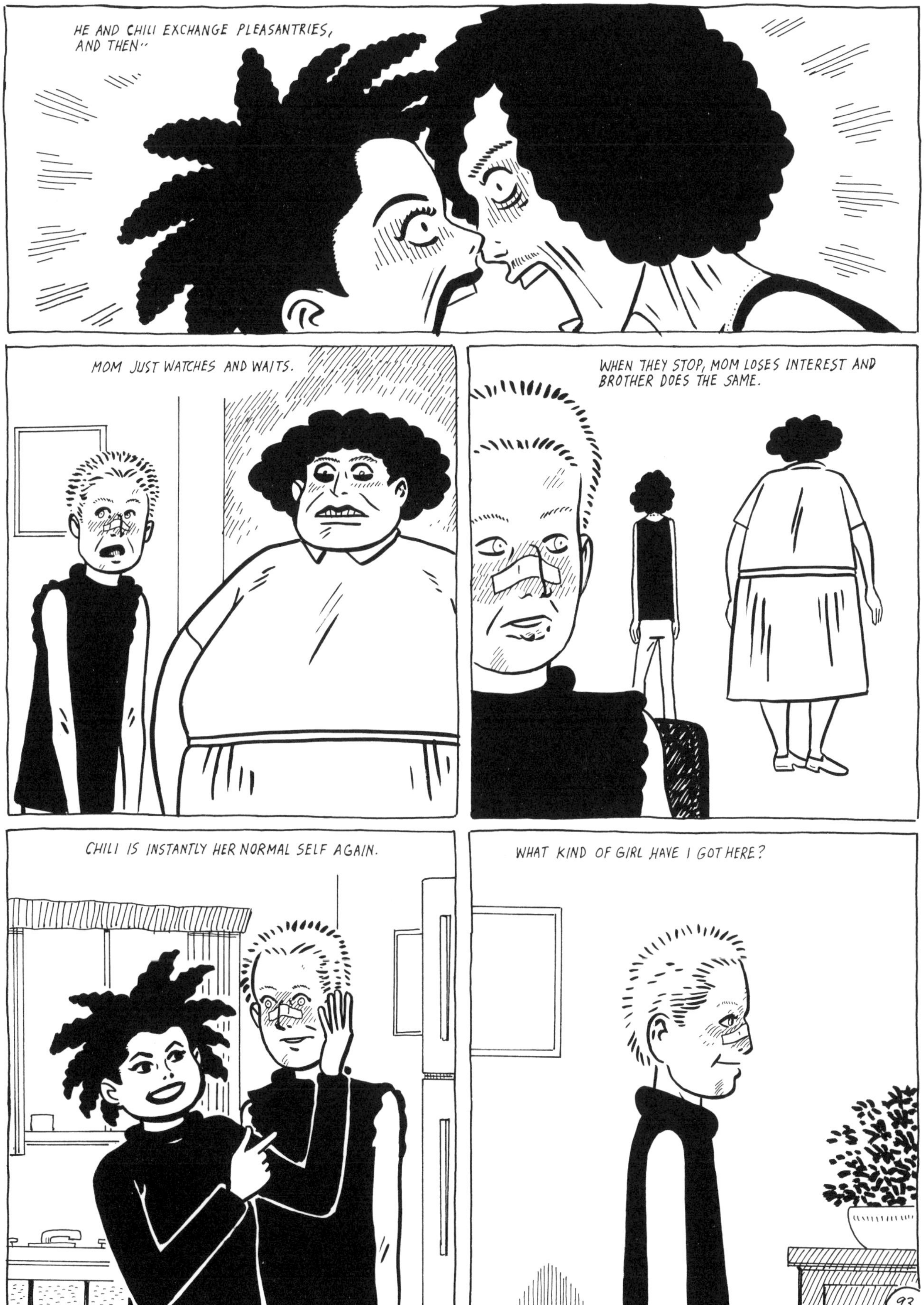
HE AND CHILI EXCHANGE PLEASANTRIES, AND THEN..
MOM JUST WATCHES AND WAITS.
WHEN THEY STOP, MOM LOSES INTEREST AND BROTHER DOES THE SAME.
CHILI IS INSTANTLY HER NORMAL SELF AGAIN.
WHAT KIND OF GIRL HAVE I GOT HERE?

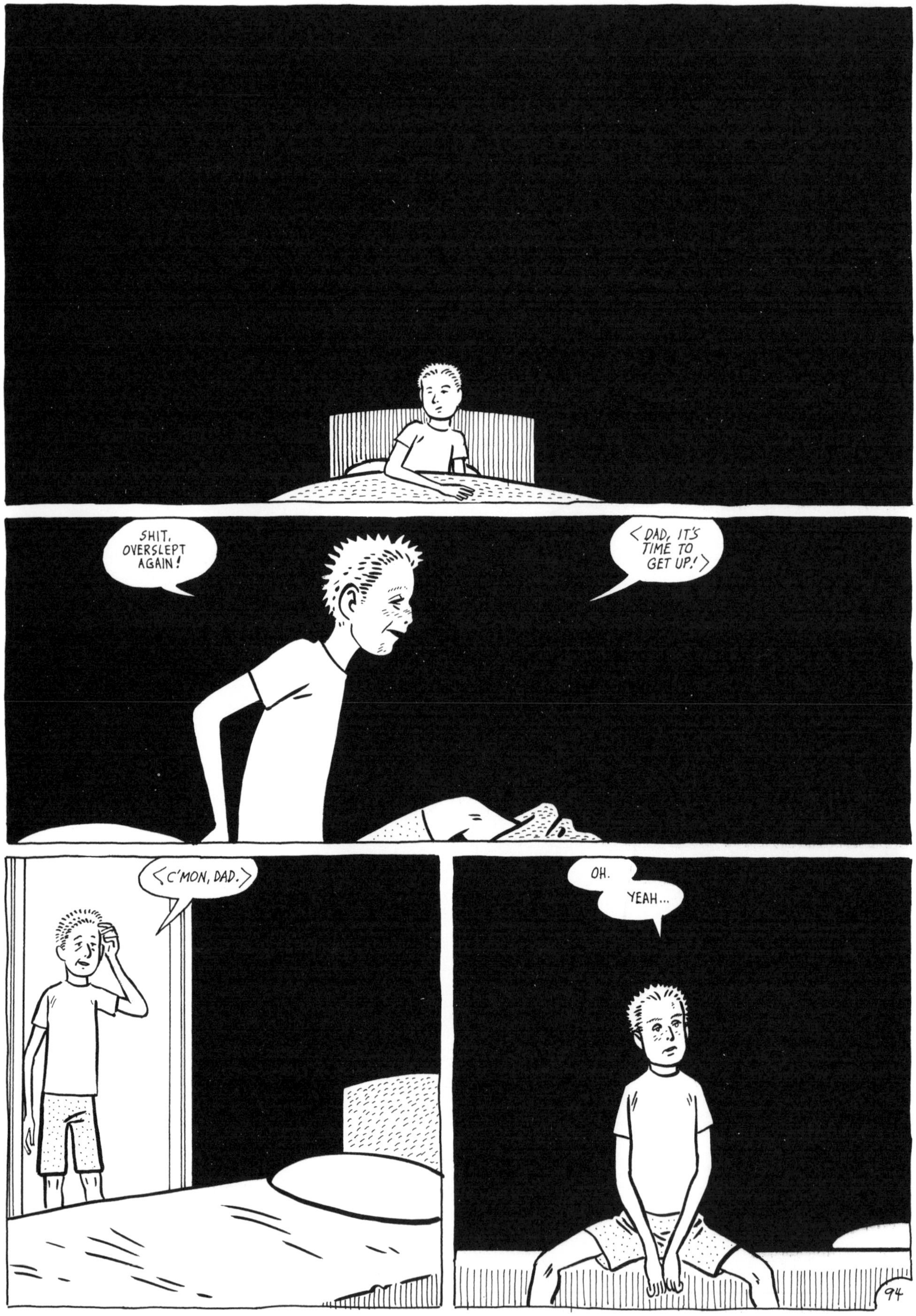
SHIT, OVERSLEPT AGAIN!
< DAD, IT'S TIME TO GET UP! >
< C'MON, DAD. >
OH.
YEAH...

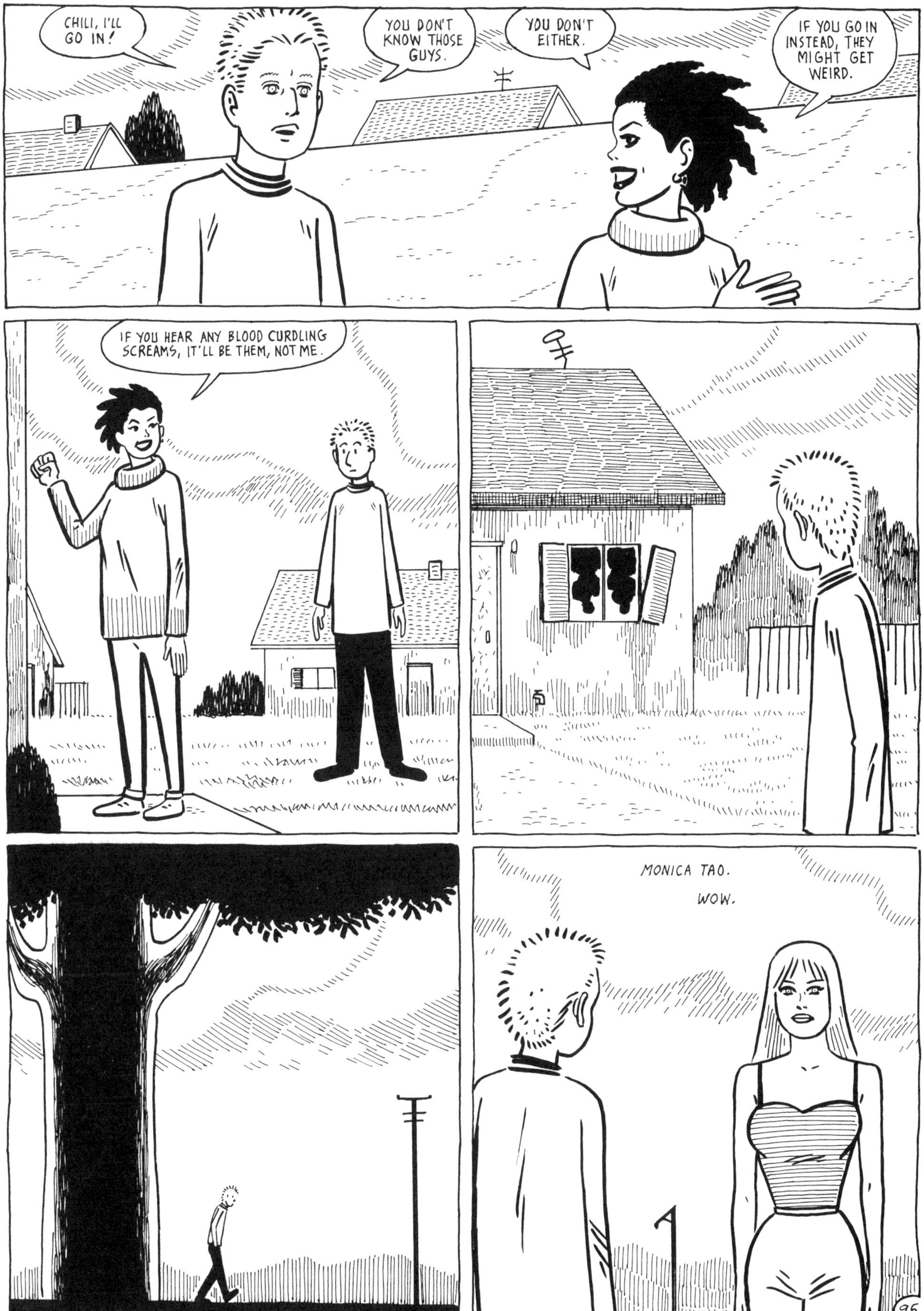
CHILI, I'LL GO IN!
YOU DON'T KNOW THOSE GUYS.
YOU DON'T EITHER.
IF YOU GO IN INSTEAD, THEY MIGHT GET WEIRD.
IF YOU HEAR ANY BLOOD CURDLING SCREAMS, IT'LL BE THEM, NOT ME.
MONICA TAO.
WOW.

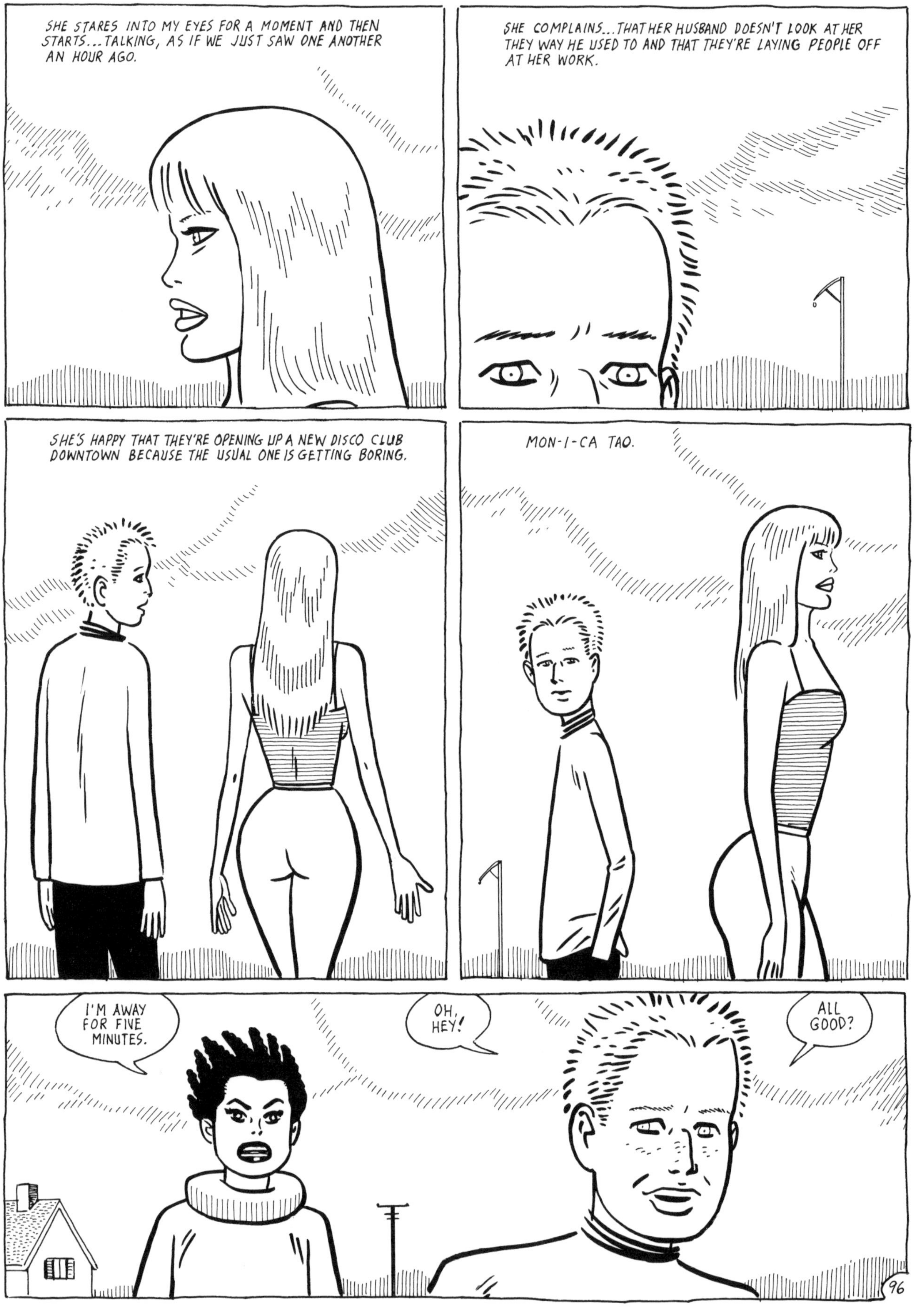
SHE STARES INTO MY EYES FOR A MOMENT AND THEN STARTS... TALKING, AS IF WE JUST SAW ONE ANOTHER AN HOUR AGO.
SHE COMPLAINS... THAT HER HUSBAND DOESN'T LOOK AT HER THEY WAY HE USED TO AND THAT THEY'RE LAYING PEOPLE OFF AT HER WORK.
SHE'S HAPPY THAT THEY'RE OPENING UP A NEW DISCO CLUB DOWNTOWN BECAUSE THE USUAL ONE IS GETTING BORING.
MON-I-CA TAO.
I'M AWAY FOR FIVE MINUTES.
OH, HEY!
ALL GOOD?

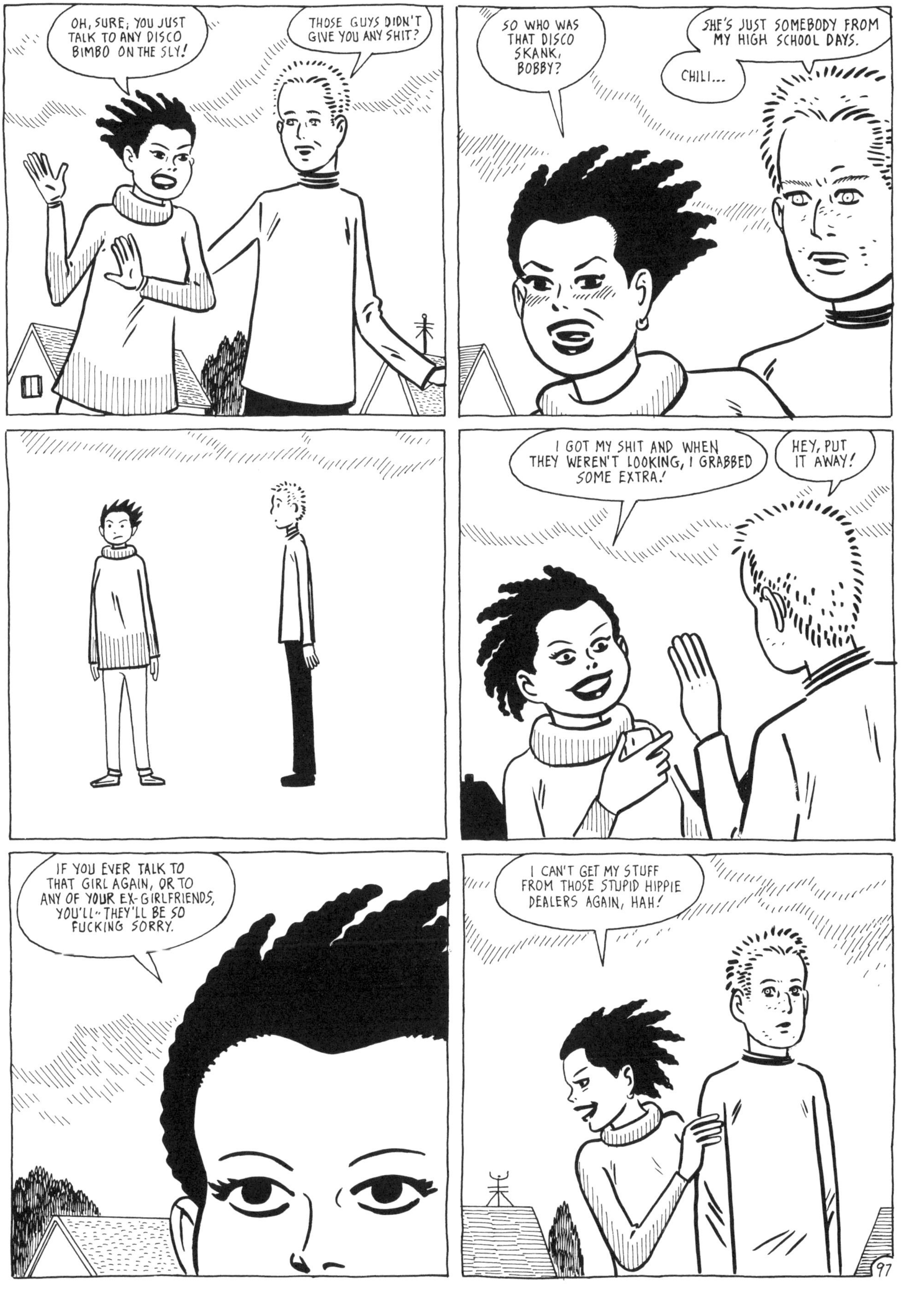
OH, SURE; YOU JUST TALK TO ANY DISCO BIMBO ON THE SLY!
THOSE GUYS DIDN'T GIVE YOU ANY SHIT?
SO WHO WAS THAT DISCO SKANK, BOBBY?
SHE'S JUST SOMEBODY FROM MY HIGH SCHOOL DAYS.
CHILI...
I GOT MY SHIT AND WHEN THEY WEREN'T LOOKING, I GRABBED SOME EXTRA!
HEY, PUT IT AWAY!
IF YOU EVER TALK TO THAT GIRL AGAIN, OR TO ANY OF YOUR EX-GIRLFRIENDS, YOU'LL-- THEY'LL BE SO FUCKING SORRY.
I CAN'T GET MY STUFF FROM THOSE STUPID HIPPIE DEALERS AGAIN, HAH!

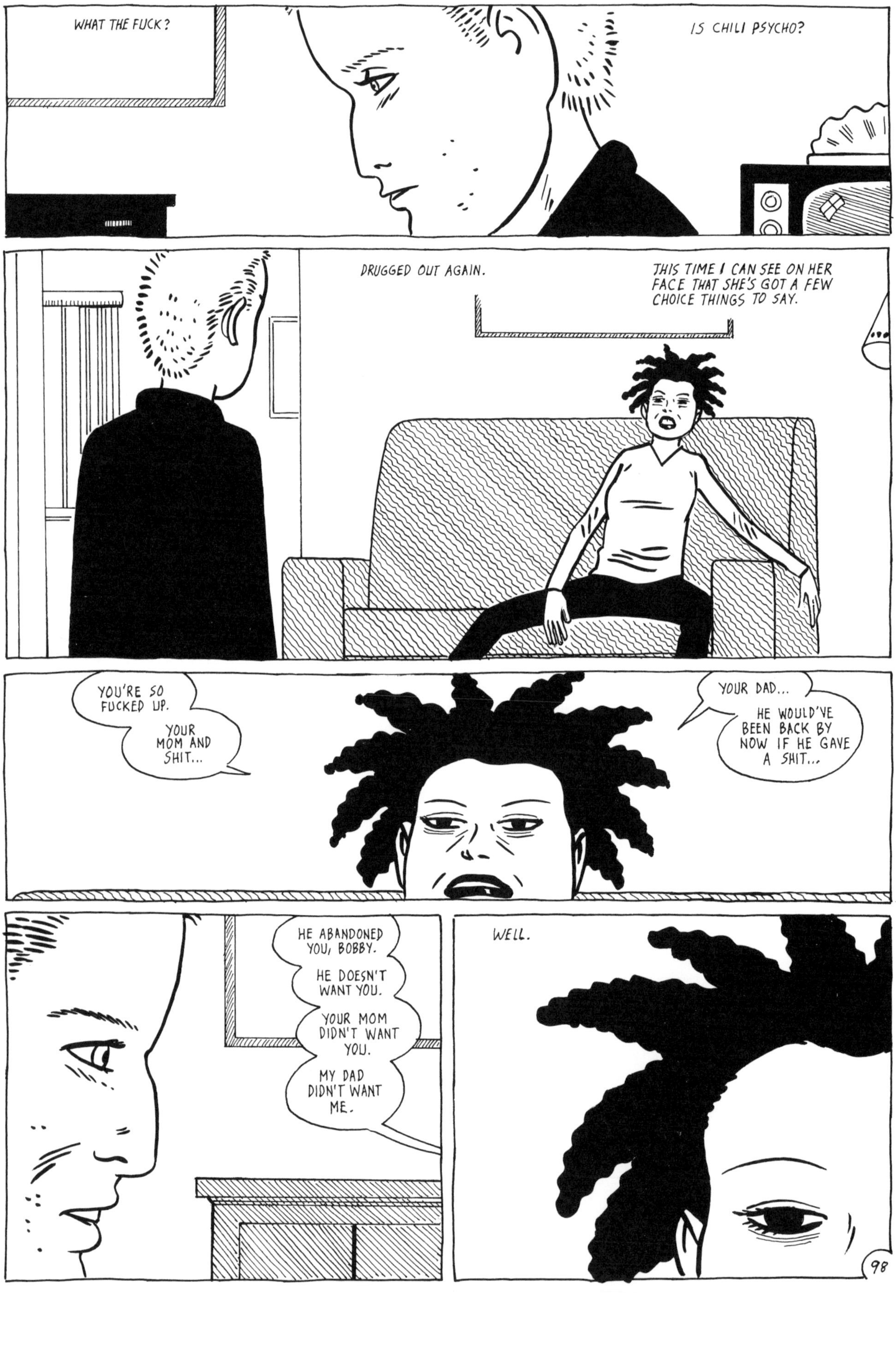
WHAT THE FUCK?
IS CHILI PSYCHO?
DRUGGED OUT AGAIN.
THIS TIME I CAN SEE ON HER FACE THAT SHE'S GOT A FEW CHOICE THINGS TO SAY.
YOU'RE SO FUCKED UP.
YOUR MOM AND SHIT...
YOUR DAD...
HE WOULD'VE BEEN BACK BY NOW IF HE GAVE A SHIT...
HE ABANDONED YOU, BOBBY.
HE DOESN'T WANT YOU.
YOUR MOM DIDN'T WANT YOU.
MY DAD DIDN'T WANT ME.
WELL.

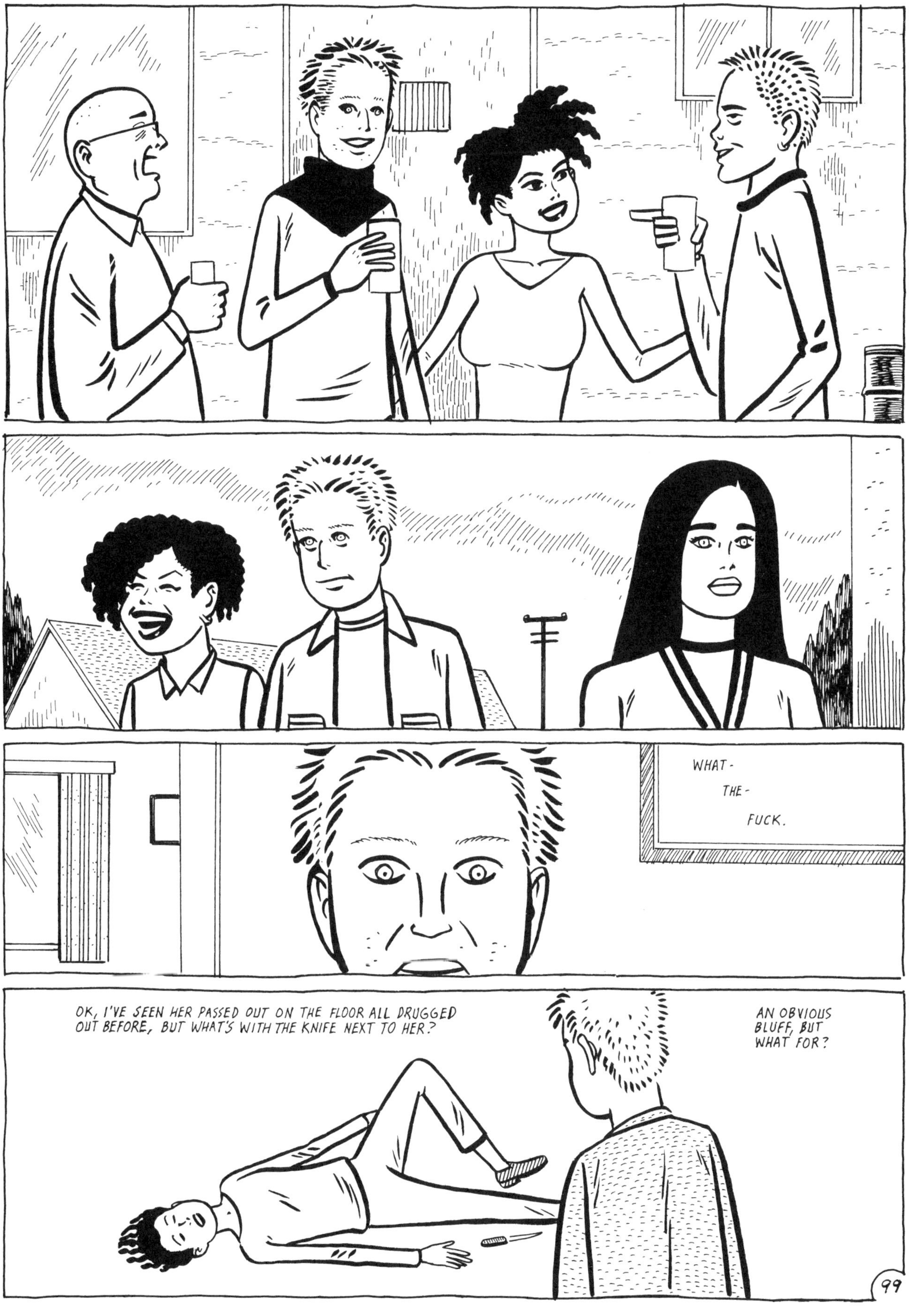
WHAT-
THE-
FUCK.
OK, I'VE SEEN HER PASSED OUT ON THE FLOOR ALL DRUGGED OUT BEFORE, BUT WHAT'S WITH THE KNIFE NEXT TO HER?
AN OBVIOUS BLUFF, BUT WHAT FOR?

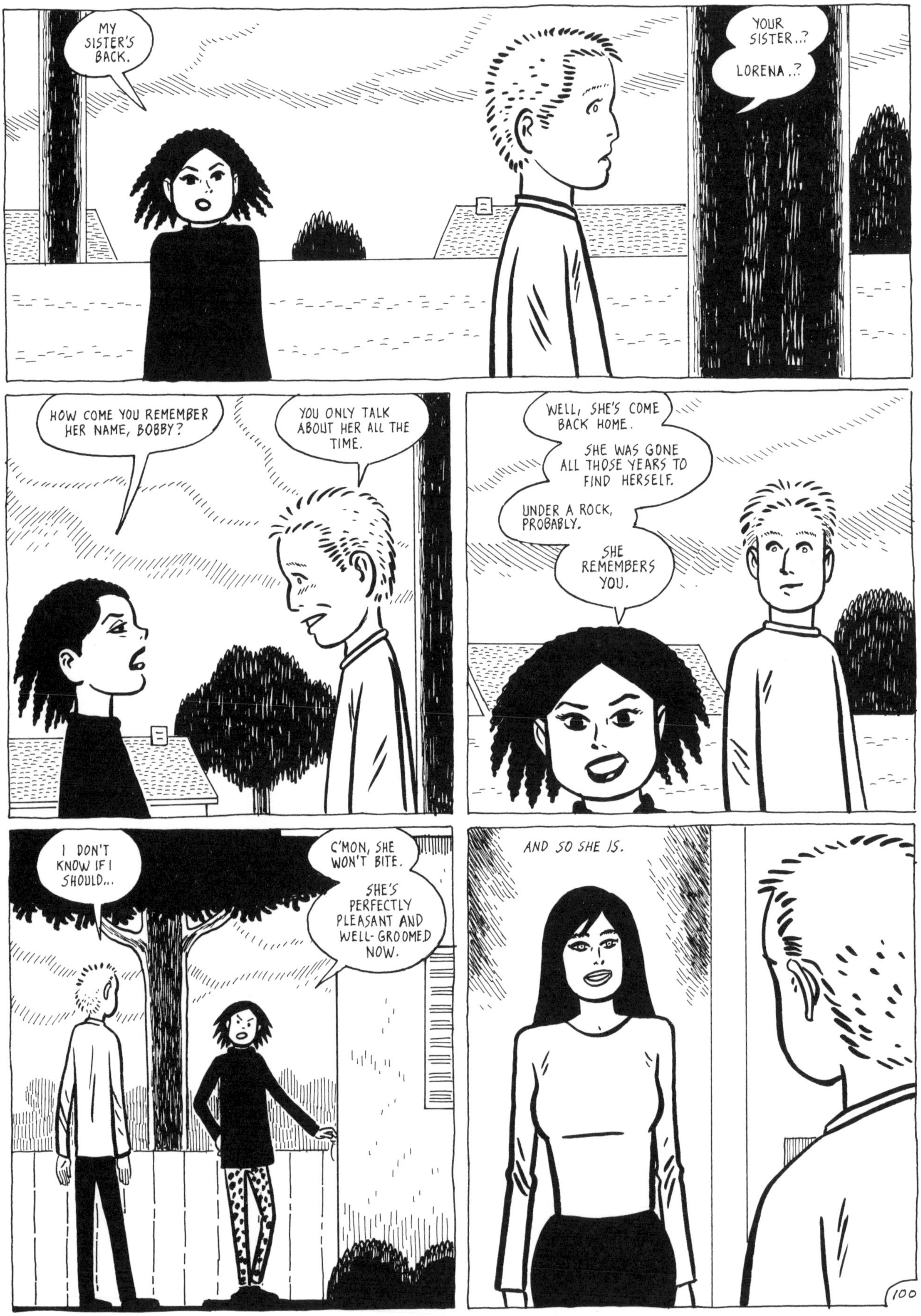
MY SISTER'S BACK.
YOUR SISTER..?
LORENA..?
HOW COME YOU REMEMBER HER NAME, BOBBY?
YOU ONLY TALK ABOUT HER ALL THE TIME.
WELL, SHE'S COME BACK HOME.
SHE WAS GONE ALL THOSE YEARS TO FIND HERSELF.
UNDER A ROCK, PROBABLY.
SHE REMEMBERS YOU.
I DON'T KNOW IF I SHOULD...
C'MON, SHE WON'T BITE.
SHE'S PERFECTLY PLEASANT AND WELL-GROOMED NOW.
AND SO SHE IS.

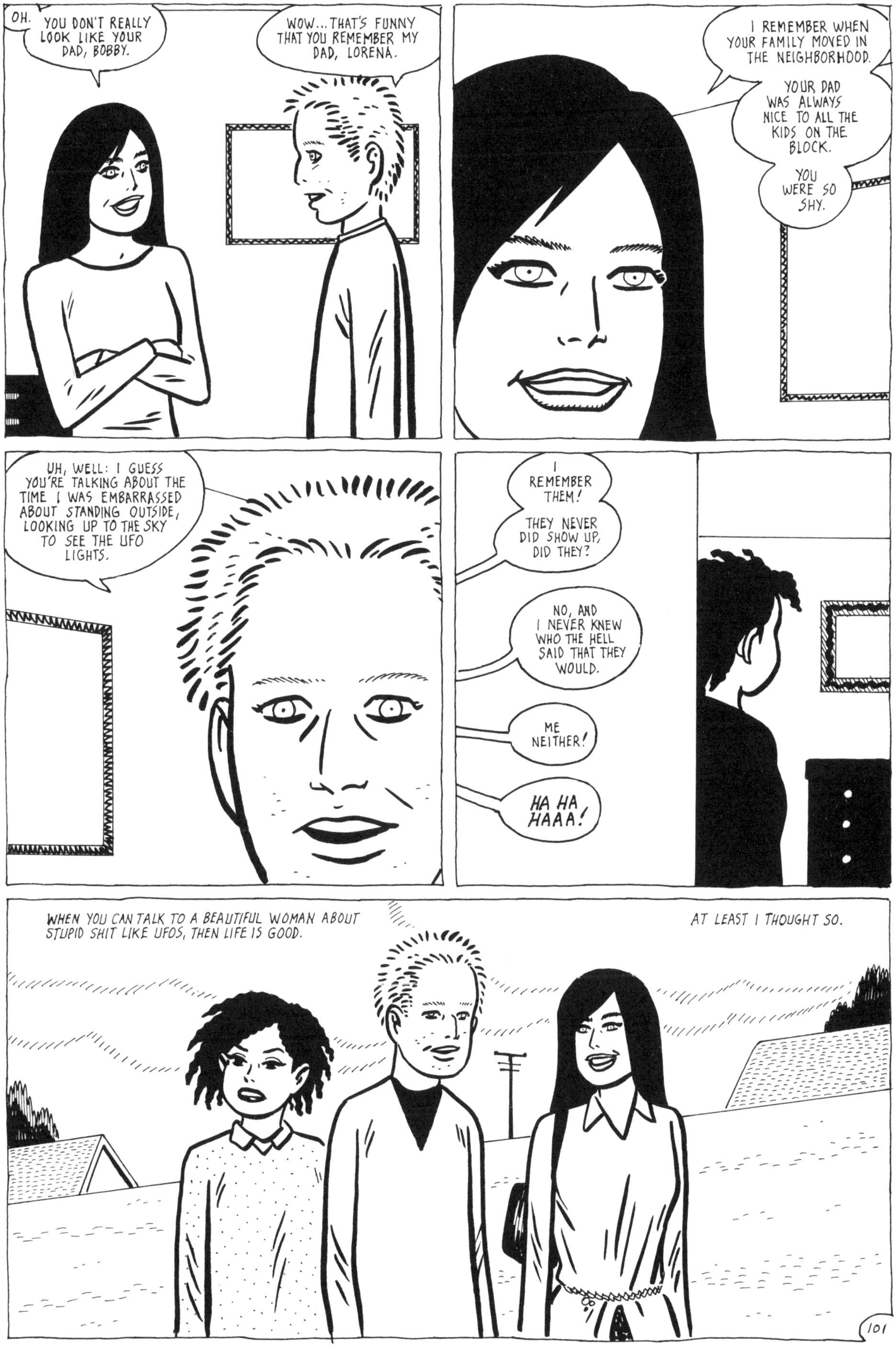
OH.
YOU DON'T REALLY LOOK LIKE YOUR DAD, BOBBY.
WOW... THAT'S FUNNY THAT YOU REMEMBER MY DAD, LORENA.
I REMEMBER WHEN YOUR FAMILY MOVED IN THE NEIGHBORHOOD.
YOUR DAD WAS ALWAYS NICE TO ALL THE KIDS ON THE BLOCK.
YOU WERE SO SHY.
UH, WELL: I GUESS YOU'RE TALKING ABOUT THE TIME I WAS EMBARRASSED ABOUT STANDING OUTSIDE, LOOKING UP TO THE SKY TO SEE THE UFO LIGHTS.
I REMEMBER THEM!
THEY NEVER DID SHOW UP, DID THEY?
NO, AND I NEVER KNEW WHO THE HELL SAID THAT THEY WOULD.
ME NEITHER!
HA HA HAAA!
WHEN YOU CAN TALK TO A BEAUTIFUL WOMAN ABOUT STUPID SHIT LIKE UFOS, THEN LIFE IS GOOD.
AT LEAST I THOUGHT SO.

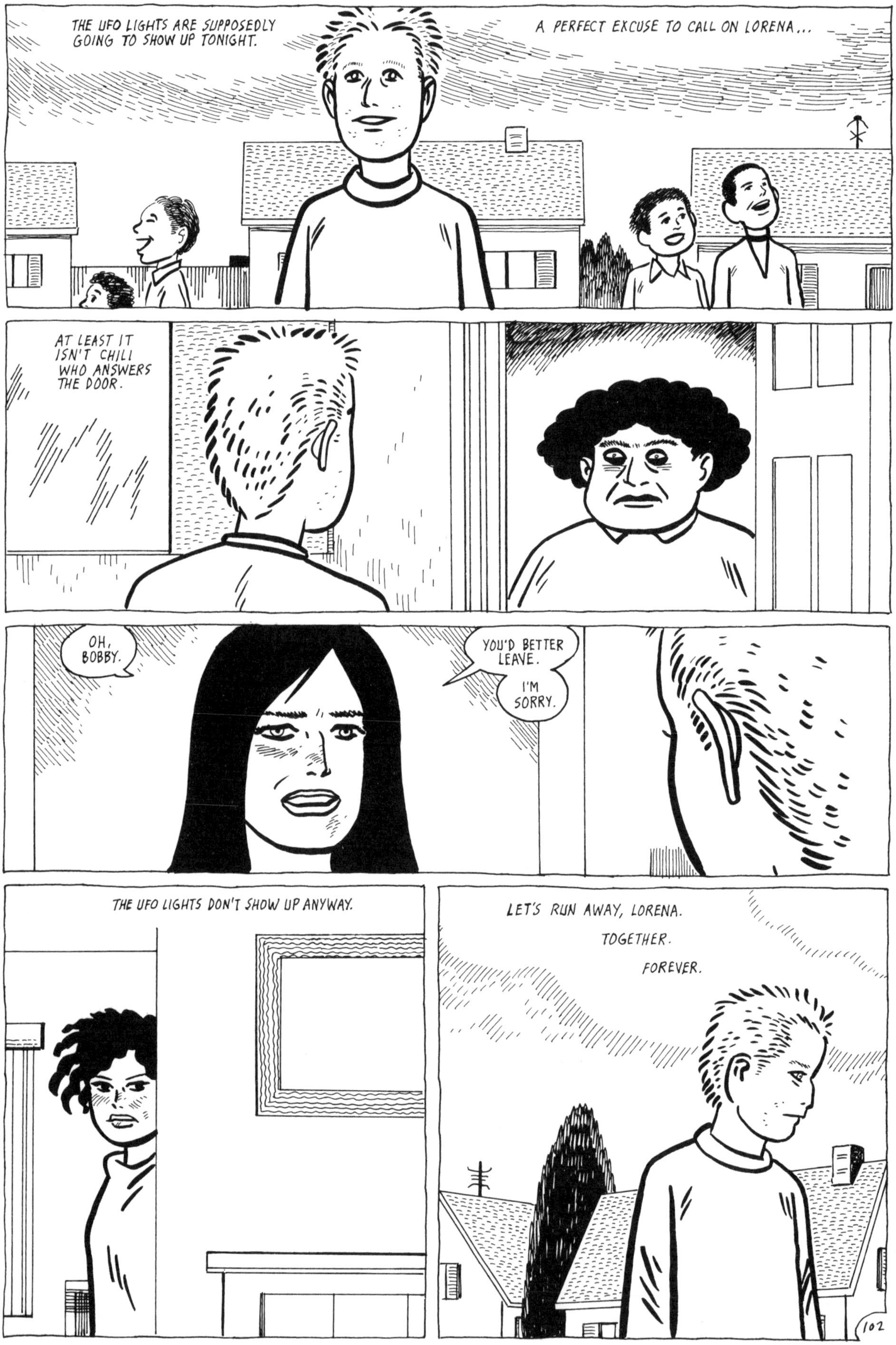
THE UFO LIGHTS ARE SUPPOSEDLY GOING TO SHOW UP TONIGHT.
A PERFECT EXCUSE TO CALL ON LORENA...
AT LEAST IT ISN'T CHILI WHO ANSWERS THE DOOR.
OH, BOBBY.
YOU'D BETTER LEAVE.
I'M SORRY.
THE UFO LIGHTS DON'T SHOW UP ANYWAY.
LET'S RUN AWAY, LORENA.
TOGETHER.
FOREVER.

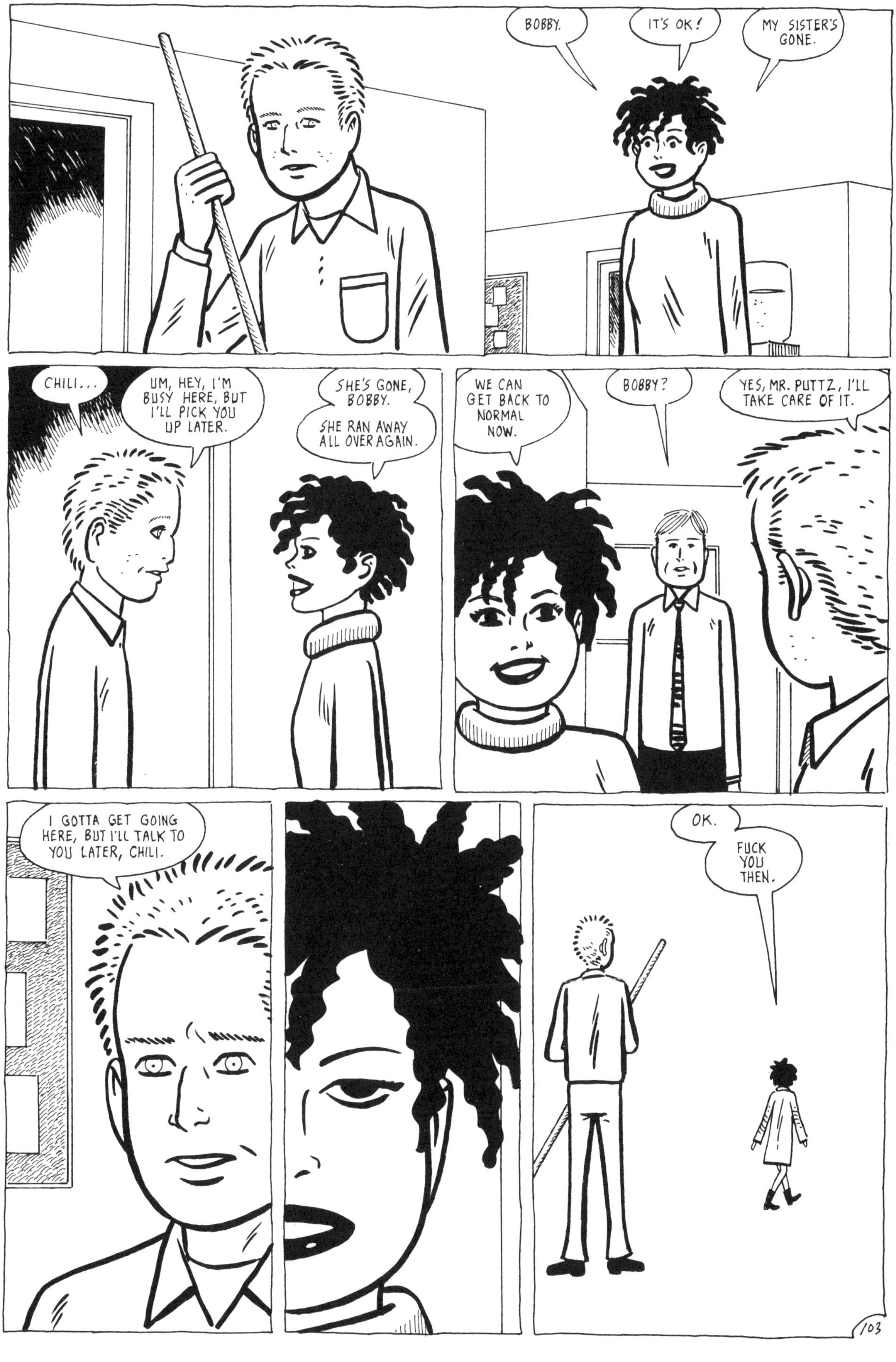
BOBBY.
IT'S OK!
MY SISTER'S GONE.
CHILI...
UM, HEY, I'M BUSY HERE, BUT I'LL PICK YOU UP LATER.
SHE'S GONE, BOBBY.
SHE RAN AWAY ALL OVER AGAIN.
WE CAN GET BACK TO NORMAL NOW.
BOBBY?
YES, MR. PUTTZ, I'LL TAKE CARE OF IT.
I GOTTA GET GOING HERE, BUT I'LL TALK TO YOU LATER, CHILI.
OK.
FUCK YOU THEN.

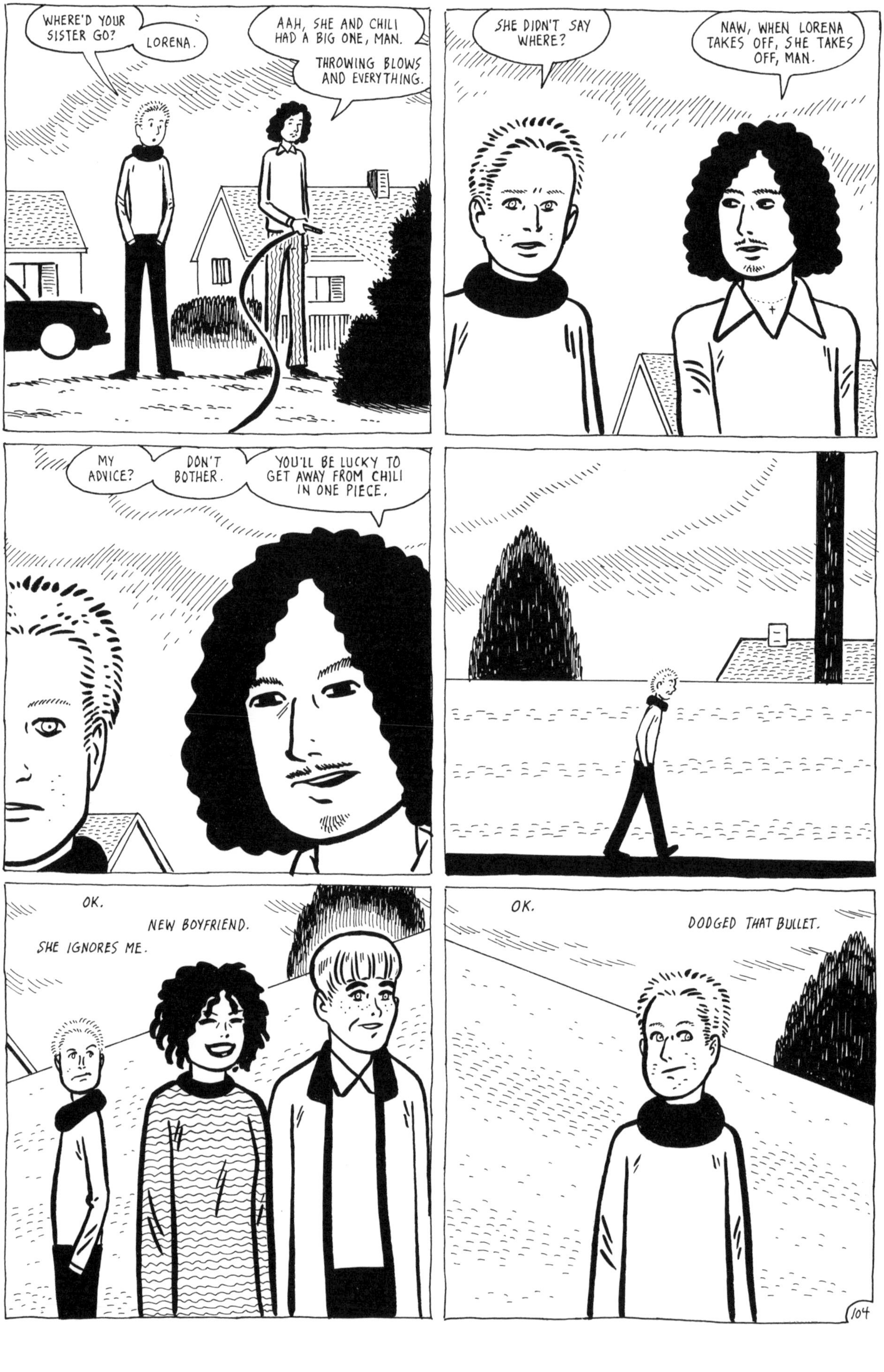
WHERE'D YOUR SISTER GO?
LORENA.
AAH, SHE AND CHILI HAD A BIG ONE, MAN.
THROWING BLOWS AND EVERYTHING.
SHE DIDN'T SAY WHERE?
NAW, WHEN LORENA TAKES OFF, SHE TAKES OFF, MAN.
MY ADVICE?
DON'T BOTHER.
YOU'LL BE LUCKY TO GET AWAY FROM CHILI IN ONE PIECE.
OK.
NEW BOYFRIEND.
SHE IGNORES ME.
OK.
DODGED THAT BULLET.

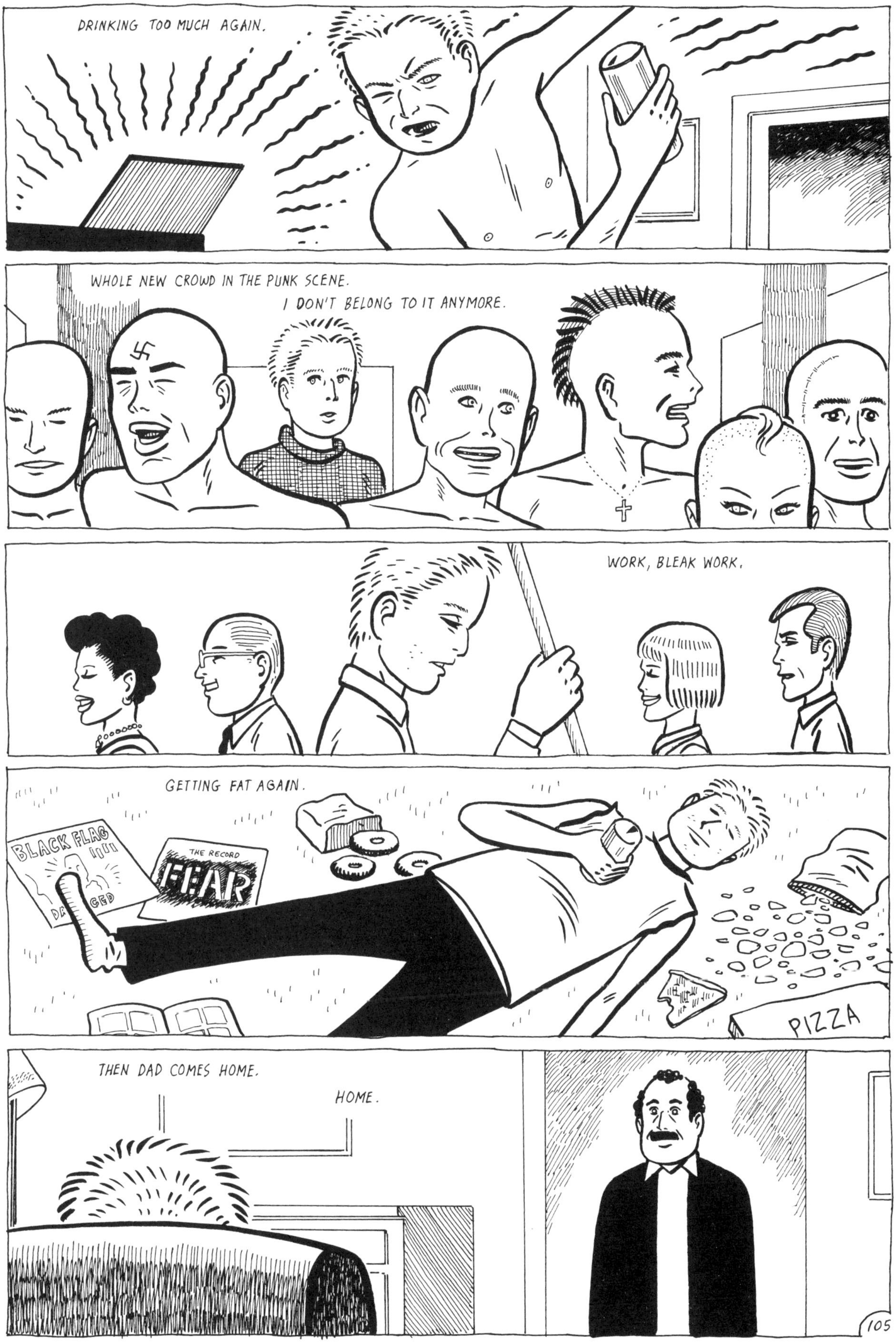
DRINKING TOO MUCH AGAIN.
WHOLE NEW CROWD IN THE PUNK SCENE.
I DON'T BELONG TO IT ANYMORE.
WORK, BLEAK WORK.
GETTING FAT AGAIN.
BLACK FLAG
THE RECORD
FEAR
PIZZA
THEN DAD COMES HOME.
HOME.

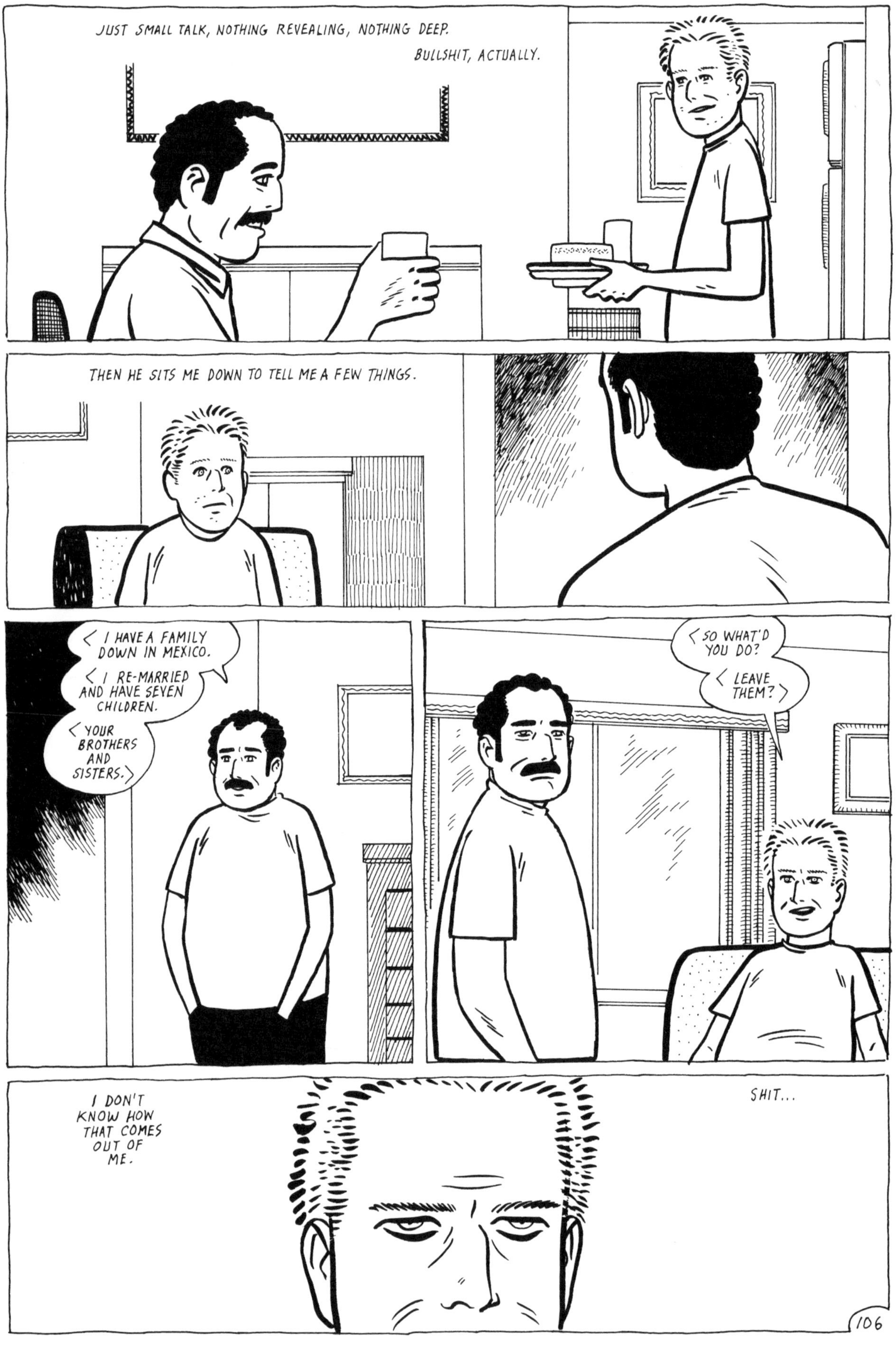
JUST SMALL TALK, NOTHING REVEALING, NOTHING DEEP.
BULLSHIT, ACTUALLY.
THEN HE SITS ME DOWN TO TELL ME A FEW THINGS.
< I HAVE A FAMILY DOWN IN MEXICO.
< I RE-MARRIED AND HAVE SEVEN CHILDREN.
< YOUR BROTHERS AND SISTERS. >
< SO WHAT'D YOU DO?
< LEAVE THEM? >
I DON'T KNOW HOW THAT COMES OUT OF ME.
SHIT...

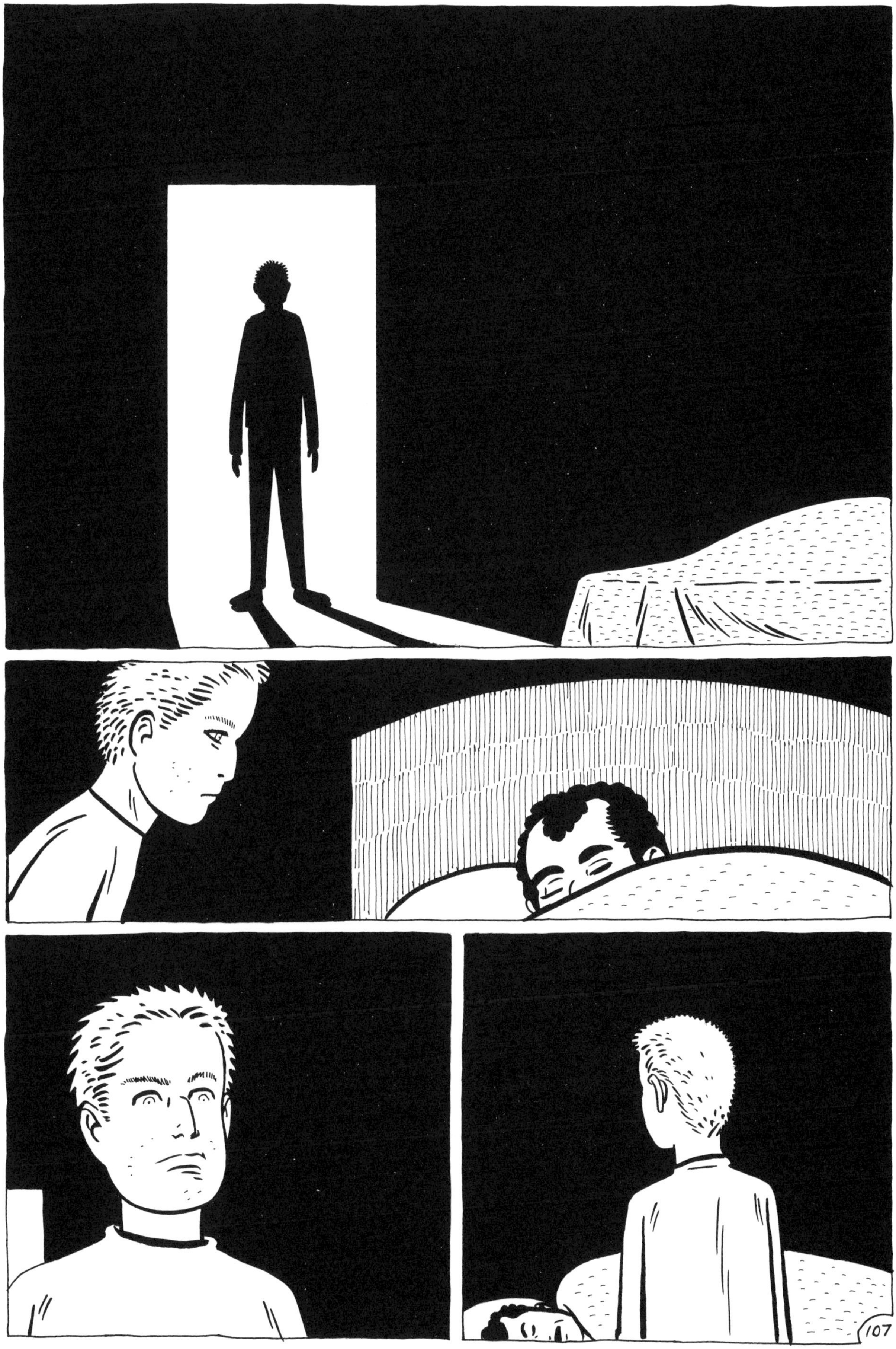

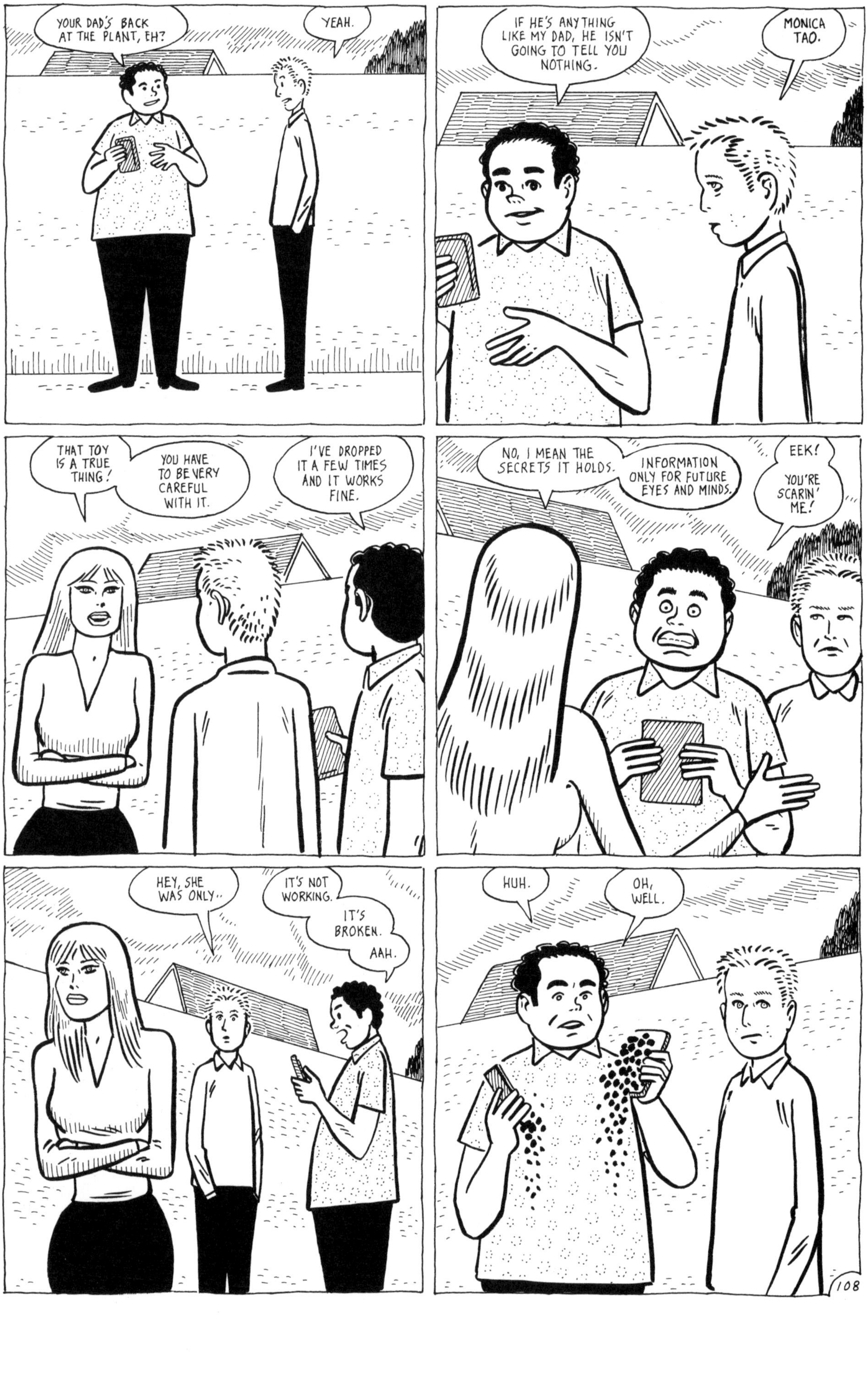
YOUR DAD'S BACK AT THE PLANT, EH?
YEAH.
IF HE'S ANYTHING LIKE MY DAD, HE ISN'T GOING TO TELL YOU NOTHING.
MONICA TAO.
THAT TOY IS A TRUE THING!
YOU HAVE TO BE VERY CAREFUL WITH IT.
I'VE DROPPED IT A FEW TIMES AND IT WORKS FINE.
NO, I MEAN THE SECRETS IT HOLDS.
INFORMATION ONLY FOR FUTURE EYES AND MINDS.
EEK!
YOU'RE SCARIN' ME!
HEY, SHE WAS ONLY..
IT'S NOT WORKING.
IT'S BROKEN.
AAH.
HUH.
OH, WELL.
108

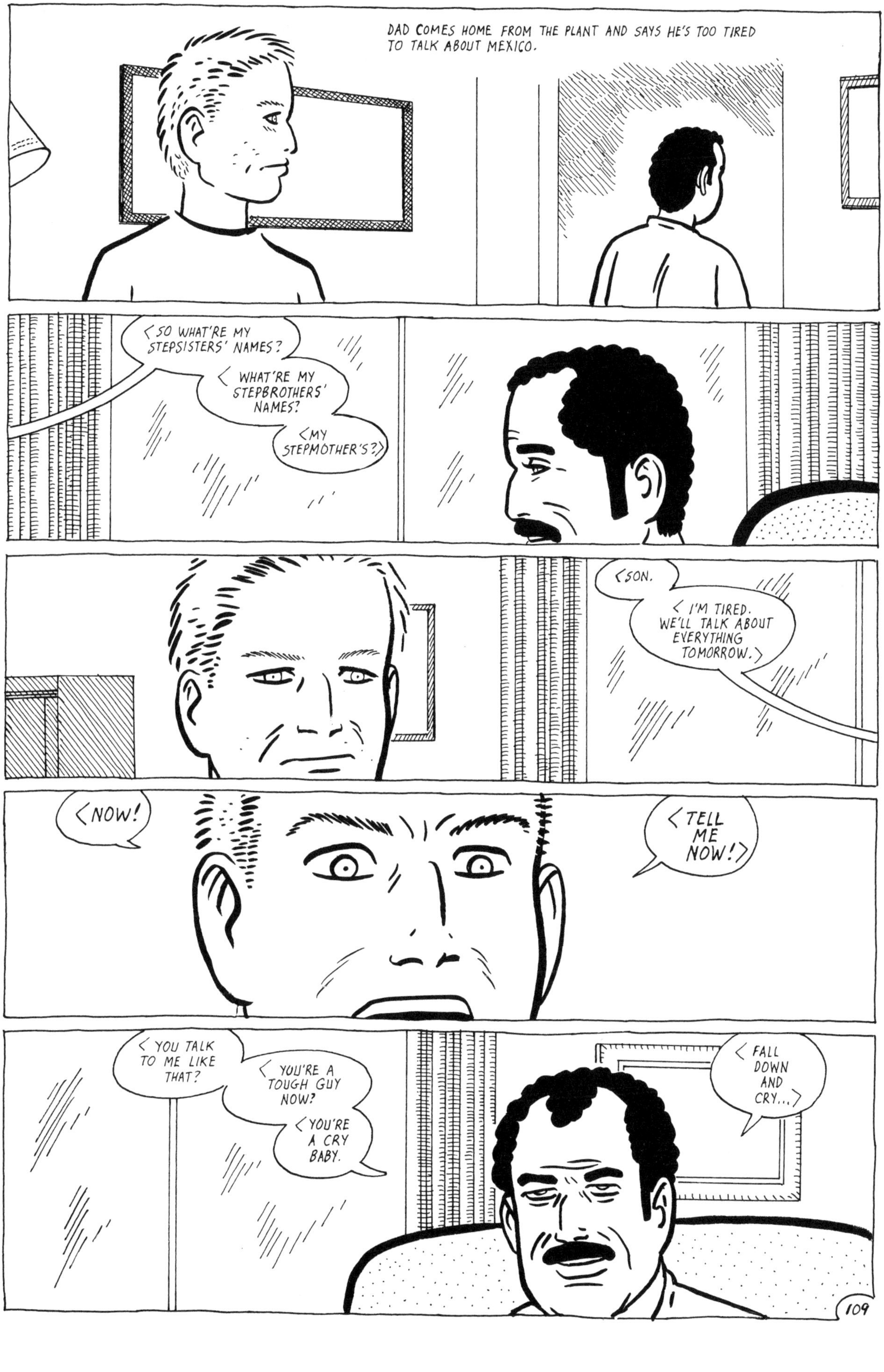
DAD COMES HOME FROM THE PLANT AND SAYS HE'S TOO TIRED TO TALK ABOUT MEXICO.
<SO WHAT'RE MY STEPSISTERS' NAMES?
<WHAT'RE MY STEPBROTHERS' NAMES?
<MY STEPMOTHER'S?>
<SON.
<I'M TIRED. WE'LL TALK ABOUT EVERYTHING TOMORROW.>
<NOW!
<TELL ME NOW!>
<YOU TALK TO ME LIKE THAT?
<YOU'RE A TOUGH GUY NOW?
<YOU'RE A CRY BABY.
<FALL DOWN AND CRY...>

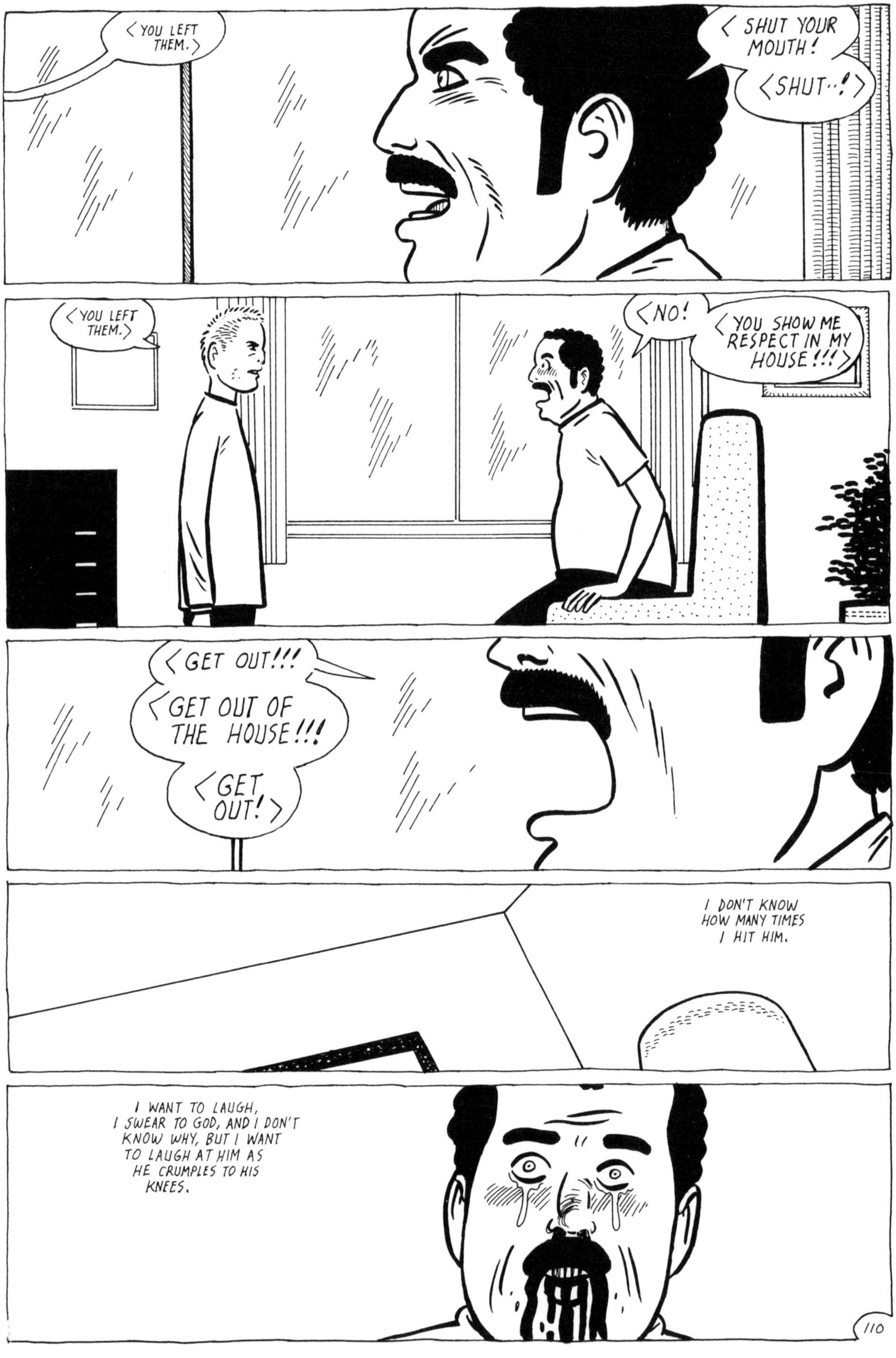

< YOU LEFT THEM. >
< SHUT YOUR MOUTH!
< SHUT..! >
< YOU LEFT THEM. >
< NO!
< YOU SHOW ME RESPECT IN MY HOUSE!!! >
< GET OUT!!!
< GET OUT OF THE HOUSE!!!
< GET OUT! >
I DON'T KNOW HOW MANY TIMES I HIT HIM.
I WANT TO LAUGH, I SWEAR TO GOD, AND I DON'T KNOW WHY, BUT I WANT TO LAUGH AT HIM AS HE CRUMPLES TO HIS KNEES.

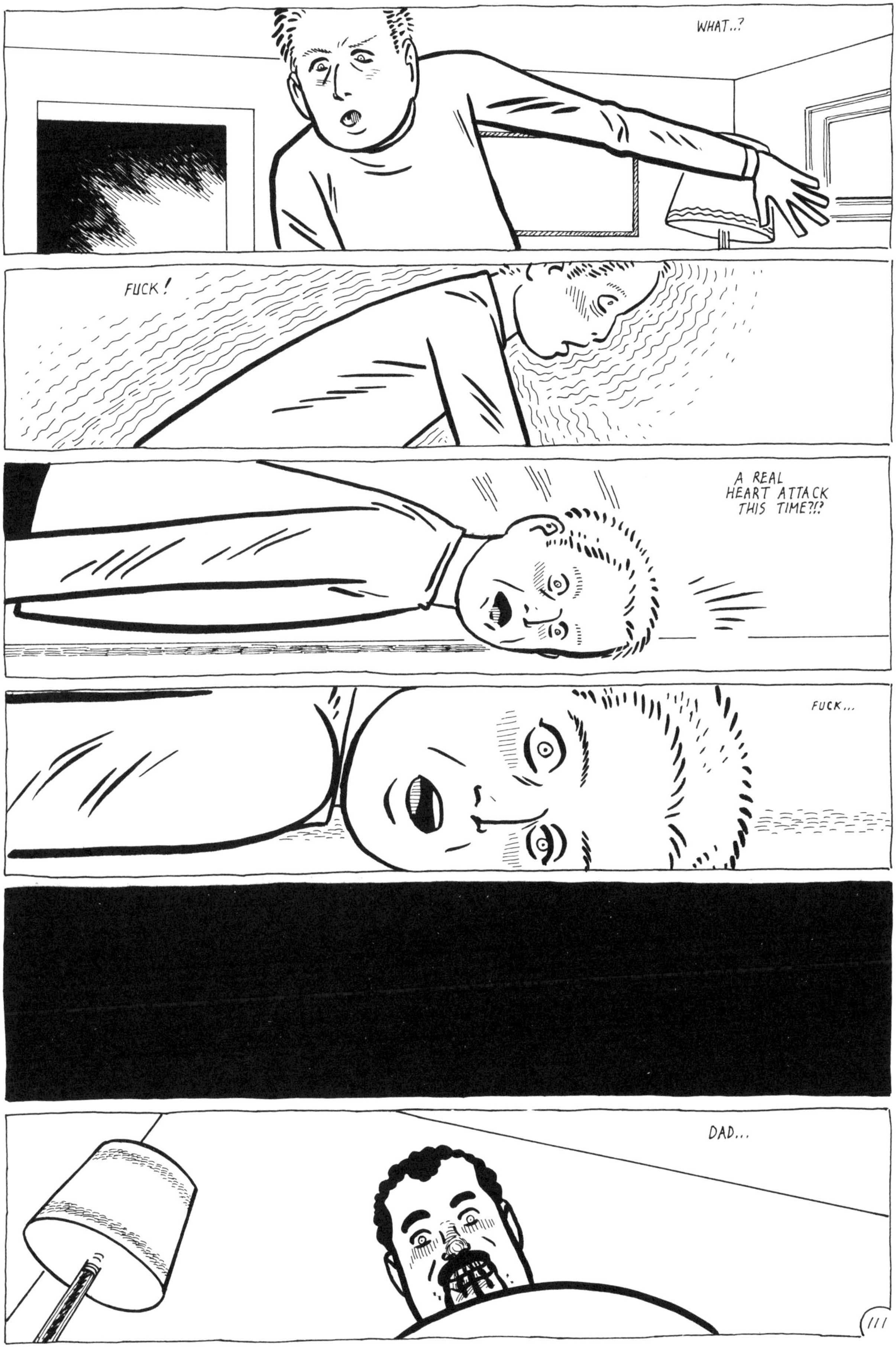
WHAT..?
FUCK!
A REAL HEART ATTACK THIS TIME?!?
FUCK...
DAD...

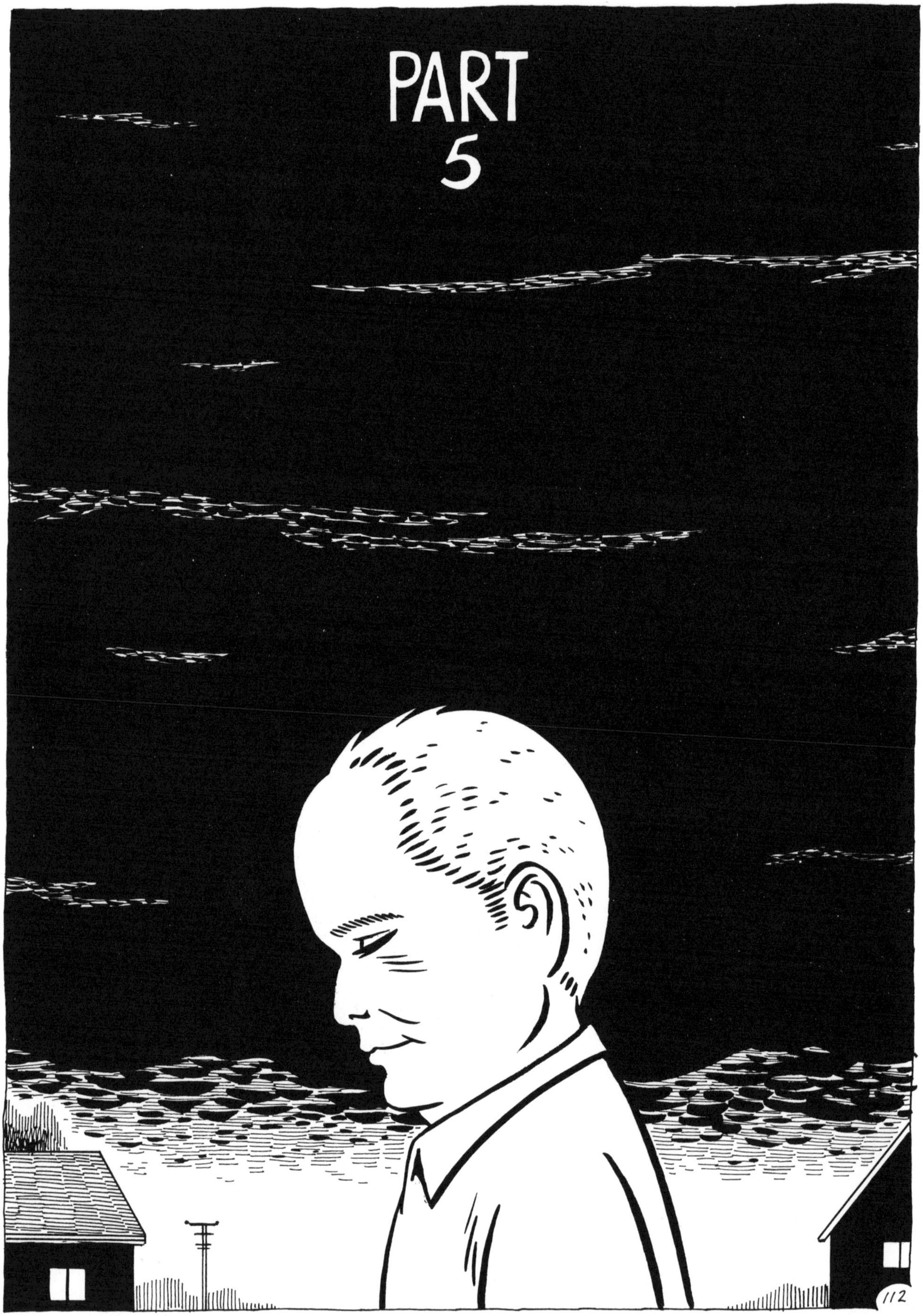
PART
5

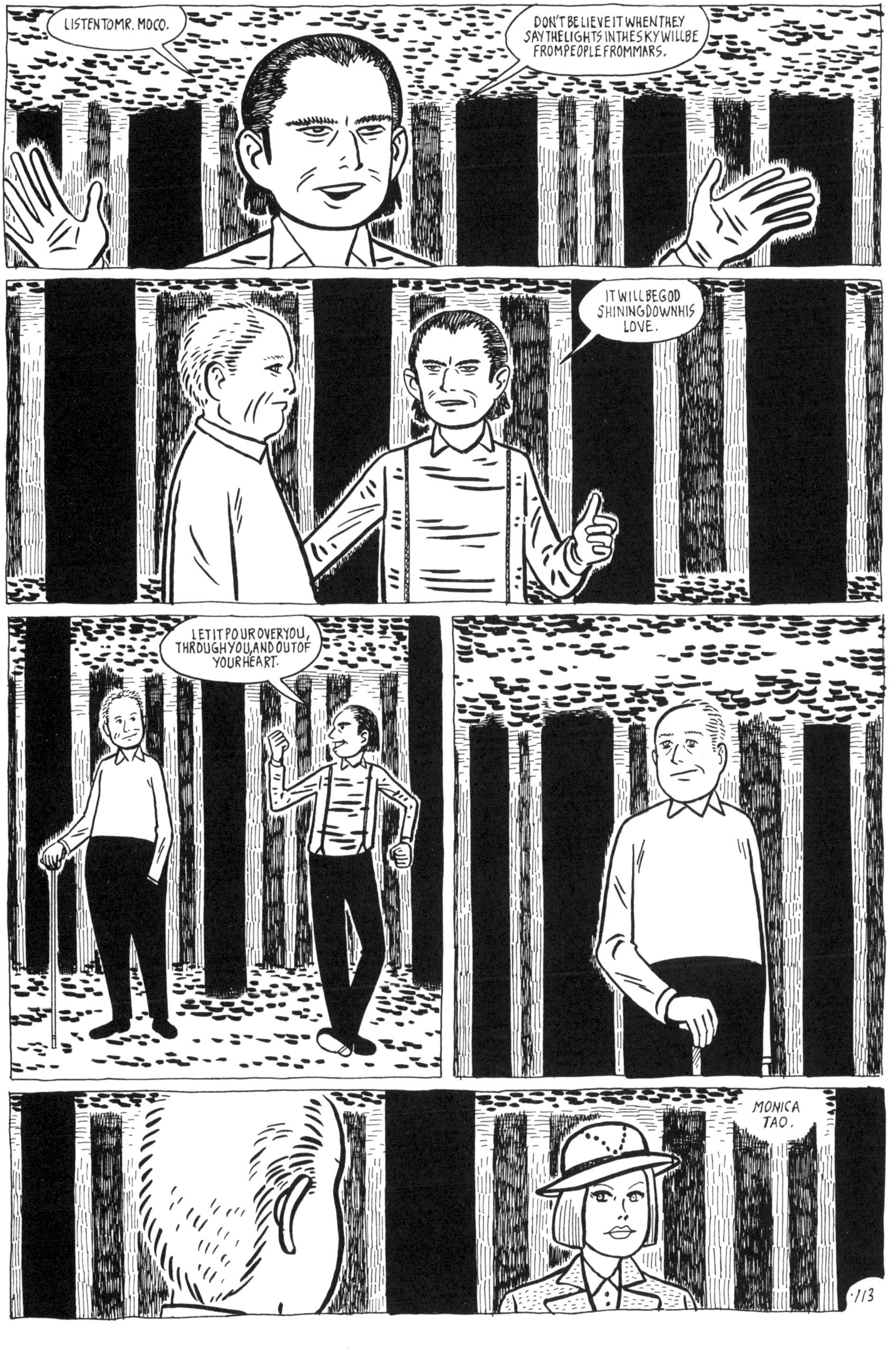
LISTEN TO MR. MOCO.
DON'T BELIEVE IT WHEN THEY SAY THE LIGHTS IN THE SKY WILL BE FROM PEOPLE FROM MARS.
IT WILL BE GOD SHINING DOWN HIS LOVE.
LET IT POUR OVER YOU, THROUGH YOU, AND OUT OF YOUR HEART.
MONICA TAO.

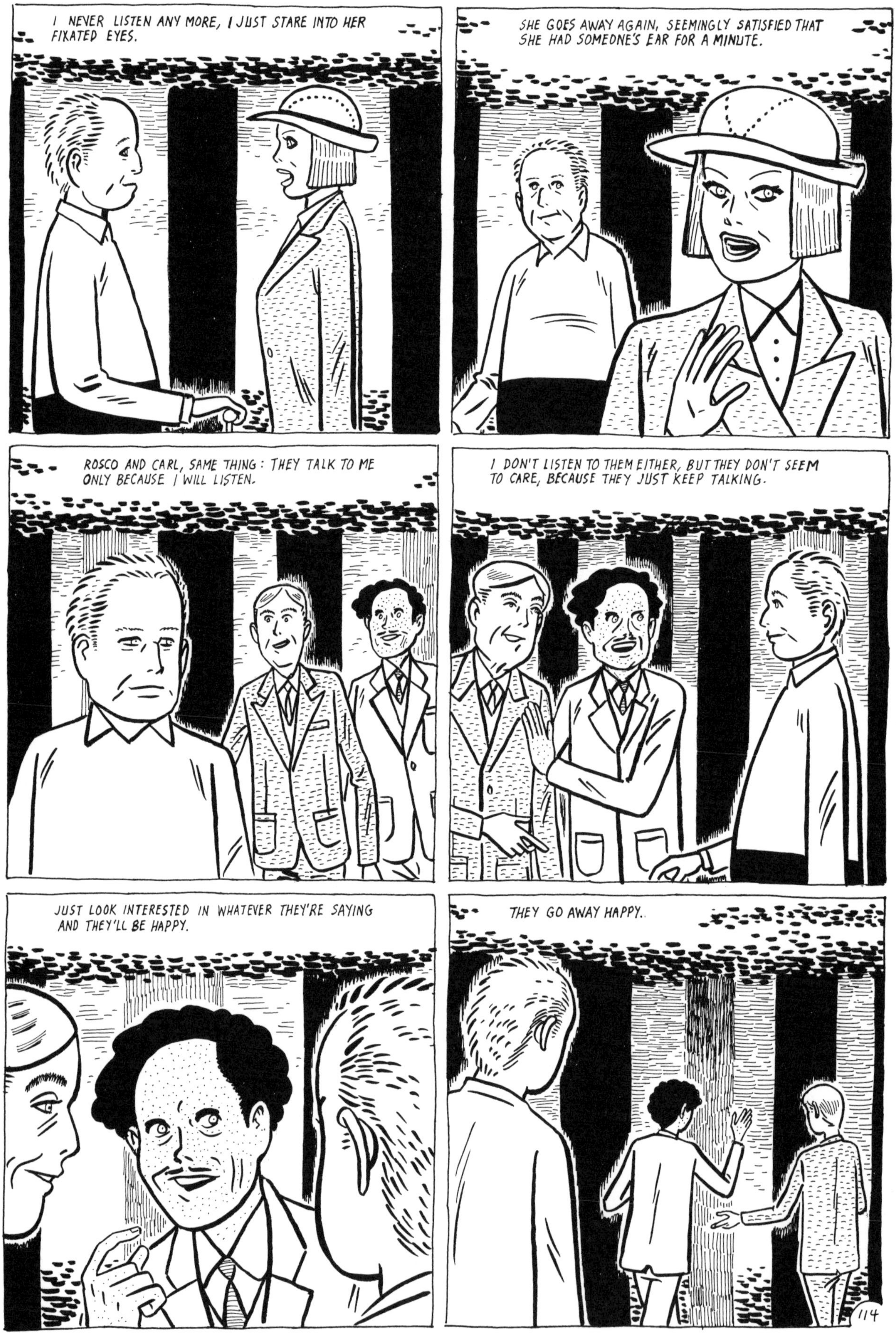
I NEVER LISTEN ANY MORE, I JUST STARE INTO HER FIXATED EYES.
SHE GOES AWAY AGAIN, SEEMINGLY SATISFIED THAT SHE HAD SOMEONE'S EAR FOR A MINUTE.
ROSCO AND CARL, SAME THING: THEY TALK TO ME ONLY BECAUSE I WILL LISTEN.
I DON'T LISTEN TO THEM EITHER, BUT THEY DON'T SEEM TO CARE, BECAUSE THEY JUST KEEP TALKING.
JUST LOOK INTERESTED IN WHATEVER THEY'RE SAYING AND THEY'LL BE HAPPY.
THEY GO AWAY HAPPY..

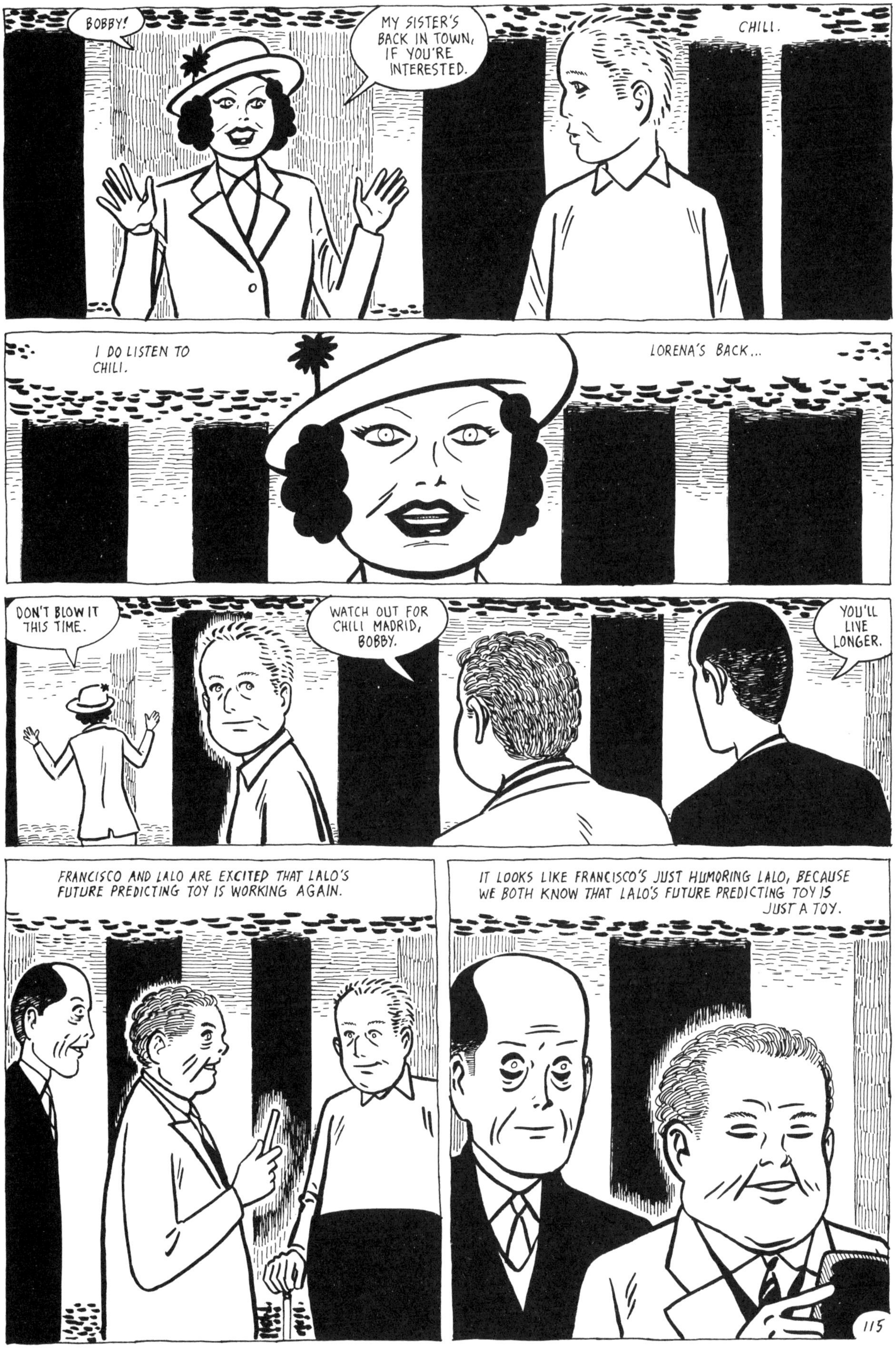

BOBBY!
MY SISTER'S BACK IN TOWN, IF YOU'RE INTERESTED.
CHILI.
I DO LISTEN TO CHILI.
LORENA'S BACK...
DON'T BLOW IT THIS TIME.
WATCH OUT FOR CHILI MADRID, BOBBY.
YOU'LL LIVE LONGER.
FRANCISCO AND LALO ARE EXCITED THAT LALO'S FUTURE PREDICTING TOY IS WORKING AGAIN.
IT LOOKS LIKE FRANCISCO'S JUST HUMORING LALO, BECAUSE WE BOTH KNOW THAT LALO'S FUTURE PREDICTING TOY IS JUST A TOY.

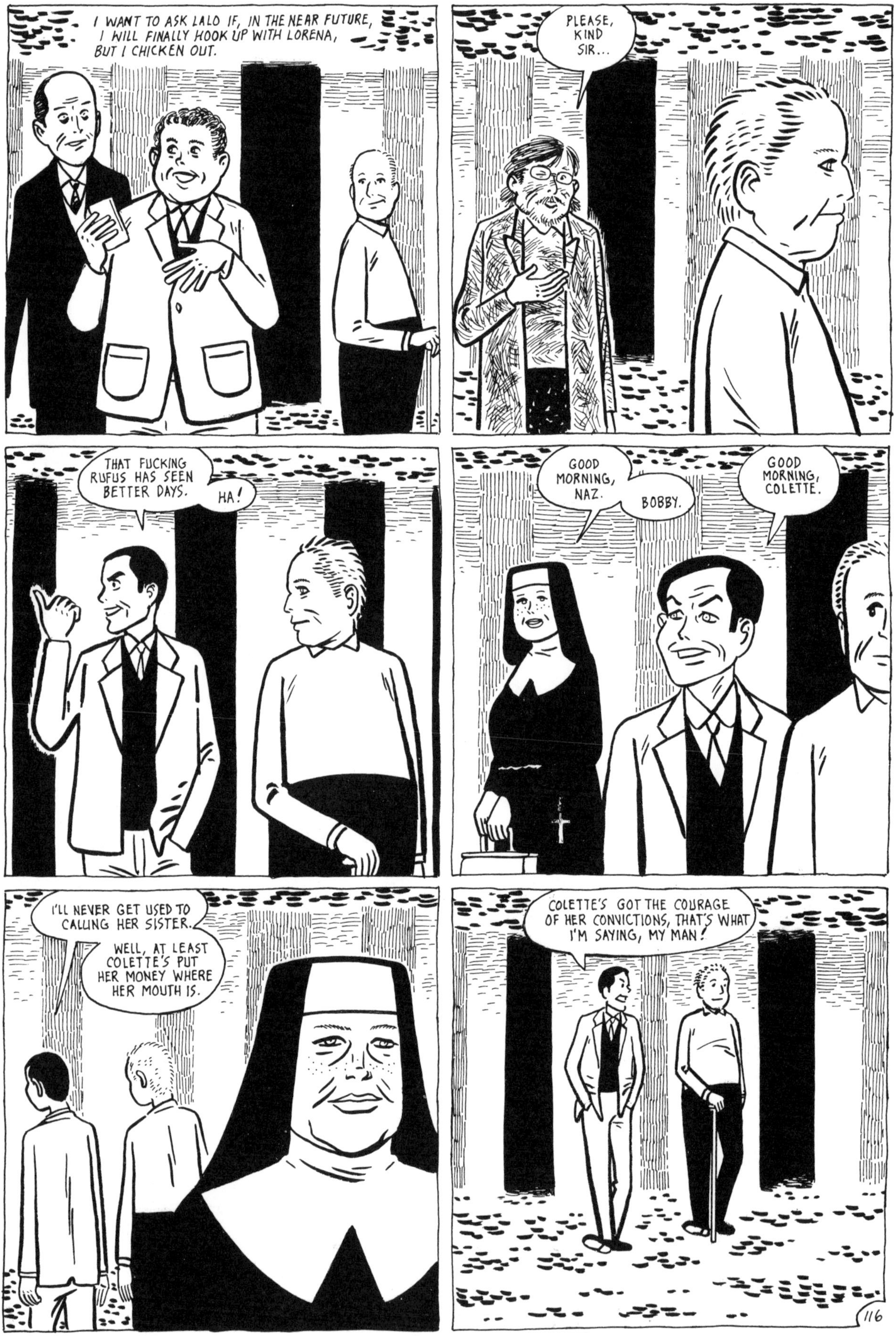
I WANT TO ASK LALO IF, IN THE NEAR FUTURE, I WILL FINALLY HOOK UP WITH LORENA, BUT I CHICKEN OUT.
PLEASE, KIND SIR...
THAT FUCKING RUFUS HAS SEEN BETTER DAYS.
HA!
GOOD MORNING, NAZ.
BOBBY.
GOOD MORNING, COLETTE.
I'LL NEVER GET USED TO CALLING HER SISTER.
WELL, AT LEAST COLETTE'S PUT HER MONEY WHERE HER MOUTH IS.
COLETTE'S GOT THE COURAGE OF HER CONVICTIONS, THAT'S WHAT I'M SAYING, MY MAN!

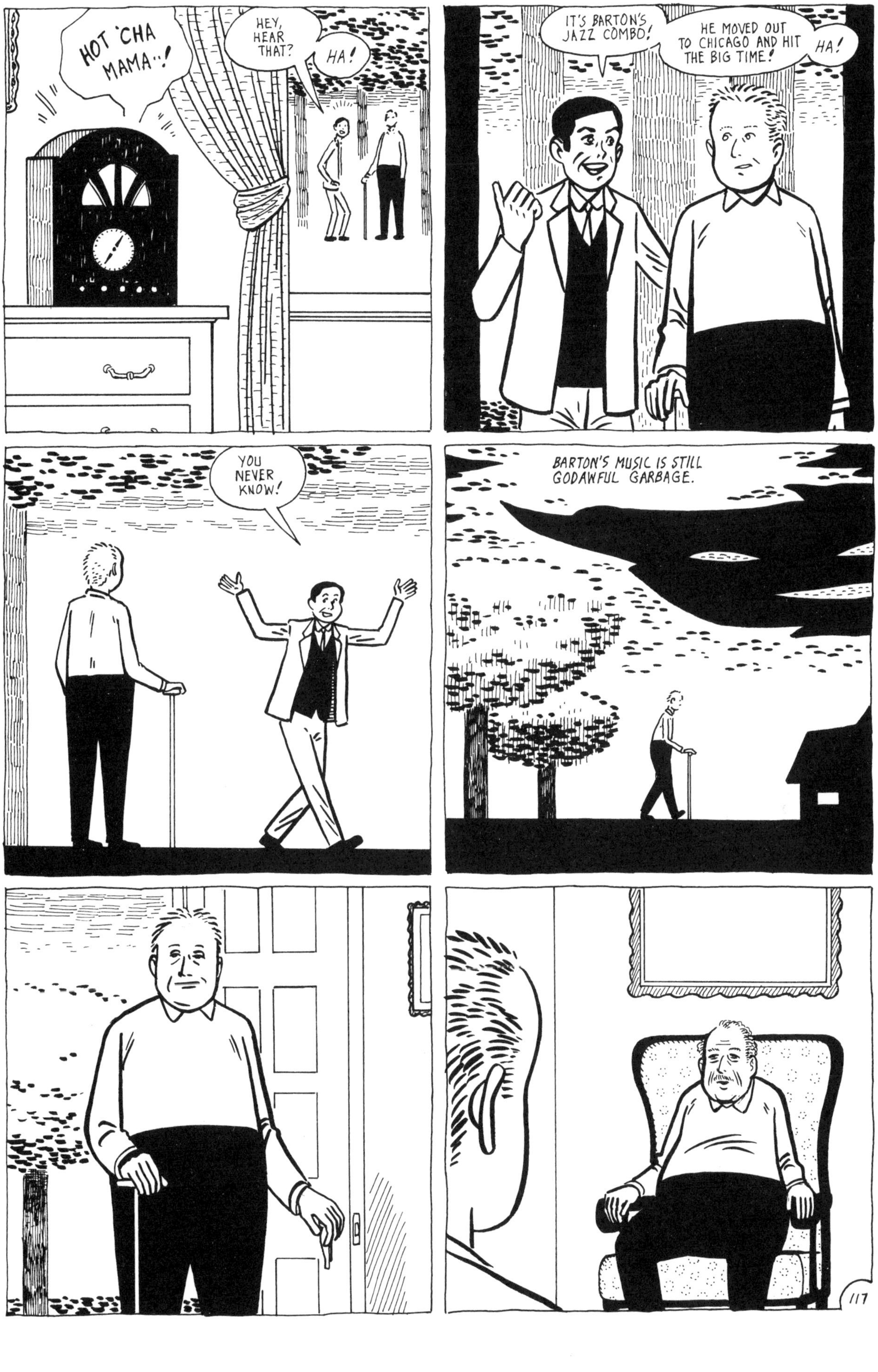
HOT 'CHA MAMA..!
HEY, HEAR THAT?
HA!
IT'S BARTON'S JAZZ COMBO!
HE MOVED OUT TO CHICAGO AND HIT THE BIG TIME!
HA!
YOU NEVER KNOW!
BARTON'S MUSIC IS STILL GODAWFUL GARBAGE.

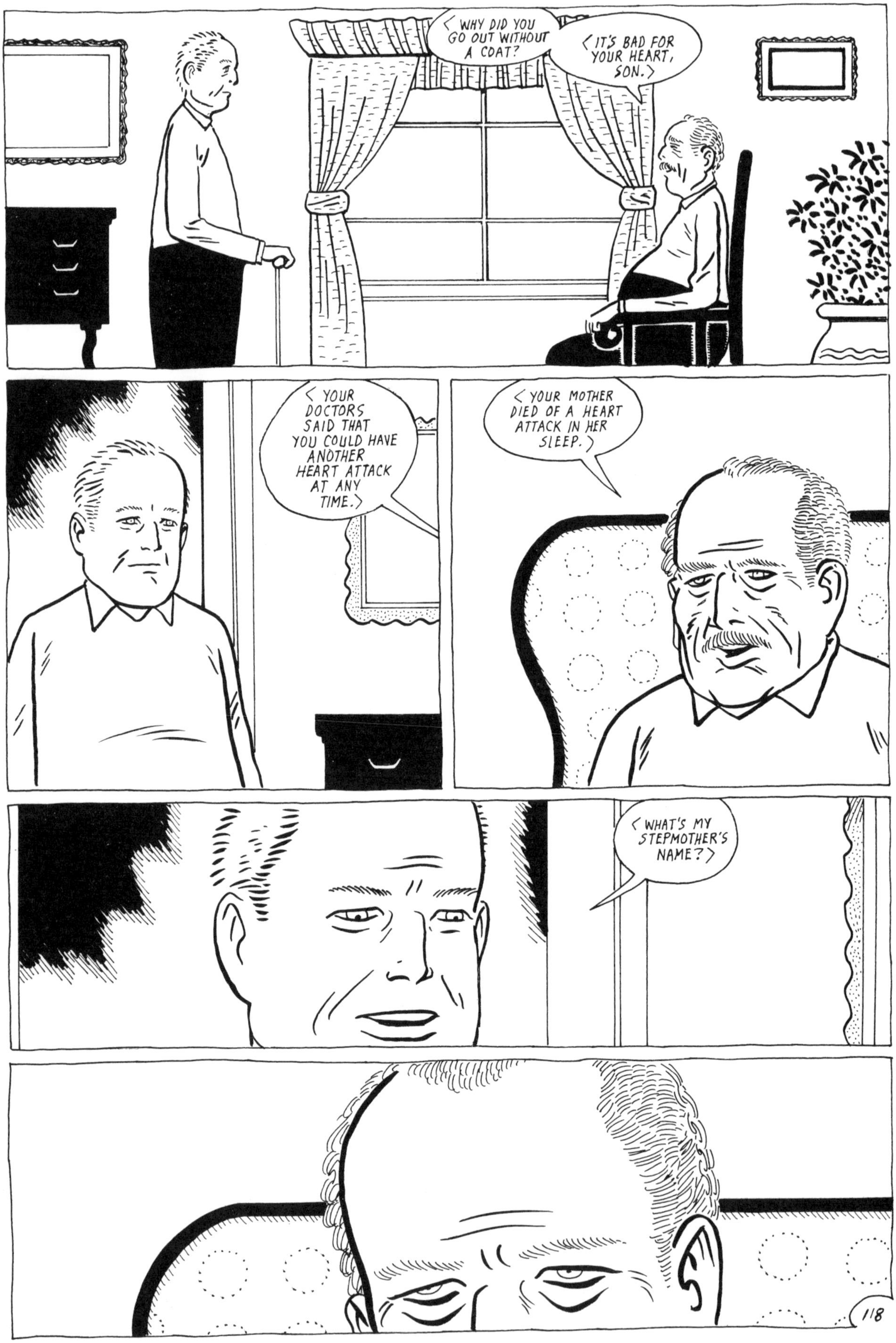
< WHY DID YOU GO OUT WITHOUT A COAT?
< IT'S BAD FOR YOUR HEART, SON. >
< YOUR DOCTORS SAID THAT YOU COULD HAVE ANOTHER HEART ATTACK AT ANY TIME. >
< YOUR MOTHER DIED OF A HEART ATTACK IN HER SLEEP. >
< WHAT'S MY STEPMOTHER'S NAME? >

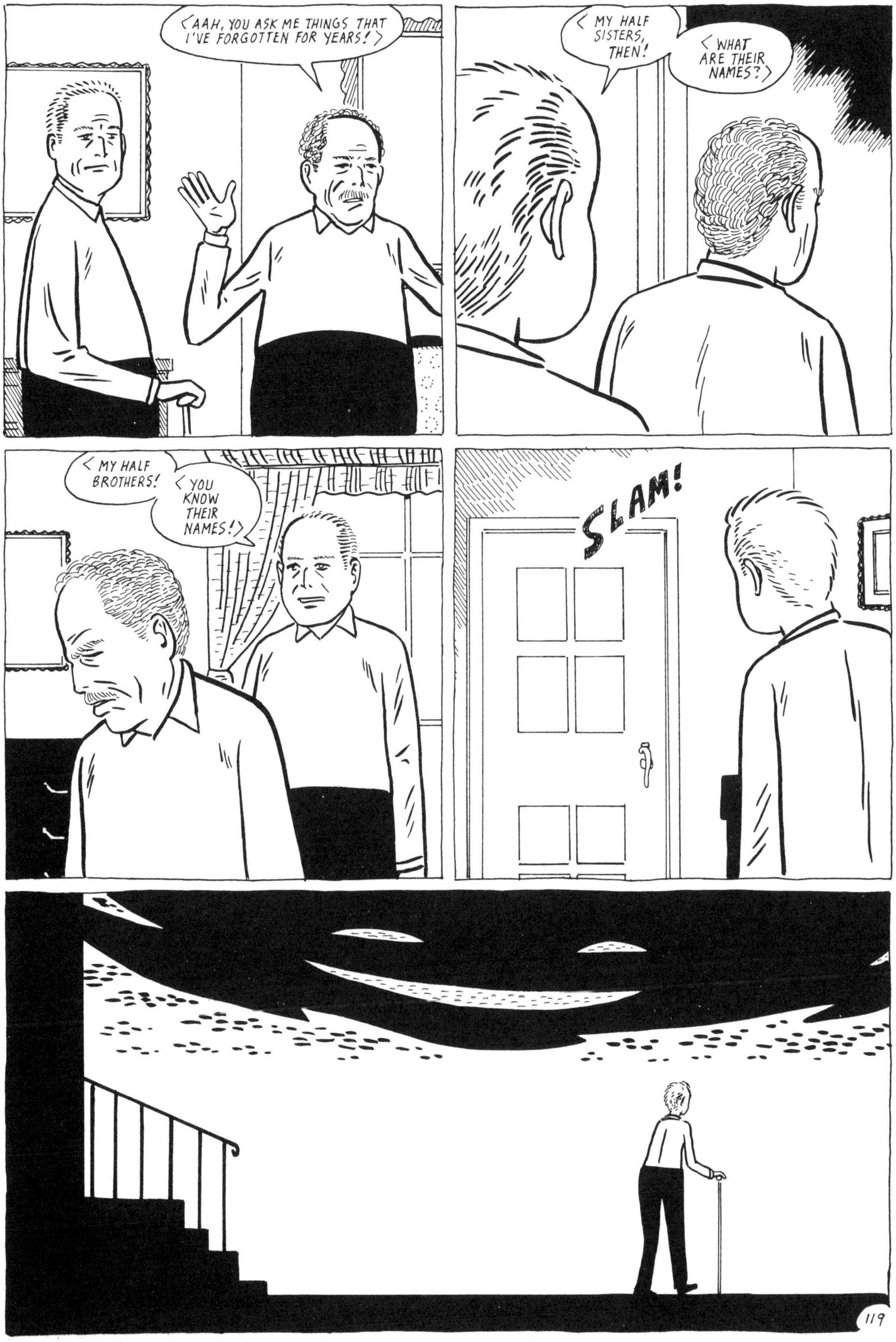
<AAH, YOU ASK ME THINGS THAT I'VE FORGOTTEN FOR YEARS!>
< MY HALF SISTERS, THEN!
< WHAT ARE THEIR NAMES?>
< MY HALF BROTHERS!
< YOU KNOW THEIR NAMES!>
SLAM!

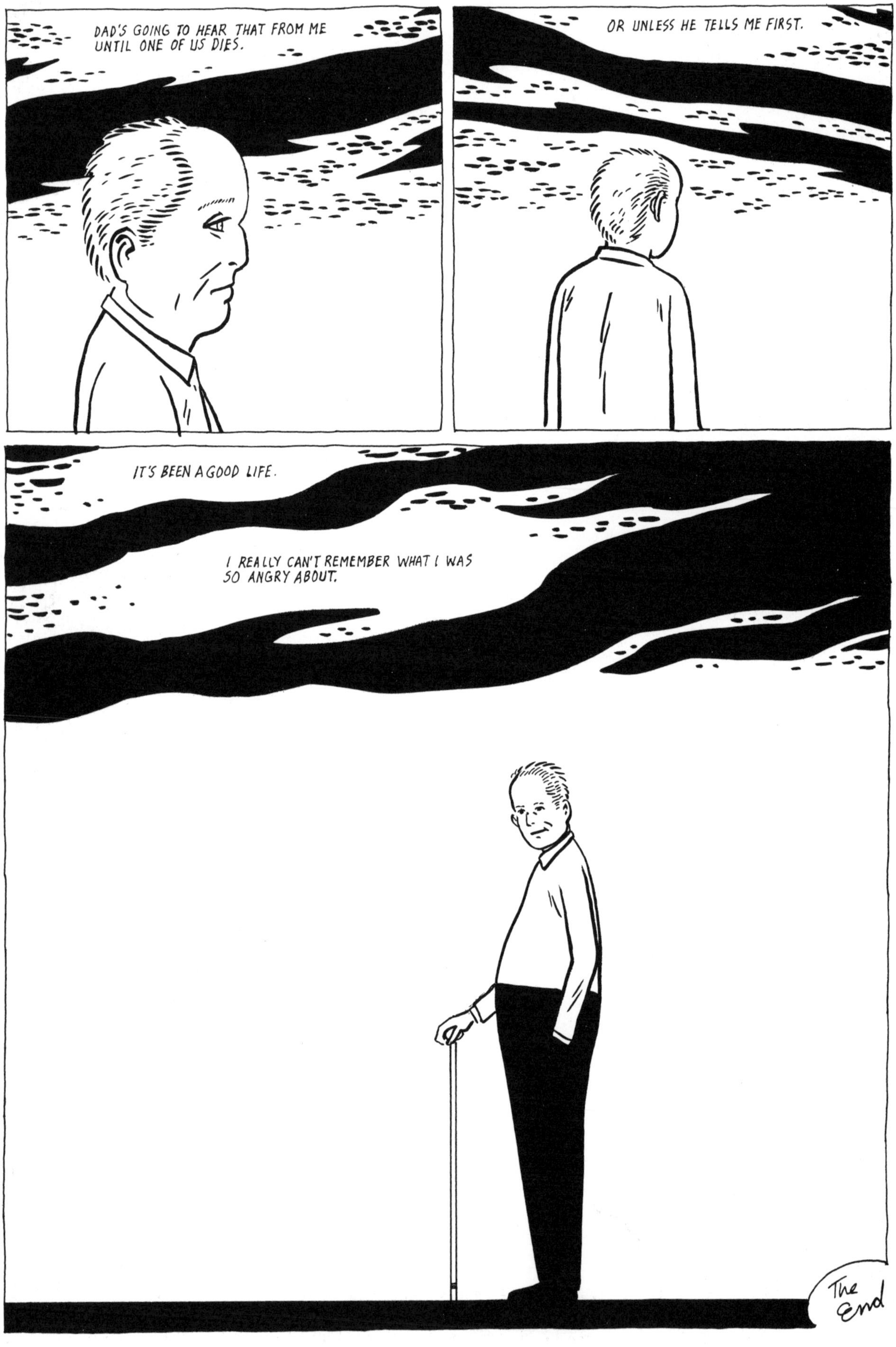
DAD'S GOING TO HEAR THAT FROM ME UNTIL ONE OF US DIES.
OR UNLESS HE TELLS ME FIRST.
IT'S BEEN A GOOD LIFE.
I REALLY CAN'T REMEMBER WHAT I WAS SO ANGRY ABOUT.
The End

GILBERT HERNANDEZ WAS BORN IN 1957 IN OXNARD, CALIFORNIA.
HE HAS BEEN THE CO-CREATOR OF *LOVE AND ROCKETS* FOR OVER THIRTY
YEARS. *BUMPERHEAD* IS HIS SECOND BOOK FOR DRAWN & QUARTERLY,
FOLLOWING *MARBLE SEASON*.

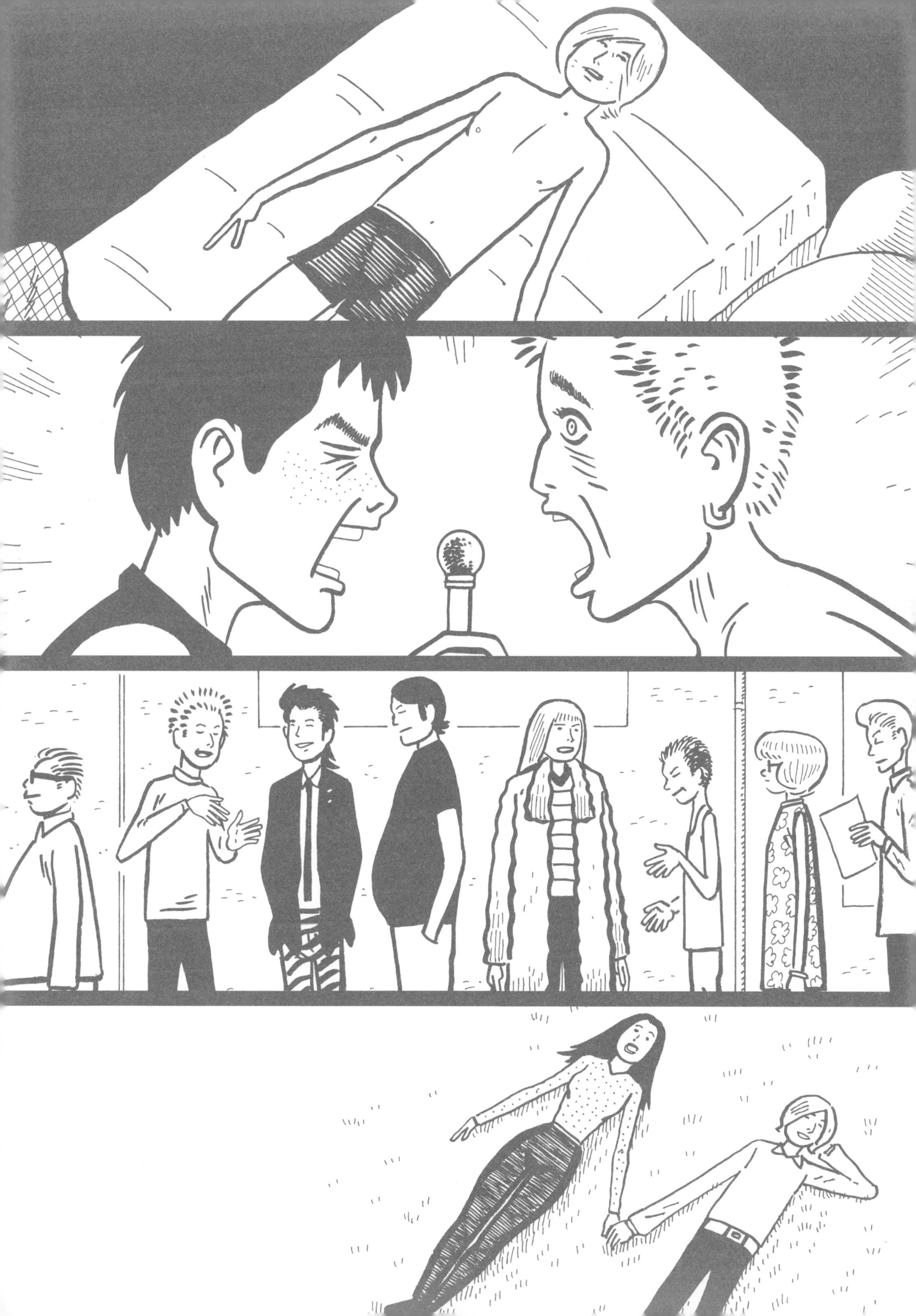

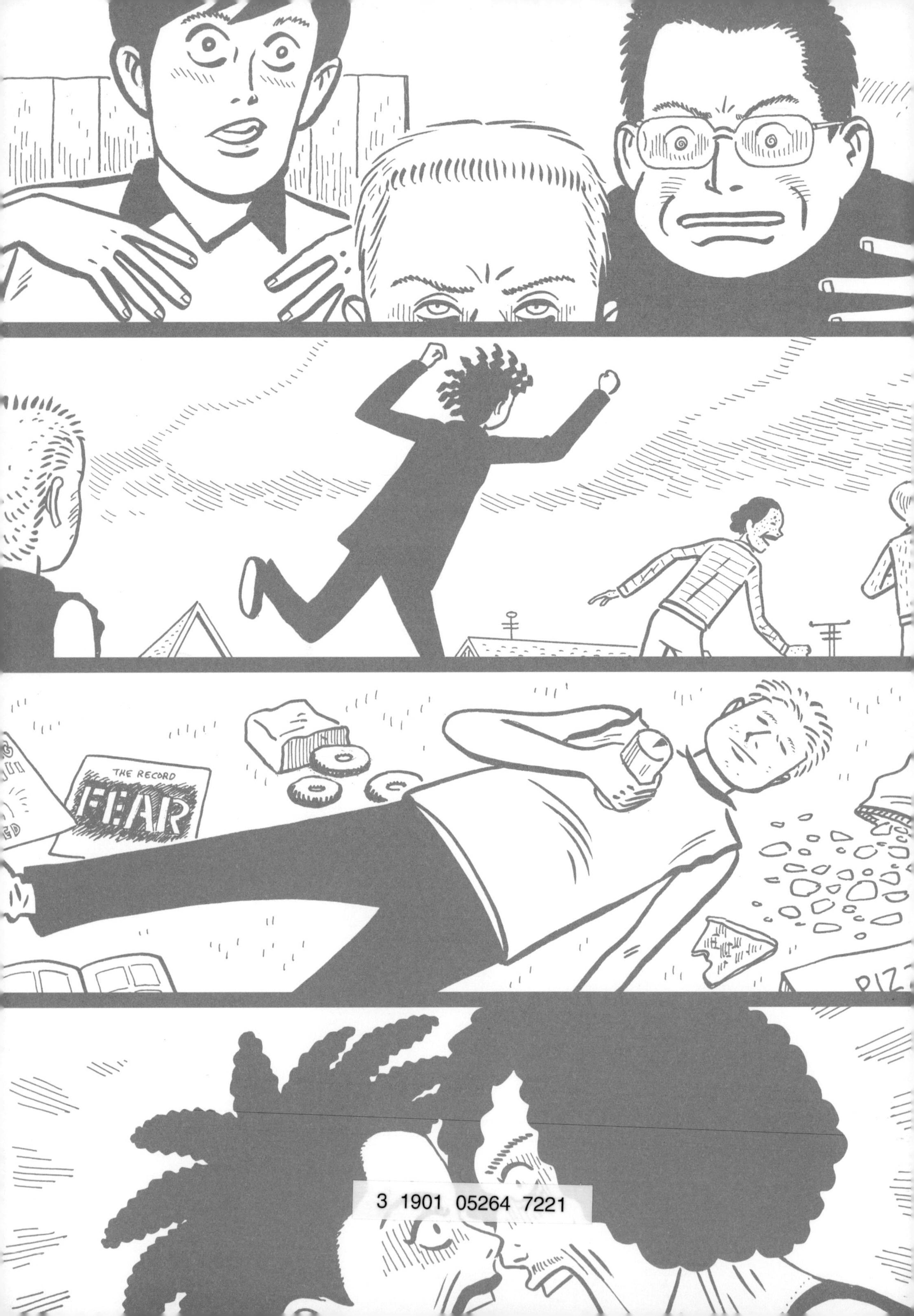
THE RECORD
FEAR